From Ibn Sina to Sindbad

From Ibn Sina to Sindbad

A GUIDED READER TO CLASSICS OF ARABIC LITERATURE

David DiMeo and Inas Hassan

The American University in Cairo Press
Cairo New York

First published in 2023 by
The American University in Cairo Press
113 Sharia Kasr el Aini, Cairo, Egypt
420 Lexington Avenue, Suite 1644, New York, NY 10170
www.aucpress.com

ISBN 978 1 649 03173 0

Library of Congress Cataloging-in-Publication Data

Names: DiMeo, David Fred, author. | Hassan, Inas, author.
Title: From Ibn Sina to Sindbad : a guided reader to classics of Arabic literature / David DiMeo and Inas Hassan.
Identifiers: LCCN 2023009695 | ISBN 9781649031730 (trade paperback) | ISBN 9781649033079 (adobe pdf)
Subjects: LCSH: Arabic language--Readers--Literature. | Arabic language--Readers--Civilization, Arab. | Arabic language--Textbooks for foreign speakers--English. | Civilization, Arab. | Arabic literature. | LCGFT: Readers (Publications)
Classification: LCC PJ6311 .D555 2023 | DDC 492.786/421--dc23/eng/20230405

1 2 3 4 5 27 26 25 24 23

Designed by David G. Hanna

Contents

Introduction vii

1. Biography of the Prophet—Ma'mar ibn Rashid 1
2. *Adab*—al-Jahiz 13
3. Philosophy—al-Kindi 25
4. Ethnicity in Islam—Ibn Qutayba 37
5. Government and Leadership—Ibn 'Abd Rabbih 49
6. Anthropology and Religion—al-Biruni 59
7. Education—Ibn Sina 71
8. Religion vs. Philosophy I—al-Ghazali 83
9. Religion vs. Philosophy II—Ibn Rushd 97
10. Impressions of Europeans—Usama ibn Munqidh 109
11. Women in the Caliphal Court—Ibn al-Sa'i 119
12. Travel Literature—Ibn Battuta 131
13. History—Ibn Khaldun 143
14. Popular Storytelling—*The Arabian Nights* 155
15. Fantasy and Adventure—*Sindbad the Sailor* 169
16. Moral Literature—Ibn al-Muqaffa', *Kalila wa-Dimna* 185

17. The *Maqamat*—al-Hariri 199

18. Philosophical Novel—Ibn Tufayl, *Hayy ibn Yaqdhan* 215

19. Satire—Abu al-'Alaa' al-Ma'arri 229

20. Animal Rights—Ikhwan al-Safa 241

Glossary 253

Resources for Further Study 279

Introduction

From Ibn Sina to Sindbad: A Guided Reader to Classics of Arabic Literature makes some of the greatest works of the Golden Age of Arab civilization accessible to Arabic students working at the mid- to high-advanced level of proficiency, while also providing a ready curriculum for teachers of advanced Arabic. It introduces students to Classical Arabic literature through detailed, but guided, studies of works spanning prose genres from travel writing to philosophy, science, religion, humor and imaginative fiction. Students will read the actual texts of the original writers, supplemented with supporting explanatory material to make the texts accessible to students at the fourth year of Arabic study. From there, students will progress through an extensive series of exercises to test their comprehension, develop interpretive and critical reading skills, and apply the linguistic structures to their own speaking and writing.

This book will help develop more than just language proficiency, offering an introduction to the leading themes of an important period in Arab culture and world history. The Golden Age of Islam undoubtedly marks one of the greatest epochs in human achievement, recorded in a wealth of literature that has influenced civilization in Asia, Africa, and Europe. The Arab Golden Age consolidated and advanced the ancient scholarship of the Greeks, Romans, Hindus, and Persians, as well as early Christianity, and reached new heights in disciplines ranging from mathematics, medicine, ethics, philosophy, and cosmology to fiction. This body of knowledge would pass into Medieval Europe and be directly responsible for the intellectual flourishing of the Renaissance. In the space of twenty lessons, we have tried to cover as wide a range as possible of prose genres, incorporating the most influential works of the most prominent writers of the Golden Age. The great battle between Rationalism and Revelation, which dominated Golden Age intellectual culture, is captured in the works of Ibn Rushd, Ibn Sina, and al-Ghazali. The relationship of Islam to Christian and pagan thought, discussed by al-Kindi, is found here as well as the Muslim views of other civilizations as recorded by Ibn Munqidh, Ibn Battuta, and al-Biruni. Ethics of kings toward subjects and humans toward animals are treated by Ibn 'Abd Rabbih and the Ikhwan al-Safa, and the controversial relationship of Arabness to Islam in the work of Ibn Qutayba. Along with these non-fiction works are found imaginative fiction for the masses and the elite of The Arabian Nights, *Kalila wa-Dimna,* and The *Maqamat.* These lessons can be presented in any order, as the student or teacher sees fit.

Additionally, as all of the writers in this collection were making claims and arguments, many of which would shape the nature of Arab civilization, we have designed the exercises to stress the argumentation aspect of the texts and students' appreciation of them. Throughout the presentations and exercises, students will be challenged to identify the different sides of the argument, evaluate their merits, and, ultimately, state their own opinions. We intend this text to greatly aid students in developing their persuasive and critical skills in Arabic, and in general.

With these considerations in mind, each lesson is divided into several parts, as described below. The sequence of activities guides the reader from comprehension activities through more abstract reasoning and interpretation and then on to presentational activities. The sequence will be useful for organizing classroom activities as well. The descriptions below explain the intended use of each section.

Introduction. Each chapter begins with a summary in Arabic of the background and importance of the text to be studied. Given that many of the excerpts presented are parts of extended debates, background and context are important for interpreting the readings. Readers may not have in-depth backgrounds in Classical Arabic literature, and indeed, few readers would be familiar with all of the texts included here. From this section, students will have a solid understanding of why the given text was so influential. What was the implication of Ibn Rushd's critique of al-Ghazali's argument, for example? What was Ibn Tufayl trying to prove by his story of a child raised by a deer on a remote island, and why did this story inspire countless commentaries in Europe?

Prediction and Scanning. To develop critical reading skills, these exercises ask students to predict, based on the introduction they have just read, what the texts are likely to say or not say. Then readers will skim through the text to find indicators toward the answers. This builds students' skill at quick reading and pre-reading.

From the Writings. Key excerpts in the words of the originals are presented with sufficient explanatory notes to situate them contextually. Here, students will not rely on paraphrases, but the actual words of the writers, and thus gain an appreciation for their style and skill. Each sentence is numbered, and key or difficult terms and phrases linked to explanatory definitions. The writings are presented separately from the vocabulary terms (although keyed to them) to encourage readers to complete as much of the text on their own as they can and to attempt to figure out unfamiliar words from roots and context. If necessary, they may refer to the vocabulary list, or consult it afterward to check themselves.

Vocabulary. Presented in the order they appear in the text, both unfamiliar vocabulary and key names and titles can be found in this section. The consolidated glossary at the end of the book lists all terms from all lessons in alphabetical order. As mentioned above, the vocabulary list is presented after the reading to encourage readers to complete the text without reference to the vocabulary, but offers definitions for some of the less familiar terms if needed. After having read the text, students are encouraged to check the vocabulary lists to confirm or check the accuracy of their derivations.

Comprehension Questions. This section begins with questions to test students' general understanding of the text, then moves on to questions that prompt students to identify idioms and phrases based on their existing knowledge of Arabic. This is a bridge step aimed primarily at facilitating readers' consolidation and organization of knowledge derived from the texts in preparation for further application.

Interpreting the Text. These questions, in Arabic, prompt students to read between the lines, applying their knowledge of history and the background notes given for the texts. They are often "why" questions, such as "Why does Ibn Qutayba acknowledge the past glory of Persian civilization?" These questions can form the springboard for class discussions or serve as useful short answer questions for tests that emphasize critical reading and reasoning.

Style and Technique. The next three sections are designed to prepare students for the production/presentation phase of the lesson. Following the comprehension and interpretation activities, these sections provide additional detail on how the writers express their ideas and present their arguments. The first section discusses stylistic devices that will better enable students to read this text and other Classical texts and understand how the writers use techniques to express themselves. It is also designed to give students practice in applying their knowledge of the language and culture to effective reading strategies. These sections will help students not only understand the text but develop their own writing or speaking skills, which will be used in the final activities.

Using Grammar and Structure Clues. Classical usage may be very different from what students of Modern Arabic are familiar with. This section, included for texts that have particularly challenging grammar structures, focuses on grammatical constructions that may be unfamiliar and also provides students with structures they can use in their own writing and speaking.

Using Cultural and Context Clues. Classical texts are heavily embedded in the historical context in which they were written. To understand any of these texts, students will need to recognize historical, religious, and literary allusions that would have been clear to the original audience but may not be to a modern one. This section will help to deepen students' understanding of the arguments being made and thus enable them to better discuss the issues involved. It builds on the background notes provided before the text, but goes much deeper into points that can be better understood now that students have read the texts.

Analysis and Argument. This is the first presentational exercise, building on the students' understanding of the issues discussed in the readings and bolstered by the techniques they have studied. This is also a preparation for the final presentation activity. Nearly all the writers in this collection were making arguments, often controversial ones, that affected Arab and Muslim civilization. None were accepted universally, and some produced vigorous counterarguments. In these exercises, we have focused on students not merely understanding these arguments but being able to debate their merits themselves.

Writing Exercises. In the fiction lessons, which are more heavily oriented to style than to argument, we present exercises that will enable students to apply the idioms and techniques they have just read to their own writing. This will also help prepare students for the final activity.

Research and Presentation. This section serves as the independent, presentational exercise for each lesson. Here, students will prepare a written or oral argument on a key controversy of the reading. In each chapter, students are provided with specific debating and argumentation terms that can be used to argue any position. Thus, over the course of the lessons, they will greatly strengthen their persuasive skills in Arabic. This exercise is intended as the culmination of each lesson. Readers will also find a list of resources they can use for more in-depth research in the next section.

Resources for Further Study. This section includes a number of online and print resources that readers can use to further their study of the authors featured in this book. These include links to the full texts from which these excerpts came, to other works by the same authors, and to background information on the subjects and writers. These can be used for research projects, to enhance the "Research and Presentation" exercises above, or for independent study.

Classical Arabic literature need not be daunting for students nor involve an excessively difficult "jump" from intermediate texts. The sequence of exercises presented here will guide students to become increasingly more confident and independent readers of Arabic literature.

The Golden Age awaits you!

1

Biography of the Prophet—Ma'mar ibn Rashid

الدرس الأول – معمر بن راشد

«كتاب المغازي» من أقدم كتب السيرة النبوية التي وصلت إلينا في العصر الحديث. مؤلف الكتاب هو مَعْمَر بن راشد (٩٦هـ/ ٧١٤م - ١٥٣هـ/ ٧٧٠م). كان معمر عالمًا مشهورًا وعبدًا فارسيًّا من البصرة في جنوب العراق، وكان دائم الترحال يبيع السلع للقبائل. وبفضل تجارته مع بلاط الخلفاء الأمويين، تعرّف على ابن شهاب الزهري، أحد أعظم الباحثين المسلمين من أبناء جيله الذي أصبح معمر تلميذه فيما بعد. معظم ما ورد في كتاب المغازي من قصص شفوية وروايات مما أخذه معمر وتعلمه على يد شيخه ومعلمه الزهري. وقد جمع عبد الرزّاق بن همام الصنعاني (أحد أبرز تلامذة معمر بن راشد) هذه الروايات ودوّنها في القرن الثاني الهجري. ويُعدّ كتاب المغازي قيمة تراثية وتحفة فنية نادرة؛ فهو من أمهات الكتب التي سَردت لنا سيرة النبي (ﷺ) وسيرة صحابته الكرام، كما أنه باكورة أعمال أدب المغازي وثقافة التدوين.

Prediction and Scanning

Based on the context and background given above, record your predictions as to whether you expect to find the issues listed below addressed in the text. Be prepared to discuss your predictions with classmates. Then, reading through the excerpts in the next section quickly, without the use of a dictionary, indicate whether your prediction was correct and where (in which lines) you found the answer. Be prepared to discuss the results with your classmates.

الدلالة	التوقُّع	العبارة
		وَقعَ الاختيار على النبي محمد (ﷺ) صدفةً ليكون حَكَماً في خصومة قبيلة قريش.
		حكم الرسول (ﷺ) لصالح قبيلته قريش في وضع حجر الزاوية في الكعبة.
		شعر النبي محمد (ﷺ) بالخوف عندما رأى جبريل عليه السلام وأمَرَه بأن يقرأ.
		كان ورقة بن نوفل ابن عمّ خديجة يعلم أنّ نبيًّا سيأتي في آخر الزمان وأنه سيتعرض للأذى من عشيرته.

From the Writings of Maʿmar ibn Rashid

كتاب المغازي، الفصل الأول

Before his prophethood began, Muhammad ﷺ was chosen by the tribes to place the cornerstone of the Kaʿba, in which he demonstrates his leadership abilities:

(١) لما بلغ رسول الله (صلّى الله عليه وسلّم) الحُلُم، أجْمَرَت امرأة الكعبة، فطارت

شرارة مـن مجمرهـا في ثيـاب الكعبـة، فأحرقتهـا ووهـت. (٢) فتشـاورت قريـش في هدمها وهابـوا هدمهـا. فقـال لهـم الوليـد بـن المغـيرة: مـا تريـدون بهدمهـا، الإصـلاح تريـدون أم الإسـاءة؟ (٣) فقالـوا: بـل الإصـلاح! قـال: فـإنّ الله لا يهلـك المصلـح. (٤) قالـوا: فمـن الـذي يعلوهـا فيهدمهـا؟ قـال الوليـد: أنـا أعلوهـا فأهدمهـا! . . . (٥) فبلغـوا موضـع الركـن. (٦) اختصمـت قريـش في الركـن، أيّ القبائـل ترفعـه؟ حتـى كاد يشـجر بينهـم. (٧) فقالـوا: تعالـوا نحكّـم أوّل مـن يطلـع علينـا مـن هـذه السـكّة. (٨) فاصطلحـوا عـلى ذلـك، فطلـع عليهـم رسـول الله (صـلّى الله عليـه وسـلّم) . . . (٩) فحكّمـوه فأمـر بالركـن، فوضـع في ثـوب. (١٠) ثـم أمـر بسـيّد كل قبيلـة، فأعطـاه بناحيـة الثـوب. (١١) ثـم ارتقـى ورفعـوا إليـه الركـن، فـكان هـو يضعـه.

Ibn Rashid describes the first revelation to come to the Prophet ﷺ:

(١٢) أوّل مـا بُـدِئ بـه رسـول الله (صـلّى الله عليـه وسـلّم) مـن الوحـي الرؤيـا الصادقـة فـكان لا يـرى رؤيـا إلاّ جـاءت مثـل فلـق الصبـح. (١٣) ثـمّ حبّـب إليـه الخـلاء، فـكان يـأتي حـراءً فيتحنّـث فيـه (١٤) وهـو التعبّـد بالليـالي ذوات العـدد، ويتـزوّد لذلـك. (١٥) ثـمّ يرجـع إلى خديجـة، فتـزوّد لمثلهـا. (١٦) فحينـما جـاءه الحـقّ، وهـو في غـار حـراء (١٧) فجـاءه الملَـك. فقـال لـه: اقـرأ! . . . (١٨) فقـال رسـول الله (صـلّى الله عليـه وسـلّم): قلـتُ مـا أنـا بقـارئ. (١٩) فأخـذني، فغطّنـي حتـى بلـغ منـي الجهـد. (٢٠) ثـم أرسـلني، فقـال: «اقْـرَأْ بِاسْـمِ رَبِّـكَ الَّـذِي خَلَـقَ» حتـى بلـغ «مَـا لَمْ يَعْلَـمْ».[1]

Following this revelation, Muhammad ﷺ returns to his wife, Khadija:

(٢١) فرجـع بهـا ترجُـف بَـوادِرُه حتـى دخـل عـلى خديجـة. (٢٢) فقـال: زمّلـوني! فزمّلـوه حتـى ذهـب عنـه الـروع. (٢٣) فقـال لخديجـة: مـا لي؟ وأخبرهـا بالخـبر، فقـال: قـد خشـيت عـليّ! (٢٤) فقالـت: كلا! والله، لا يخزيـك الله أبـدًا. (٢٥) إنـك لتصـل الرحـم وتصـدق الحديـث وتقـري الضيـف وتعـين عـلى نوائـب الحـقّ!

After receiving the first revelation, the Prophet ﷺ traveled to a Christian relative:

(٢٦) ثـم انطلقـت بـه خديجـة حتـى أتـت بـه ورقـة ابـن نوفـل . . . (٢٧) وهـو ابـن عـمّ

1 Qur'an 96:1,5

خديجة . . . وكان تنصّر في الجاهلية وكان يكتب الكتاب العربي. (٢٨) فكتب بالعربية من الإنجيل ما شاء الله أن يكتب. (٢٩) فقالت خديجة: أي ابن عمّي! اسمع من ابن أخيك! (٣٠) فقال ورقة: ابن أخي؟ ما ترى؟ (٣٢) فقال رسول الله (صلّى الله عليه وسلّم) ما رأى. (٣٣) فقال ورقة: هذا الناموس الذي أنزل على موسى عليه السلام! (٣٤) يا ليتني فيه جذعًا حين يخرجك قومك! (٣٥) فقال رسول الله (صلّى الله عليه وسلّم): أَوَمُخرجيّ هم؟ (٣١) فقال ورقة: نعم، لم يأتِ أحد بما أتيت به إلّا عودِي وأوذِي. (٣٢) وإنْ يدركني يومك، أنصرك نصرًا مؤزرًا. (٣٣) ثم لم ينشب ورقة أن تُوفي.

Vocabulary

حُلُم	puberty
أجمر	to burn incense
شرارة	spark
وَهَى	to weaken
هدم	to demolish
هاب	to dread, fear
إساءة	sin, offense, misuse
علا	to climb (to go up high)
اختصم	to quarrel
شجر	to fight
سكّة	road, way
فلق	break of dawn
خلاء	isolation
تحنّث	practice religious piety
تعبّد	to engage in worship
تزوّد	to provision
غار حراء	the cave of Hira' (outside Mecca)
غطى	to envelop (here: to crush)
جهد	exertion (here: exhaustion, fatigue)

بادرة ج. بوادر	stirring, sign
ارتجف/ رجف	to shake, shudder
زَمّل	to cover, wrap (Classical use)
خشي على	to be afraid, worried for someone
أخزى	to disgrace
صَدَقَ	to tell the truth
قرى	to treat hospitably
تنصّر[2]	to become a Christian
إنجيل	the Gospel, the Bible
الناموس	the Archangel Gabriel
موسى	Moses
جَذَع	young man
عُودِيَ	to be antagonized by someone
أُوذِيَ	to be hurt or harmed by someone
مؤزرًا	aided, supported
لم ينشب	didn't take long, didn't delay

Comprehension Exercises

Answer the following questions in complete Arabic sentences, according to the author's opinions:

١. كيف حلّ رسول الله (ﷺ) الاختصام بين قبائل مكة حول موضع ركن الكعبة؟

____

____

2 See Cultural and Contextual Clues section below.

٢. كيف كان يتعبد الرسول (ﷺ)؟

---

٣. أين هبط الوحي على الرسول (ﷺ)؟

---

٤. كيف أبلغ الرسول (ﷺ) زوجته خديجة بخبر الوحي؟ وماذا فعلت؟

---

٥. مَن ورقة بن نوفل؟ وكيف فَسّر رؤيا الرسول (ﷺ)؟

Interpreting the Text

١. ما صور العدالة في حُكم رسول الله (ﷺ) في قضية ركن الكعبة؟

---

٢. ما علامات النبوة التي تحلّى بها رسول الله (ﷺ)؟

---

٣. ما معنى قول النبي (ﷺ) «ما أنا بقارئ»؟

---

٤. ما موقف السيدة خديجة عند نزول الوحي؟ وما الحكمة منه؟

---

٥. هل يُعدُّ ورقة بن نوفل من الصحابة؟

Style and Technique

1. In line 6, the verb كادَ (conjugated كِدتُ/ يَـكادُ) belongs to a special set of verbs known as أخـوات كادَ (similar to the concept of أخـوات كانَ). One of the functions of these verbs is as أفعـال المقاربـة (verbs of approaching). These verbs take a verbal sentence as predicate or خـبر and indicate that the action is about to happen, or on the verge of happening. When used in the past tense, as in this case, they indicate that the condition almost or nearly occurred.

Other verbs in this group include أوشك (to be on the verge of, very often used in a prepositional phrase – على وشك) and كرب (to be near to doing something).

I almost died!	كِدتُ أموت!
The government is on the verge of collapse.	الحكومة أوشكت على السقوط.
My patience almost ran out.	كَرِبَ صبري أنْ ينفذ.

2. The section from lines 12 to 20 makes extensive use of the connector ف. This particle has multiple uses that translate differently in English. Recognizing the use in each case is important in understanding the narrative in this section. ف can mean "then," indicating an immediately following action. As such, it narrates events in rapid succession to show urgency and intensity. The sequence from 18 to 20 uses this function to show the rapid, frightening interaction between the Angel Gabriel and the Prophet (ﷺ). This particle can also show cause, meaning "and so" or "so then." This is what is meant in line 13, for example, when the Prophet (ﷺ) is described as taking up habitual actions after the first revelation comes. Here, a rapid sequence of individual actions is not intended. ف can also provide elaborating information as is the case in line 12, which describes in general how all the revelations came. It can also be a particle of resumption, indicating that a previous thought that was interrupted is now continuing. This is the use in line 16, where the *haal* construction[3] وهو في غار حراء, which tells us where the Prophet (ﷺ) was, interrupts the narrative action, and the second ف resumes it.
3. The word ذوات in line 14 is the plural of ذات, which, like its masculine counterpart ذو causes difficulty for English speakers. These words are nouns, typically used in *idaafa*, which translate literally as "possessor of . . . ," although a literal translation would be quite

---

3 See Lesson 14 for more on the *haal* construction.

awkward in English. The use here is fairly typical: الليـالي ذوات العـدد means "nights having number," or in more idiomatic translation "many nights."

4. In the narrative in lines 12–20, following the referent pronouns can be tricky. In line 14, the Prophet (ﷺ) is described as spending many nights in devotion in the cave. We are then told in line 15 he would habitually return to his wife and provision himself لمثلها. Context tells us that the هـا refers to the nights and that he was provisioning himself for more "nights like those." Referring to Khadija in this case would not make sense.
5. The particle قَـد in line 23 has several uses in the past tense. It can mean an action was already completed before another action took place:

   مثال: عندما وصل الأستاذ إلى الصف كان سمير قد ذهب.

   It can mean an action was *about* to take place:

   مثال: قد بدأت المؤتمر.

   It can also be used for emphasis, as is the case here – "you *certainly* must have been worried about me (قـد خشـيت علـيّ)!" Note that its present tense meaning—something *might* happen—is completely different.
6. The particle لَيْـتَ in line 24 has the meaning of "if only" and expresses an unobtainable wish. It is often used with يـا. This is one of the particles known as أخـوات إنّ (*inna* and her sisters). These are followed immediately by a noun or pronoun (as is the case here) which is the subject of the wish and will be in the accusative case. In this example, Waraqa is wishing "If only I were a young man" when the persecution he predicts begins.

Using Cultural and Contextual Clues to Understand the Text

1. The Ka'ba (the black structure at the center of the Grand Mosque in Mecca) is known to have been a center of pagan worship and

pilgrimage before Islam. In Islamic tradition, the Ka'ba is believed to have been established by Abraham and his son Ishmael and that true worshipers of God (known as Hanifs, or الحنفيّة) preserved it as a center of monotheistic religion until its corruption. The leader of the Quraysh in this account, al-Walid bin Mughira, one of the richest merchants in Mecca, was an early opponent of Islam and one of the five main offenders of Muhammad(ﷺ) . Despite his reference to God, he is interested in repairing the Ka'ba for pagan worship.

2. Lines 15–20 refer to the Angel Gabriel (جبريل), who revealed the Qur'an to the Prophet Muhammad (ﷺ), although he is not mentioned by name. The word المَلَك here is the reference to him. The Angel Gabriel is mentioned by name in only three verses of the Qur'an. In other verses, mention is made without his name. Other details about the Angel Gabriel come to us through Prophetic traditions (Hadith).
3. In line 20, the author quotes only verses 1 and 5 of the 96th sura, with حتى بلغ (until he reached) in between. Here, he means that the angel recited all five verses. These five verses are the first revelation to Muhammad (ﷺ).
4. Waraqa ibn Nawfal was a cousin of Khadija and a more distant relative of Muhammad (ﷺ)—thus referred to here as a cousin of both. He is traditionally believed to have been one of four men of Mecca who rejected paganism and sought true monotheism. Waraqa emerged from that experience as a Christian priest (possibly an Assyrian Christian). The incident described here closely follows the Hadith of the event related by 'A'isha, the last wife of the Prophet (ﷺ). He is thus respected as the first man to confirm Muhammad's (ﷺ) prophethood.
5. The verb تنصّر (line 27) is related to نصراني (plural نصارى), a term used in the Qur'an to refer to Christians. It was a common Arabic word for "Christian" used by authors of the Classical era. This term is generally considered offensive today, however, as the term مسيحي is preferred.

Analysis and Argument

Discuss the following questions based on the evidence in these excerpts and your knowledge of the historical events.

١. هل سمي عصر ما قبل الإسلام بالعصر الجاهلي لجهل العرب وقتها بالعلم والدين أم لجهلهم بالأخلاق والقِيم؟
٢. ناقشوا باختصار ظهور الإسلام وتعاليمه وأثر هذه التعاليم في المجتمع العربي قديمًا وحديثًا.
٣. يكشف الحوار بين محمد (ﷺ) وورقة بن نوفل عن علاقة خاصة بين المسيحية والإسلام، حلّلوا هذه المقولة.
٤. لماذا كان معظم الرُّسل والأنبياء ضحايا للظلم والعدوان؟ اذكروا بعض الأمثلة.
٥. شاهدوا الفيلم العربي التاريخي «فَجْر الإسلام» على يوتيوب وقارنوا بين قصة الفيلم وما قرأتموه في «كتاب المغازي»

Research and Presentation

From the reading and your background knowledge, you should have a general idea of the thrust of this text. Based on this, prepare a 2–3-minute presentation to reflect on the following topic:

نزول الإسلام في الجزيرة العربية وأثره في الحضارات

To prepare your presentation, incorporate some of the following expressions:

to make a comparison between . . . and . . .	وازَنَ بين . . . وبين . . .
the weight of the evidence, the preponderance of the evidence	رُجْحان الأدلة
argument, evidence	حُجّة
conclusion, deduction	استنتاج

2

Adab—al-Jahiz

الدرس الثاني – الجاحظ

أبو عثمانَ عمرو بن بحرِ بنِ محبوب، المُلقَّبُ بالجاحِظ (١٥٩هـ/ ٧٧٦م – ٢٥٥هـ/ ٨٦٨م). وُلد في البصرةِ بالعراق ولُقّبَ بالجاحظ لجحوظ عينيه، كما أنّه يُلقّب بإمام أدباء العصر العباسي الثاني. نشأ الجاحظ يتيمًا وفقيرًا، ولكنه أصبح غنيًّا بعلمه. فقد طلَبَ العلمَ في سِن مبكرة، وتَتلْمذ على يد جهابذة علماء اللغة في عصره. وكان الجاحظ حاد الذكاء، ذا جلدٍ وصرامةٍ وقدرةٍ فائقة على الكلام. كما تميزَ بسرعة البديهة وبأسلوبه البارع الرصين في كتبه ومؤلفاته. كتاب البخلاء من أروع مؤلّفات الجاحظ وتتجلى فيه روح الفكاهة والسخرية التي كان يتميز بها. وللكتاب قيمة علمية وأدبية كبيرة؛ فهو يغوص في طبائع النفس البشرية وأسرارها وسلوكها، كما يحتوي على أسماء أعلام ومشاهير ذلك العصر وأسماء المدن والبلدان وصفات أهلها، علاوة على كثير من الأبيات الشعرية وقطوف الأحاديث النادرة. وبينما كان الجاحظ جالسًا في مكتبتِه في يوم من الأيام سقط على رأسه صفٌّ مِنَ الكُتبِ وفاضت روحه[1] أسفل كتبه التي عاش عمره شغوفًا بها.

Prediction and Scanning

Based on the context and background given above, record your predictions as to whether you expect to find the issues listed below addressed in the text. Be prepared to discuss your predictions with classmates. Then, reading through the excerpts in the next section quickly, without the use of a dictionary, indicate whether your predictions were correct

1 تُوفي = he passed away

and where (in which lines) you found the answers. Be prepared to discuss the results with your classmates.

الدلالة	التوقُّع	العبارة
		يركز الكاتب نقده على شعب معين.
		موضوع كتاب البخلاء فكاهي ساخر.
		يعـرض الجاحـظ قصصًـا عـن البخـل، خاصـة البخـل بالطعـام.
		يسـتخدم الكاتـب ألفاظًـا حسـيّة قريبـة مـن العاميـة في رواياتـه.

From the Writings of al-Jahiz

كتاب البخلاء

Al-Jahiz singles out the citizens of Khurasan, and particularly the city of Merv (in present-day Turkmenistan) as examples of poor behavior. As is common in humor, he uses a contrived "Mervite" (مـروَزي) as his straw man for stories of miserliness and false propriety:

(١) يقـول المـروَزيُّ للزائـر إذا أتـاه، وللجليـس إذا طـال جلوسـه: تغديـتَ اليـوم؟ (٢) فـإن قـال: نعـم، قـال: لـو لا أنـك تغديـتَ لغدّيتـك بغـداء طيّـب. (٣) وإن قـال: لا، قـال: لـو كنـتَ تغدّيـتَ لسـقيتك خمسـة أقـداح. (٤) فـلا يصـيرُ في يـده عـلى الوجهـين قليـل ولا كثـير.

Another of his many caricatures of the typical Mervite contrasts the behavior of an Iraqi—someone from the heart of the Abbasid Empire—with his Mervite friend:

(٥) أنّ رجلًا من أهل مرو كان لا يزال يحجّ ويتّجر، وينزل على رجل من أهل العراق، فيُكرمُهُ ويكفيه مؤنته. (٦) ثم كان كثيرًا ما يقول لذلك العراقي: ليتَ أني قد رأيتك بمرو، حتى أكافئك لقديم إحسانك، وما تُجدّد لي من البرّ في كل قدمة. (٧) فأما هٰهُنا فقد أغناك الله عني . . . (٨) فعرضتْ لذلك العراقي بعد دهر طويل حاجةٌ في تلك الناحية، (٩) فكان ممّا هوّن عليه مكابدة السفر ووَحشة الاغتراب، مكان المروَزي هنالك. (١٠) فلمَّا قَدِم مضى نحوه في ثياب سَفره وفي عمامته وقَلَنسُوته وكسائه، ليحطَّ رحلَه عنده، كما يصنع الرجل بثقتِه وموضع أُنسه. (١١) فلمّا وجده قاعدًا في أصحابه، أكبَّ عليه وعانقه، فلم يره أثبته، ولا سأل به سؤال من رآه قط. (١٢) قال العراقي في نفسه: لعلّه إنكاره إيَّاي لمكان القِناع. (١٣) فرمى بقناعه، وابتدأ مُساءَلته، فكان له أنكر. (١٤) فقال: لعله أن يكون إنما أتِيَ من قِبَل العمامة، فنزعها ثم انتسب، وجدَّد مُساءَلته، فوجده أشدّ ما كان إنكارًا. (١٥) قال: لعله إنما أتى من قبل القلنسوة. (١٦) وعَلِم المروزيُّ أنه لم يبقَ شيء يتعلق به المتغافل والمتجاهل، فقال: لو خرجتَ من جِلدك لم أعرفْك!

In yet another example, a Khurasani, who need only be identified by his place of origin, is shown to be not only stingy, but rather dumb as well:

(١٧) قلتُ مرةً لجار كان لي، من أهل خراسان: أعِرْني مِقلاكم فإني أحتاجُ إليه. (١٨) قال: كان لنا مقلى ولكنه سُرق. (١٩) فاستعرتُ من جار لي آخر. (٢٠) فلم يلبث الخراساني أن سَمِع نشيش اللحم في المِقلى، وشمّ الطُّباهج. (٢١) فقال لي، كالمُغضب: ما في الأرض أعجبُ منك! لو كنتَ خبّرتني أنك تريده للحم أو لشحم لوجدني أسرع إليك به!

Many of the stories al-Jahiz relates are from famous personalities in the empire. This story is supposedly related by the great poet Abu Nuwas:

(٢٢) قال أبو نواس: كان معنا في السفينة، ونحن نريد بغداد، رجلٌ من أهل خُراسان، وكان من عُقلائهم وفقهائهم. (٢٣) فكان يأكل وحده. (٢٤) فقلت له: لِمَ تأكل وحدكَ؟ (٢٥) قال: ليس عليَّ في هذا الموضع مسألة. إنما المسألة عليّ من أكل

الجماعــة، لأنّ ذلــك هــو التكلُّــف. (٢٦) وأكلي وحــدي هــو الأصــل، وأكلي مــع غــيري زيــادة في الأصــل.

Vocabulary

المروَزيُّ	the Mervite (one from Merv)
أسقى	to give someone a drink
قَدَح ج. أقداح	goblet, drinking vessel
مؤنة	provisions, supplies
كفى	to meet all needs (here: to supply)
ليتَ[2]	if only . . .
برّ	charity, goodness
أغناك الله عني	May God spare you the need. (i.e., "You are not in need of my help.")
دَهْر	period of time
هوَّن	to make easy, relieve
مكابدة	hardship
وَحشة	loneliness, estrangement
عمامة	turban
قَلَنسُوة	cap
كِساء	garment, cloak
أكبَّ	to approach, embrace
إنكار	denial
القِناع	mask, veil
انتسب	to associate with (here: introduce)
تغافل	to feign or pretend inattention
تجاهل	to feign or pretend ignorance
أعار	to lend

2 For further discussion of ليتَ, see Lesson 1.

مِقلى	frying pan
استعار	to borrow
لم يلبث	did not hesitate
نشيش	sizzle
طباهج	cooking
شحم	fat, grease
عاقل ج. عقلاء	wise person, rationalist
فقيه ج. فقهاء	legal scholar
تكلّف	to burden, to assume a responsibility
أصل	here: the norm, the natural state

Comprehension Exercises

A. Answer the following questions in complete Arabic sentences, based on the excerpts:

١. لماذا سأل المروزي زائره عن الغداء (١-٤)؟

____

____

٢. هل كان المروزي صادقًا في دعوته[3] لصديقه (٥-١٦)؟

____

____

3 Invitation

٣. لماذا نزع العراقي عمامته وقَلَنسُوته (٥-١٦)؟

____

____

٤. هل سُرِقَ مِقلى الخراساني (١٧-٢١)؟

____

____

٥. لماذا كان يفضّل الخراساني تناول الطعام وحده في السفينة (٢٢-٢٦)؟

____

____

B. Are the following statements true in the opinion of the author? If not, why?

١. أهل خراسان من أكرم الناس.

____

____

٢. إعارة الأدوات المنزلية إلى الجيران عادة سائدة في المجتمع العربي.

____

____

٣. الضيافة والكرم من القيم الحميدة التي توارثها[4] العرب.

٤. الطعام جزء مهم من هوية العرب وثقافتهم.

٥. يختلف أهل خراسان في عاداتهم وسلوكهم عن المجتمع العربي.

Interpreting the Text

١. ما الطريف[5] في حكايات الجاحظ من وجهة نظركم؟

4 To inherit
5 Quaint

٢. في القصة الأولى، ماذا كانت أولويات المروزي؟

---

٣. في القصة الثانية، لماذا اعتقد العراقي أنّ المروزي لا يتذكره؟

---

٤. في القصة الثالثة، لماذا نَدِم[6] الخراساني على كذبته؟

---

٥. ما مفهوم التكلف من وجهة نظر الخراساني؟ هل توافقونَه الرأي؟

Style and Technique

1. In line 7, the compound هَهُنـا combines two words. هـا is an attention getter (حـرف تنبيـه) and is not completely necessary. هنـا is the familiar demonstrative pronoun (اسـم إشـارة للقريـب) meaning "here." This compound can also be found written in some texts as هـا هنـا. The preposition فـ is introducing the second half of the

6 To regret

topic-comment statement: أما . . . فـ. The whole sentence is a rather fancy way of saying "But here, you don't need any help," coming after the miser's very fake declaration of the generosity he would offer his friend if they were in Merv.

2. In line 11, the word قَطُّ functions as an adverb, meaning "ever." It is used with negatives to indicate that something absolutely never happened. In this case, the miser is acting as if he has never seen the Iraqi before, with the emphasis on "never." Without voweling, this word will look like the word قَطْ meaning "exactly," "at this point, and no more," better known from the compound فَقَط, which has the same meaning.
3. One of the functions of the Form VI verb (تفاعَل) is to add a sense of insincerity to the meaning of the basic Form I verb. Line 16 includes two examples of this in their participle form: متغافل, from the basic root غفل meaning to neglect or be inattentive to, has the Form VI meaning to pretend not to be aware of something; متجاهل, from the familiar root جهل, to be ignorant, has the Form VI meaning to pretend not to know, both of which the miserly Mervite is doing to his friend. The other major function of this form is a reciprocal action (i.e., two or more subjects interacting or sharing the same action). Even without knowing the dictionary definition of this word, the root, pattern and the context make clear what is happening.
4. 4. The word نشيش (verb نَشّ) in line 20 is an example of an onomatopoeia, resembling the sound of food sizzling. These are common in Arabic and frequently occur with roots that do not have three unique consonants. A particularly common pattern involves a repeated sequence of two consonants: بَرْبَر (to jabber incoherently, to be a barbarian) which replicates the sound of babbling; وَشْوَش (to whisper), which sounds like whispering; شَخْشَخ (to rattle). Looking at the context and the sound will often reveal these.
5. In line 21, the miser is described as speaking كالمغضب. Literally, this is saying "as the one who is angered." This fits with the depiction

of Khurasanis throughout as not only miserly and dishonest, but completely selfish and unaware of how they are perceived. The story makes it clear that the narrator has been wronged and the Khurasani is the guilty party, but here, he reacts as (كـ) the (ال) one and only offended party.

6. As Abu Nuwas uses it in line 22, the verb نريـد means "we were heading toward." While the meaning "to want" is more familiar, this verb also means "to seek or head to." The context—having just said they were on a boat—makes this evident.
7. The compound لِمَ in line 24 is a shortened form of لِمَا. Like the more familiar لماذا, it is a way of asking "why?" This should not be confused with لَمْ, which would look the same without diacritical marks, but which means "did not." The fatha mark in this case is given to clarify, although the context would also make it clear. The Khurasani is eating by himself, so لَمْ would not work in this situation as it would be saying he didn't.

Using Cultural and Contextual Clues to Understand the Text

1. While the Arabic term *al-Adab* (الأدب) is commonly used to refer to literature in general, the term originally refers to the behaviors and knowledge expected of respected members of society. *Adab* writing in the Classical period refers to a specific genre to teach these behaviors. *The Misers* is a leading example of this type of literature, in this case teaching proper behaviors of generosity through the mode of parody of bad examples.
2. The Persian region of Khurasan (today northeastern Iran, northwestern Afghanistan) was noted for its fierce warriors. These gained influence in the Abbasid empire when al-Ma'mun used them to defeat his brother, the caliph al-Amin, and seize power in 813. From this point on, Khurasani, and more generally Turkish, military figures would displace the traditional Arab elite in Bagh-

dad. As the influence of Arabs with roots in the peninsula declined, there was an increasing nostalgia for traditional Arab culture (see Ibn Qutayba, Chapter Four). Al-Jahiz, who extolled the military virtues of the Khurasanis, nonetheless criticizes their manners, in contrast to the legendary generosity and hospitality of the Arabs.

3. Many of these stories involve the idea of "saving face." Throughout *The Misers*, culprits attempt to hide blatantly ungenerous actions with transparent excuses and politeness, although the true lack of hospitality is obvious (the first anecdote in this chapter is an example). Al-Jahiz highlights the ineffectiveness of this type of tactic (as in the first example, where the Mervite's poor hospitality is well known, despite his attempt to hide it with excuses). This reflects a very superficial understanding of face saving, to which al-Jahiz objects.

Analysis and Argument

Al-Jahiz paints a clear picture of good and bad behavior through his use of humor. How would you evaluate his argument based on what you know of cultural expectations in his time and yours?

١. يقولون إن الجاحظ كان يفضل التصريح[7] على التلويح[8] في كتاباته، ما رأيكم؟
٢. هل أسلوب السخرية[9] «التهكّم» وسيلة فعالة لنقد العادات السيئة؟ لماذا؟
٣. هل يختلف مفهوم الضيافة وآدابها في مجتمعاتنا الآن عمّا أورده الجاحظ في قصصه؟ اذكروا بعض الأمثلة.
٤. ابحثوا في يوتيوب عن النسخة المسموعة لكتاب «البخلاء» واستمعوا إلى مقتطف منه أو قصة جديدة، واكتبوا ملخصًا عنها.

7 Explicit
8 Hinting, implying
9 Mockery, parody

Research and Presentation

Based on your reading of al-Jahiz's book, prepare a three-minute presentation on the following statement and question:

كتب المؤلف الفرنسي موليير عن ظاهرة البخل مسرحيته الشهيرة «البخيل» في عام ١٦٦٨م، أي بعد حوالي ثمانية قرون من كتاب «البخلاء» للجاحظ. وقد انتهج موليير الطريقة الكاريكاتيرية نفسها التي صوّر بها الجاحظ البخل والبخلاء.
فهل ثمة علاقة ومغزى[10] وراء ذلك؟

You may use some terms that may be useful for this analysis:

to compare	عقد مقارنة بين
a private matter	مسألة خاصة
universal value	قيمة عامة
to give preference to	فَضَّلَ
to be given precedence	تُعطى الأولوية

10 Significance

3

Philosophy—al-Kindi

الدرس الثالث – الكندي

أبو يوسف يعقوب بن إسحاق الكندي (١٨٥هـ/ ٨٠٥م - ٢٥٦هـ/ ٨٧٣م) علاّمة عربي مسلم، ولد في مدينة الكوفة في العراق التي كانت مهدًا للحضارة العربية حينها. كان الكندي موسوعة في العلم وبحرًا في المعرفة، وعالمًا قلما يجود الزمان بمثله. قال عنه أحد المستشرقين الفرنسيين إنه واحد من أنبغ اثني عشر عبقريًا في التاريخ. تفوّق الكندي في دراسة الفلك والفلسفة والكيمياء والفيزياء والطب والرياضيات والموسيقى وعلم النفس والمنطق أو علم الكلام. كما كان من أوائل العلماء الذين أطلعوا العرب والمسلمين على علوم الفلسفة اليونانية القديمة واجتهد في التوفيق بين الفلسفة والعلوم الإسلامية الأخرى، وبخاصة العلوم الدينية. وقد أثرى الكندي البحث العلمي بمئات المؤلفات التي اندثرت ولم يبق منها سوى العشرات. يلقب الكندي بأبي الفلسفة العربية أو فيلسوف العرب، نظرا لكونه من أعظم الفلاسفة ذوي الأصول العربية ولدوره الرائد في تعريف العرب والمسلمين بعلمي الفلسفة والمنطق.

Prediction and Scanning

Based on the context and background given above, record your predictions as to whether you expect the author to agree with the following statements. Be prepared to discuss your predictions with classmates. Then, reading through the excerpts in the next section quickly, without the use of a dictionary, indicate whether your predictions were correct and where (in which lines) you found the answers. Again, be prepared to discuss the results with your classmates.

الدلالة	التوقُّع	العبارة
		يجب علينا احترام الفلاسفة والمفكرين من الحضارات القديمة.
		لا يستطيع أحد أن يفهم حقيقة الأشياء حولنا بمعزل عن الدين.
		دراسة الفلسفة القديمة ونظرياتها لزامٌ على الجميع سواء اتفقوا أم اختلفوا معها.
		حاول الكندي التوفيق بين العقل والنقل وبين الدين والفلسفة.

From the Writings of al-Kindi

في الفلسفة الأولى، الفن الأول

Al-Kindi begins by discussing what the proper attitude to the philosophers of previous (i.e., non-Muslim) civilizations should be:

(١) ومن أوجب الحق ألا نذم أحدًا ممن كان أحد أسباب منافعنا الصغار الهزلية، (٢) فكيف بالذين هم أكثر أسباب منافعنا العظام الحقيقية الجدية. (٣) فإنهم وإن قصروا عن بعض الحق، فقد كانوا لنا أنسابًا وشركاء فيما أفادونا من ثمار فكرهم، التي صارت لنا سبلًا وآلات مؤدية إلى علم كثير مما قصروا من نيل حقيقته. (٤) وسيما إذ هو بَيّن عندنا، وعند المبرزين من المتفلسفين قبلنا من غير أهل لساننا، إنه لم ينل الحق، بما يستأهل الحق أحد من الناس بجهد طلبه، ولا أحاط به جميعهم، (٥) بل كل واحد منهم إما لم ينل منه شيئًا، وإما نال منه شيئًا يسيرًا بالإضافة إلى ما يستأهل الحق. (٦) فإذا جمع يسير ما نال كل واحد من النائلين من الحق منهم اجتمع من ذلك شيء له قدر جليل.

He then continues on his main project of explaining how earlier pagan philosophers discovered universal truth, despite lacking the religious truth:

(٧) أما أرسطوطاليس مبرز اليونانيين في الفلسفة، فقال: ينبغي أن نشكر آباء الذين أتوا بشيء من الحق، إذ كانوا سبب كونهم، فضلًا عن أنهم سبب لهم. (٨) وإذ هم سبب لنا إلى نيل الحق. (٩) فما أحسن ما قال في ذلك. (١٠) وينبغي لنا ألّا نستحي من استحسان الحق، واقتناء الحق من أين أتى، وإن أتى من الأجناس القاصية عنا، والأمم المباينة، فإنه لا شيء أولى بطالب الحق من الحق. (١١) وليس يبخس الحق، ولا يصغر بقائله ولا بالآتي به. (١٢) ولا أحد بخس الحق؛ بل كان يشرفه الحق.

He explains why it is a duty for all seekers of truth to pursue this knowledge, even from pagan sources:

(١٣) فواجب إذن التمسك بهذه القنية النفيسة عند ذوي الحق، وأن نسعى في طلبها بغاية جهدنا، (١٤) وذلك باضطرار يجب على ألسنة المضادين لها اقتناؤها، (١٥) وذلك أنهم لا يخلون من أن يقولوا إن اقتناءها يجب أو لا يجب، (١٦) فإن قالوا إنه يجب وجب طلبها عليهم، وإن قالوا إنها لا يجب وجب عليهم أن يحضروا علّة ذلك، (١٧) وأن يعطوا على ذلك برهانًا، وإعطاء العلة والبرهان من قُنية علم الأشياء بحقائقها. (١٨) فواجب إذن طلب هذه القُنية بألسنتهم، والتمسك بها اضطرار عليهم.

Al-Kindi launches a harsh reproof of the religious and political figures of his day who opposed his exploration of ancient philosophy:

(١٩) نلزم في كتابنا هذا عاداتنا في جميع موضوعاتنا من إحضار ما قاله القدماء توقيا سوء تأويل كثير من المتسمين بالنظر في دهرنا من أهل الغربة عن الحق، وإن تتوجوا بتيجان الحق من غير استحقاق: لضيق فطنتهم عن أساليب الحق، وقلة معرفتهم بما يستحق ذو الجلالة في الرأي والاجتهاد في الأنفاع العامة للكل، (٢٠) الشاملة لهم، ولدرانة الحسد المتمكن من أنفسهم البهيمية والحاجب بسدف سجوفه أبصار فكرهم عن نور الحق، (٢١) ووضعهم ذوي الفضائل الإنسانية—التي قصروا عن نيلها وكانوا منها في الأطراف الشاسعة—لموضع الأعداء الحربية الواترة

(٢٢) ذبًّا عن كراسيهم المزورة التي نصبوها عن غير استحقاق (٢٣) بل للترؤُّس والتجارة بالدين وهم عدماء الدين، لأن من تجر بشيء باعه، ومن باع شيئًا لم يكن له، (٢٤) فمن تجر بالدين لم يكن له، ويحق أن يتعرى من الدين من عاند قُنية علم الأشياء بحقائقها وسماها كفرًا.

Vocabulary

ذمّ	to revile, disparage
قصر	to lack, fall short of
أنساب	predecessors, lineage
يستأهل	to merit, deserve
أحاط	to grasp, encompass
نال	to obtain
أرسطوطاليس	Aristotle
استحى	to be ashamed
استحسان	approval, acclaim
اقتناء	acquisition
قاصٍ/ القاصي	distant
بخس	to depreciate, disparage
قُنية	acquisition
نفيس	precious
مضادّون لـ	adversaries of
لا يخلون	they cannot avoid (i.e., they must)
حصر	to narrow, restrict (here, meaning to identify)
عِلّة	reason
تاج ج. تيجان	crown
فطنة	astuteness, understanding
درانة	withered pasture
بهيمي	beastly, animal
سدف	to darken
سجوف	veils, curtains

شاسع	remote
ذب	to defend

Comprehension Exercises

Answer the following questions in complete Arabic sentences, according to the author's opinions:

١. ما موقف الكاتب من الفلاسفة القدماء؟

____

____

٢. ماذا قال أرسطوطاليس عن شيوخه[1]؟

____

____

٣. ما النصيحة التي يجب اتباعها عند تقييم دور الفلاسفة؟

____

____

1 Masters

٤. لماذا يحتاج معارضو الفلسفة القديمة إلى دراستها وفهمها؟

٥. بماذا اتّهم الكاتب بعض الزعماء الدينيين في عصره؟

Interpreting the Text

١. ما الطريق الصحيح لمعرفة الحقّ من وجهة نظر الكندي؟

٢. في رأيكم، ما سبب كتابة الكندي لهذا النص؟

٣. ما الفرق بين المعرفة الدينية والمعارف الدنيوية؟

٤. لماذا استشهد الكندي بأقوال الفيلسوف أرسطوطاليس؟ وعلامَ يدلّ ذلك؟

٥. ما المنهج الذي اقترحه الكندي للمُثقّف المسلم في عصره؟

Style and Technique

1. At the end of line 10, al-Kindi is using أولى بـ... من as a comparative meaning "of greater worth, taking precedence." The preposition بـ in this case means "for" and is attached to طالب الحق meaning the seeker of truth. Putting this together, the statement means that nothing takes precedence, for the seeker of truth, over the truth itself.
2. The structure of the argument in line 14–18 can be difficult to identify due to its subtleties and the repetition of synonyms. The use of the phrase وذلك refers to his statement in line 13 about the necessity of accepting this inherited knowledge and pursuing it wholeheartedly. Having made his claim in line 13, al-Kindi then argues that even the opponents (المضادين لها) must accept it (اقتناؤها), according to their own logic, or tongues (على ألسنة). The two synonyms for "necessary" in proximity in line 14 refer to different things. The first, باضطرار, means "it is necessarily true that . . . "; the second, يجب, refers to the things that he said in line 13 were necessary. In line 15, he is giving the scholars two choices—either they embrace the knowledge as necessary or provide an argument why it isn't. Line 16 discusses the two options, using the particle

إنْ (if) to introduce both. English commonly uses a "then" to introduce the result of "if." This is often expressed in Arabic with the connector فـ, but in this case, it is implied, coming in between يجب and وجب in both statements. Line 18 then summarizes his point.

3. Al-Kindi makes extensive use in the last section of the phrase من غير استحقاق. The phrase you may recognize from the roots as meaning "undeservedly." Rather than using an adverb or adjective construction, which might be simpler (وهم ليسوا مستحقين), he is using the *masdar* form (استحقاق, worthiness). The word غير, as you likely recognize, means "other than" and is frequently used in the sense of "not." Here, he is saying they have received their honors from a position of unworthiness, or a lack of worthiness. A simpler, less stylistic way of saying this would be بدون استحقاق. This way is slightly less direct. Similar uses of this construction include من غير معرفة and غير جائز.

Using Cultural and Contextual Clues to Understand the Text

1. Al-Kindi lived at a time when the introduction of (primarily Greek) writings from non-Muslim civilizations into the Caliphate began on a large scale. This was largely due to the lands that were conquered in the first century of Islam. Al-Kindi was a leader in the translation movement and was appointed by the caliph to the famous "House of Wisdom"—the royal library and research center. This movement faced opposition from religious traditionalists, who opposed the inclusion of ideas created by essentially pagan sources, and rationalists, and advocated using original reasoning to derive knowledge. Al-Kindi is addressing both camps in this work.
2. Medieval Philosophy could be a surprisingly dangerous field of endeavor. As the leading thinkers received the financial support of the caliphs and had enormous political influence, the competition between them could be quite vicious. Al-Kindi was appointed by

the caliph al-Ma'mun (813–33) but was eventually beaten and dismissed by the caliph al-Mutawakkil (847–61), because of intrigues by a rival group of philosophers. Al-Kindi would spend the rest of his life without a political office, being very bitter and disdainful of those intellectuals who held high positions. His harsh critiques in the last section of this reading are directed at those.

Analysis and Argument

A. Do you think al-Kindi would agree or disagree with the following statements, and why or why not?

١. الترجمة ركيزة[2] أساسية في تعلّم اللغات الحديثة والقديمة.

____

____

٢. من الممكن أن تتوافق التعاليم الدينية مع العلمانية.

____

____

2 Pillar

٣. يمكن التغاضي[3] عن انحدار[4] مستوى الأمانة العلمية عند الباحثين.

____

____

٤. تتطلّب النزاهة العلمية احترام الحقوق الفكرية والعلمية والأدبية للباحثين الآخرين.

____

____

٥. الناقد الجيد هو من يعرض رأيه بموضوعية وبعد دراسة دقيقة متأنية[5] للموضوع.

____

____

B. Discuss your opinions on the following questions raised by al-Kindi's writing:

١. يؤمن الكندي بأهمية دراسة أعمال المفكرين بلغتهم الأصلية. هل دراسة العلوم باللغة الأصلية تؤدي إلى فهم أفضل؟ كيف ذلك؟
٢. يشدّد الكندي على ضرورة احترام أفكار السلف حتى وإن أخطؤوا. كيف يوازن الباحث بين هذا الرأي والتفكير النقدي ونتائجه الإبداعية؟
٣. ينتقد الكندي المثقفين والعلماء الذين يشاركون في الحياة السياسة. بينما نجد في عصرنا الحالي أنّ البحث العلمي والثقافي قد يعتمد على دعم الدولة وحكومتها. كيف يستطيع المفكر والباحث المعاصر العمل في هذا المناخ بشفافية[6] ونزاهة؟

---

3 To let pass, condone
4 Degeneration
5 Careful, caution
6 Transparency

٤. تظهر في كتابات الكندي أمثلة تكشف عن تأثره بالتيارات الفكرية الفلسفية في عصره. اذكروا بعض الأمثلة وحلّلوها.

Research and Presentation

The issues that al-Kindi discusses are not limited to his time only. We can see echoes of the same controversies today. Based on your reading and discussion of al-Kindi in this chapter, prepare a 3–4-minute Arabic presentation with your position on the following question:

هل من الممكن أن يتآلف[7] الدين بأحكامه وثوابته مع الفكر الفلسفي بتحرُّره ومتغيراته؟

To present a convincing argument, it is helpful not to paint the situation as being unambiguously one way or the other. In this case, it can be useful to argue that in some cases the assertion above is true and in others it is not, and then draw an overall conclusion. Some of the following terms may help in constructing this type of argument:

to admit, concede (a fact)	اعترف بـ
there are some exceptions	هناك بعض الاستثناءات
despite	رغم أنّ
likewise	ونظير هذا

7 To come together, co-exist in harmony

4

Ethnicity in Islam—Ibn Qutayba

الدرس الرابع – ابن قتيبة

هو أبو محمد عبد الله بن مسلم بن قتيبة (٢١٣هـ/ ٨٢٨م - ٢٧٦هـ/ ٨٩٩م) من أشهر أعلام القرن الثالث الهجري في الأدب واللغة والأخبار وعلوم القرآن والحديث. لا يُعرف بالتحديد المدينة التي وُلد بها ابن قتيبة، ولكن يرجح المؤرخون أنه ولد بالكوفة وانتقل إلى مدينة بغداد في سن صغيرة؛ حيث نشأ بها وتتلمذ على يد علمائها النوابغ. وقد شهد ابن قتيبة مجد الدولة العباسية، وعاصر صراع الثقافات العربية والفارسية وغيرها، وما نتج عنه من ظهور الحركة الشعوبية المعادية لكل ما هو عربي. كما عاش في فترة صعود الفكر المعتزلي وسقوطه، وقد كان لهذه الأحداث والتغييرات أثر بالغ على أفكاره ومؤلفاته المتنوعة. وقد عبّر ابن قتيبة عن نفسه حين قال: من أراد أن يكون عالمًا فليطلب فنًّا واحدًا، ومن أراد أن يكون أديبًا فليتسع في العلوم.

Prediction and Scanning

Based on the context and background given above, record your predictions as to whether you expect the author will agree with the following statements. Be prepared to discuss your predictions with classmates. Then, reading through the excerpts in the next section quickly, without the use of a dictionary, indicate whether your predictions were correct and where (in which lines) you found the answers. Again, be prepared to discuss the results with your classmates.

العبارة	التوقُّع	الدلالة
تميَّزَ العرب عن حكّام الفرس بما لهم من فضائل في الحكم.		
هناك حِقبة تاريخية محددة توسّع فيها الفُرس في حكمهم.		
كان لقبيلة قريش منزلة ومكانة رفيعة قبل ظهور الإسلام وبعده.		
كان للفرس والعجم حضارة عظيمة توارثها العرب بعد ذلك.		

From the Writings of Ibn Qutayba

فضل العرب والتنبيه على علومها، الجزء الأول

After reviewing the genealogy of Arabs and Persians, Ibn Qutayba concluded that they share the same ancestry from Shem, the son of Noah, but then goes on:

(١) فالعرب وفارس يتساوون في هذه الجملة، وتفضلها العرب بعدها بأنّها من ولد إسماعيل بن إبراهيم فهي أدنى من خليل الله دناوةً وأمسّ به رحمًا. (٢) ثمّ تتساوى العرب وفارس في أن الفريقين ملكوا، وتفضلها العرب بأنّ قواعد ملكها نبوّة وقواعد ملك فارس استلاب وغلبة. (٣) وتفضلها العرب بأنّ ملكها ناسخ وملك فارس منسوخ، (٤) وتفضلها بأنّ ملكها متصل بالساعة وملك فارس محدود، (٥) وتفضلها العرب بأنّ ملكها واغل في أقاصي البلاد داخل في آفاق الأرض، وملك فارس شطّيّة منه (٦) ليس فيه الشام والجزيرة ولا خراسان في أكثر مددهم ولا اليمن إلاّ في أيام وَهْرِز وسيف بن ذي يزن.

Ibn Qutayba continues with the Arabs superior history:

(٧) كان لقريش بيت الله الحرام العتيق المنصور من الجبابرة بالطير الأبابيل، (٨) لم يزالوا وُلاته وسدنته والقائمين لأموره والمعظمين لشعاره. (٩) وكان يقال لهم أهل الله وجيران الله؛ لنزولهم الحرم وجوارهم البيت. (١٠) وكان منهم بقايا من الحنفيّة يتوارثونها عن إسماعيل صلّى الله عليه وسلم (١١) منها حجّ البيت الحرام وزيارته والختان والغُسل والطلاق والعِتق وتحريم ذوات المحارم بالقرابة والرضاع والصهر. (١٢) وقد كان حاجب بن زرارة وَفَدَ على كسرى، فرأى العجم ينكحون الأخوات والبنات (١٣) فسوّلت له نفسه التأسّي بهم والدخول في ملّتهم فنكح ابنته ثم ندم على ذلك . . .

With the coming of Islam, the superiority of the Arabs is cemented:

(١٤) ثمّ أتى الله بالإسلام، فابتعث منها النبي صلّى الله عليه وسلّم سيّد الأنبياء وخاتم الرسل، وناسخ كلّ شرعة وحائز كلّ فضيلة (١٥) فنشر عددها وجمع كلمتها وأمدّها بملائكته وأيّدها بقوّته (١٦) ومكّن لها في البلاد وأوطأها رقاب الأمم، (١٧) وجعل فيها خلافة النبوّة ثمّ الإمامة خالدة تالدة حتى يأتي المسيح عليه السلام فيصلّي خلف الإمام منها فاردة لا يستطيع أحد أن يأتي بمثلها. (١٨) وخاطبها يومئذ لا عجم فيها فقال: كُنْتُم خَيْرَ أُمَّةٍ أُخْرِجَتْ لِلنَّاسِ، فلها فضل هذا الخطاب . . . (١٩) ومَن ذا مِن المسلمين يصحّ إسلامه ويصحّ عقده يقدّم على قريش أو يعادل بها. (٢٠) وقد قضى الله لها بالفضل على جميع الخليقة؛ إذ جعل الأئمة منها والإمامة فيها مقصورة عليها ألّا تكون لغيرها والإمامة هي التقدّم، (٢١) وهذا نصّ ليس فيه حيلة لمتأوّل، (٢٢) قال رسول الله صلّى الله عليه وسلّم: الأئمة من قريش.

Ibn Qutayba concedes that the Persians once had a great civilization, but this has now passed to the Arabs:

(٢٣) ولم يدّع أحد أنّه كان للعرب في دولة العجم مثل مُلكها وأموالها وعددها وسلاحها وحريرها وديباجها، (٢٤) فيحتاج أن يذكر فيلة أبرويز وجواريه وفرشه. (٢٥) وقد كان هذا لأولئك كما ذكر، (٢٦) ثمّ جعله الله لهؤلاء فابتزّوه واستلبوه والتَحَوهم كما يُلتحى القضيب، (٢٧) والناسخ لأفضل من المنسوخ.

Vocabulary

في هذه الجملة	in all of this (a reference to what he has just discussed)
دناوةٌ	closeness
أمسّ	strongest contact
نبوّة	prophethood
استلاب	pillaging
نسخ	here: to abrogate, supersede
الساعة	here: refers to the Hour of Resurrection
واغل	deep-rooted
شظيّة	a splinter, sliver
وَهْرِز	Wahrez, a Persian general who conquered Yemen
سيف بن ذي يزن	Sayf ibn Dhi Yazan, Persian rebel who fought against Ethiopians in Yemen
بيت الله الحرام	The Holy Kaʿba in Mecca
الطير الأبابيل	flock of birds
الحنفيّة	Hanifs (believed to be followers of the true religion in Arabia before the coming of Islam)
الختان	circumcision
عِتق	freeing slaves
تحريم	prohibiting
حاجب بن زرارة	Hajib ibn Zurara (an envoy sent to Korsow, in Persia)
العجم	Persians
نكح	to marry
سوّلت له نفسه	to be tempted
ندم	to regret
حائز	possessor

أوطأ	to trample
رقاب	necks
خاطب	to address, announce
متأوّل	interpreter
إمام ج. أئمة	imam
ديباج	brocade
أبرويز	Khorsow Parviz, Persian Shah
ابتزّ	to extort
التحى	to remove bark (Classical use)
القضيب	branch

Comprehension Exercises

A. Answer the following questions in complete Arabic sentences, based on the excerpts:

١. لماذا يفضّل الكاتب ملك العرب على ملك العجم؟

___

___

٢. ما التعاليم الدينية التي اتّبعتها[1] قريش قبل ظهور الإسلام؟

___

___

1 To follow

٣. ما الشيء الذي ندم عليه حاجب بن زرارة؟

____

____

٤. كيف تغيرت مكانة[2] قريش بعد ظهور الإسلام؟

____

____

٥. لماذا تميّزت قريش عن الأمم الأخرى؟

____

____

B. Are the following statements true in the opinion of the author? If not, why?

١. استمدّت[3] الإمبراطورية الفارسية قوتها من رسالتها الدينية.

____

____

2 Status
3 To derive

٢. كانت لقبيلة قريش امتيازات اجتماعية كثيرة قبل ظهور الإسلام وبعده.

---

٣. كان أهل قريش يؤدون شعيرة[4] الحج قبل الإسلام.

---

٤. الفرس يتساوون مع العرب في المكانة والمنْزِلة.

---

٥. جاء الإسلام لتصحيح المفاهيم والمعتقدات الجاهلية المغلوطة[5].

---

4 Rite
5 False

Interpreting the Text

١. ما أساس قيام الدول من وجهة نظر ابن قتيبة؟

---

٢. لماذا عقد ابن قتيبة هذه المقارنة بين العرب والفرس؟

---

٣. ما المغزى[6] من قصة حاجب بن زرارة وتجربته؟

---

٤. ماذا يقصد الكاتب بقوله: نشر عددها وجمع كلمتها؟

Style and Technique

1. In line one, Ibn Qutayba says "وتَفْضُلها العرب"; the verb here is the Form I فَضُلَ meaning: تميّز = [to be] distinguished, as in:

6 Significance

قوله تعالى:وَنُفَضِّلُ بَعْضَهَا عَلَى بَعْضٍ فِي الأُكُلِ[7]. The verb is conjugated for the feminine gender because of the word "العرب," which can be treated as masculine or feminine in Arabic because it is one of a type of plural names (اسم الجمع) that may not have a singular counterpart. Some other examples include:

روم ونساء وعرب ورهط وقوم . . . . .إلخ

2. Lines 19–21 form a long and somewhat complex rhetorical question. The question makes extensive use of the *haal* construction to elaborate on the conditions under which the question is asked. The key is to separate this information out and identify who the subject is and what the verbs are. The subject is found at the beginning with "مَن ذا من المسلمين" (who among Muslims). The next part is further refinement: "true in his faith and belief," made by two statements using variations of صحّ (to be true or healthy). The conditions we're being asked about appear in the verbs يقدّم على (put ahead of) and يعادل بـ (equal to), meaning "put ahead of or equal to the Quraysh." What follows in line 20 is a long *haal* construction citing the evidence for the excellence of the Quraysh; that is, the condition despite which one would be doing this. The word قد at the beginning of line 20 signals that these are conditions already in place, and thus the context in which the question is being asked is already firmly set. The question ends in line 21 with the final piece of refinement that the text establishing this—the Qur'an—is unambiguous. In simpler form: "What true Muslim would put anyone ahead of or equal to the Quraysh?"
3. In line 23, the pronoun attached to أنّ is what is called a "dummy pronoun" or ضمير الشأن. This is a pronoun that refers to something that has not been mentioned before, unlike the normal use for a pronoun. Because أنّ cannot grammatically be followed by a verb, if

7 Qur'an 13:4

the speaker wants to use a verb after أنّ or إنّ, they add the pronoun هُ. This pronoun is not translated, so line 23 would read "no one claims that . . ." not "no one claims that he . . ." The dummy pronoun can be thought of as representing the fact that will follow.

Using Cultural and Contextual Clues to Understand the Text

1. Ibn Qutayba makes several references to Muslim beliefs that would be easily recognized by his readers. In line 1, he cites the lineage from إسماعيل بن إبراهيم (Ishmael, son of Abraham) as proof of the Arabs' superiority. Ishmael, the son of Abraham, is believed from the Bible and Qur'an to be the progenitor of the Arab tribes, while his half-brother Isaac is the ancestor of the Israelites. Islam and Judaism differ on which son was offered as a sacrifice to God, and therefore, which branch of the family is preferred.
2. In line 5, the contrast between the Persian empire being limited and the Arabs' unlimited references the concept of Dar al-Islam, a non-Qur'anic but prevalent belief during the Caliphate in which the world is divided into two spheres or domains, one under the rule of Muslim rulers (Dar al-Islam or Dar al-Salam) and the other not (Dar al-Harb). Additionally, in line 3, he claims that the rule of the Arabs will last until الساعة, a reference to the Hour of Judgment, or the end of the world.
3. Line 10 refers to the Hanifs (الحنفيّة), which the Qur'an identifies as true believers in God before the coming of Islam, who were neither Christians nor Jews. Ibn Qutayba refers to the belief that true worship passed from Abraham to Ishmael and to the Arabs.
4. The Quraysh tribe (the tribe of the Prophet Muhammad) had been the protectors of the Ka'ba shrine in Mecca (identified here as بيت الله) before it became a center of Muslim worship. Line 7 refers to the Qur'an 105:3, in which God sends a flock of birds to defend theKa'ba.

Analysis and Argument

Ibn Qutayba has a lot to say about what makes one group superior to another. How would you evaluate his ideas, based on your knowledge of history?

١. فاضلوا بين الدولة الدينية والدولة العِلمانية من وجهة نظر ابن قتيبة وبين بعض التحولات السياسية في عصرنا الحالي.
٢. هل ترون ابن قتيبة متحيزا[8] في أحكامه وآرائه؟ لماذا؟
٣. قضية الناسخ والمنسوخ في القرآن الكريم من القضايا التي أولاها[9] علماء الدين اهتمامًا كبيرًا. ناقشوا هذه العبارة.
٤. اقرأوا سورة «قريش» من القرآن الكريم، وابحثوا عن أسباب نزولها.

Research and Presentation

Based on your understanding of Ibn Qutayba's ideas, prepare a 3–4 minute argument on the following question:

كتاب «الشعر والشعراء» من المؤلفات الأدبية القيّمة أيضًا لابن قتيبة التي ناقش فيها قضية القديم والحديث في الشعر.
ابحثوا في منحى[10] هذا الكتاب، واكتبوا ملخصًا عنه متضمنًا الآراء النقدية لابن قتيبة في هذه القضية.

You may try to use some of the following constructions in your presentation:

8 Biased
9 أولى اهتمامًا = to give special attention
10 To approach

if (had happened), then (would have happened)	لو + (past tense) ل + (past tense)
if (had happened), then (would not have happened)	لو + (past tense) ما + (past tense)
whenever (happens), then (happens)	كُلما + (past tense)، (past tense)

5

Government and Leadership—Ibn ʿAbd Rabbih

الدرس الخامس – ابن عبد ربّه

أبو عمر أحمد بن محمد بن عبد ربه الأندلسي المعروف بابن عبد ربه (٢٤٦هـ/ ٨٦٠م - ٣٢٨هـ/ ٩٤٠م). هو أديب وشاعر من أهل العلم. وقد جمع ابن عبد ربه في أثناء دراسته بين كل من الثقافة الدينية والأدبية.

كان ابن عبد ربه صديقًا مقرّبًا لعدد من الأمراء الأمويين في عصره، وكان من الشعراء المادحين لهم.

من أشهر كتبه العِقد الفريد، وهو كتاب يشتمل على الأخبار، والأنساب، والأمثال، والشعر، والعروض والموسيقى، وقد جمع فيه خلاصة ما كتب الأصمعيّ، وأبو عبيدة، والجاحظ، وابن قتيبة وغيرهم من الأدباء الكبار.

وقد اهتمّ ابن عبد ربه كثيرًا بأدب الشرق وتعمّق فيه، وعلى الرغم من أصله الأندلسي ونشأته في قرطبة فلم يذكر الأندلس ولا أهلها بكلمة في أشعاره وموشحاته التي اكتسبت شهرة واسعة.

Prediction and Scanning

Based on the context and background given above, record your predictions as to whether you expect the author will agree with the following statements. Be prepared to discuss your predictions with classmates. Then, reading through the excerpts in the next section quickly, without the use of a dictionary, indicate whether your predictions were correct and where (in which lines) you found the answers. Again, be prepared to discuss the results with your classmates.

الدلالة	التوقُّع	العبارة
		للحاكم أهمية عظمى في حياة الشعوب ومصائرها.
		الله مالك الملك، يُعزّ من يشاء ويُذلّ من يشاء.
		العدل أساس المُلك
		يجب تحديد المسؤوليات المتبادلة بين الحاكم ورعيّته.

From the Writings of Ibn ʻAbd Rabbih

العِقد الفريد، كتاب اللؤلؤة

Ibn ʻAbd Rabbih begins with a prologue about the importance of rulers:

(١) السلطان زمام الأمور، ونظام الحقوق، وقِوام الحدود (٢) والقُطب الذي عليه مدار الدين والدنيا. (٣) وهو حِمَى الله في بلاده وظلّه الممدود على عباده، (٤) به يمتنع حريمهم، وينتصر مظلومهم، وينقمع ظالمهم، ويأمن خائفهم. (٥) قالت الحكماء: إمام عادل، خير من مَطر وابل. (٦) وإمام غشوم، خير من فتنة تدوم. (٧) ولما يزَعُ الله بالسلطان أكثر مما يزع بالقرآن.

As is often the case in classical instruction manuals, the author quotes great authorities and then offers his interpretation:
(٨) وقال وهب بن مُنبِّه: فيما أنزل الله على نبيه داود (عليه السلام): إني أنا الله مالك الملوك، قلوب الملوك بيدي، (٩) فمن كان لي على طاعة جعلت الملوك عليهم رحمة، ومن كان لي على معصية جعلت الملوك عليهم نقمة. (١٠) فحق على من قلّده الله أزمَّةَ حُكمه، وملّكه أمور خلقه. (١١) واختصه بإحسانه، ومَكَّن له في

سلطانه، أن يكون من الاهتمام بمصالح رعيّته (١٢) والاعتناء بمرافق أهل طاعته، بحيث وضعه اللهّ من الكرامة، وأجْرى عليه من أسباب السعادة.

Essential to any instruction manual are the *Hadith* of the Prophet:

(١٣) وقال النبي (صلى الله عليه وسلم): عدل ساعةٍ في حكومة خيرٌ من عبادة ستين سنة. (١٤) ومن شأن الرعية قلة الرضى عن الأئمة، وتحجُّرُ العُذْر عليهم، (١٥) وإلزامُ اللائمة لهم، ورُبَّ مَلوم لا ذنب له. (١٦) ولا سبيل إلى السلامة من ألسنة العامة (١٧) إذ كان رضى جملتها وموافقةُ جماعتها مِن المعْجِز الذي لا يُدْرَك، والممتنع الذي لا يُملك.

Ibn ʿAbd Rabbih comments on the relationship between the ruler and the ruled:

(١٨) ولكلٍّ حصتُه من العدل، ومنزلته من الحكم. (١٩) فمن حقّ الإمام على رعيته أن تقضيَ عليه بالأغلب من فعله والأعمّ من حُكمه، ومن حق الرعيّة على إمامها حُسنُ القبول لظاهر طاعتها وإضرابُه صفحًا عن مكاشفتها، (٢٠) كما قال زياد لما قَدِم العراق واليًا عليها: أيها الناس، قد كان بيني وبينكم إحَن، (٢١) فجعلت ذلك دَبْرَ أذني، وتحت قدمي، (٢٢) فمَن كان مُحسنًا فليزددْ في إحسانه، (٢٣) ومن كان مسيئًا فلينزع عن إساءته. (٢٤) إني لو علمتُ أن أحدكم قتله السّل من بغضي لم أكشف له قناعًا ولم أهتك له سِترًا حتى يُبدي صفحتَه لي.

Vocabulary

زِمام ج. أَزِمّة	rein
قُطب	pole, axis
حريم	here: wives, female members of a household
انقمع	deterred
وابل	downpour, barrage
غشوم	tyrannical
وزع (يزع)	to restrain
طاعة	obedience

معصية	disobedience
نِقْمة	wrath, grudge
قلّد	to invest, appoint
اعتناء بـ	to care for, look after
رعية	subjects, citizens
إمام ج. أئمة	imam (here: leader)
تَحَجَّر	to be stiff, adamant (here: uncompromising)
عُذْر	excuse
مَنزلة	place, position
مُكاشفة	revealing
إِحَن	bad feelings, rancor
دَبْر	backside, rear
مسيء	offensive
نزع	abstain, give up
بُغض	hatred
هَتَكَ	to divulge
بدا	to reveal, expose

Comprehension Exercises

Answer the following questions in complete Arabic sentences, according to the author's opinions:

١. ما تعريف الحاكم أو الزعيم؟

____

____

٢. كيف وصف الحكماء الأئمة والقادة؟

---

٣. ما واجبات القائد تجاه شعبه؟

---

٤. بماذا[1] فضّلَ النبي (ﷺ) العدل في الحكم؟

---

٥. بمَ وَعَد القائد زياد أهل العراق؟

---

1 With what?

Interpreting the Text

١. هل هناك رسالة خَفية[2] موجهة من الحاكم إلى شعبه في نصّ ابن عبد ربه؟ ما دليلكم؟

____

____

٢. لماذا استشهد[3] الكاتب بحديث النبي داود (عليه السلام) في هذا النص؟

____

____

٣. ما المسؤوليات المتبادلة بين الحاكم وشعبه كما صوّرها ابن عبد ربه؟

____

____

٤. هل رضا الشعب وامتنانه أمر مهم للحاكم؟

____

____

2 Hidden
3 To cite a quote

٥. هل تتفقون مع مبادئ[4] زياد في حكمه؟

____

____

Style and Technique

1. In the first section, notice the use of rhythm and rhyme to give the text a poetic quality. This suits Ibn ʿAbd Rabbih's aim of making easily memorable and quotable maxims that cultured readers can use in conversation. In line 1, the sultan is described as:

   زمام الأمور
   نظام الحقوق
   قِوام الحدود

   Notice the parallel pattern of consonants and the corresponding long vowels in each phrase. Similarly in line 3: بـلاده and عبـاده. Can you identify the repeating patterns in lines 4, 5, 6, and 7?
2. In the quote from Ziad in lines 22 and 23, the preposition لِ is being used in its role of expressing a command or invitation, as if to say, "let him." In this form, it is followed by a jussive verb (thus the sukun ending), and is often preceded by فـ or و. Thus, he invites, with the force his ruling power, those who have been good to "increase" and those who have been bad to desist.
3. In several lines, Ibn ʿAbd Rabbih uses phrases incorporating the word حـقّ. While this term is most familiar as meaning "a right," it also has the meaning of an obligation (the basic meaning of the root—as in حقيقـة—is "true," meaning both rights and duties are something that are correct and true). The extended sequence beginning in line 10, for example, starts with فحـق and then uses several metaphors to describe God granting authority to someone. In

4 Principles

this case, he is saying it is the duty of those who have been put in power to act in a certain way.

4. In line 19, حـقّ is used to mean "the right." The author talks about حـقّ الرعيـة عـلى إمامهـا. The preposition عـلى in this use connotes "in regard to," such that the phrase comes to mean "the right of the governed regarding its leader . . . " or more idiomatically "the right of the governed that their leader . . . " The converse statement is made in the same line about the right of the ruler vis-à-vis the governed.
5. The Qur'anic verse in line 9 depends on the correct reading of the preposition لِ which has many different uses. Here, لي should be read as "to me." The preposition عـلى here refers to a manner of acting: عـلى الطاعـة – "with obedience." The entire phrase then means "who was obedient toward me." While كان لي would most often be read as "I had," the reading does not work here.
6. The Prophetic Hadith in line 13 begins with the word عَـدْل. Without diacritical marks, this could appear to be a noun or a verb. The parallel clause that follows, however, helps us to understand the structure of this clause. The meaning intended here is the noun "fairness," or "acting justly." سـاعة, like سـتين سـنة in the parallel clause, is used as an adverb, meaning "for an hour." Taken together, the phrase means "acting justly in governing for one hour is better than worshiping for sixty years."
7. In line 15 the author says: وتحجُّـرُ العُـذْر عليهـم. The verb تحجـر comes from the root حجـر, and the most familiar verb from this root is حَجَـر = to stone. The Form V verb used here has several meanings based on the context: to solidify, to turn to stone, or to be narrow-minded and uncompromising, which is the intended meaning in this case.

Analysis and Argument

A. Ibn 'Abd Rabbih has strong ideas about the nature of political authority. How well do you think these ideas hold up today?

١. قال ابن عبد ربه إنّ ما يزعُ الله بالسلطان أكثر مما يزع بالقرآن (٧). ناقشوا باختصار مسألة خلط الدين بالسياسة بين الماضي والحاضر. هناك كاتب معاصر يُعرّف السياسة بأنها فنّ السفالة[5] الأنيقة؟ ما رأيكم في هذا التعريف؟
٢. قال الكاتب إنّه من شأن الرعية قلة الرضا عن الأئمة. (١٤). هل تؤيدون هذه الفكرة؟ وضحوا بالدليل؟
٣. تكلم ابن عبد ربه عن مفهوم الطاعة التي يجب أن يتبعها الشعب مع حاكمه (١٩). حلّلوا هذا المفهوم ومدى تأثيره على نظام الحكم والعلاقة بين الحاكم والمحكوم؟
٤. تعبير «بوق السلطة»[6] من التعابير السياسية السلبية الشائعة؟ مَن يستحق هذا اللقب؟

B. Do you think Ibn ʿAbd Rabbih would agree or disagree with the following statements, and why or why not?

١. يجب الفصل الكامل بين الدين والدولة في الحكم من أجل رفاهية المجتمع وأمنه.

____

____

٢. يجب على الحاكم تلبية احتياجات شعبه ومطالبهم.

____

____

٣. العلماء هم حلقة الوصل[7] بين الحاكم والمحكوم.

____

____

5 Baseness
6 One who supports the ruler at all times
7 Connection

٤. الشعوب لا ترضى في الأغلب عن حكامها مهما قدّم الحاكم من خدمات.

٥. يجب أن يتميّز الحاكم بالحزم والشدة والصرامة.

Research and Presentation

You now have a fairly solid idea of Ibn 'Abd Rabbih's picture of good governance. Write a short piece on the following question:

هل هناك نظام حُكْم مثالي في عصرنا الحديث؟ عللوا إجاباتكم.

An argument of this type would make extensive use of the counterfactual "if"—لـــو. Review the structure of this type of statement. لـــو is always followed by the past tense, while the ف can introduce a result clause in the present or future, which would be appropriate for a hypothetical visit that hasn't yet happened:

لو + past ف present or future

You may also borrow Ibn 'Abd Rabbih's own structures, like:
is better than = خير من

6

Anthropology and Religion—al-Biruni

الدرس السادس – البيروني

محمد بن أحمد أبو الريحان البيروني الخوارزمي (٣٦٢هـ/ ٩٧٣م - ٤٤٠هـ/ ١٠٤٨م) وُلِد في مدينة خوارزم التي كان لها دور بارز في التاريخ الإسلامي. أما لقبه، البيروني، فيعني بلغة أهل مدينة خوارزم الغريب، لأنه كان دائم الترحال والسفر. كان البيروني فيلسوفًا ومؤرخًا ورحالة وجغرافيًّا ولغويًّا ورياضيًّا وفلكيًّا وشاعرًا وعالمًا في الفيزياء، وله مؤلفات كثيرة وأبحاث قيّمة في علوم شتّى. كان البيروني على دراية واسعة بعدة لغات منها اللغة الخوارزمية والفارسية والعربية واليونانية والسنسكريتية والعبرية والسريانية. قضى البيروني أغلب أوقاته في غزنة (كابول في أفغانستان الآن)، وعمل في بلاط السلطان محمود الغزني وكان المنجّم[1] الرسمي للدولة. كما أنّه رافق السلطان الغزني في حملاته العسكرية في الهند وألّف خلالها كتابه المشهور عن ثقافات الهند. يُعرف البيروني بلقب مؤسس الهنديات أو علم الهند، كما يُعرف بلقب الأستاذ، لوصفه الاستثنائي للهند في بدايات القرن الحادي عشر. كما اشتهر بدراساته وأبحاثه الموضوعية عن عادات وعقائد الأمم والمجتمعات.

Prediction and Scanning

Based on the context and background given above, record your predictions as to whether you expect the author will agree with the following statements. Be prepared to discuss your predictions with classmates.

1 Astrologer

Then, reading through the excerpts in the next section quickly, without the use of a dictionary, indicate whether your predictions were correct and where (in which lines) you found the answers. Again, be prepared to discuss the results with your classmates.

العبارة	التوقُّع	الدلالة
تُعدّ صعوبة اللغة الهندية من العقبات التي تحول دون فهم ثقافة هذه الأمّة.		
تختلف المعتقدات والطقوس الدينية الهندية اختلافًا كليًّا عن معتقدات الكتب السماوية.		
تطابقت المعتقدات اليونانية القديمة مع المعتقدات الهندية التي رصدها البيروني في حينها.		
آمنَ الهنود بوحدانية الله.		

From the Writings of al-Biruni

في تحقيق ما للهند، الجزء الأول

Al-Biruni begins his treatise by describing the vast differences between the Arabs and the people of India. The first issue he addresses is language:

(١)]الصعوبات[أوّلها اللغة . . . (٢) ومتى رامها أحد لإزالة المباينة لم يسهل ذلك لأنها في ذاتها طويلة عريضة تشابه العربية. (٣) يتسمّى الشيء الواحد فيها بعدّة أسامٍ مقتضبة ومشتقّة، (٤) وبوقوع الاسم الواحد على عدّة مسميات محْوِجة في

المقاصد إلى زيادة صفات، (٥) إذ لا يفرق بينها إلاّ ذو الفطنة لموضع الكلام وقياس المعنى إلى الوراء والأمام. (٦) ويتفخرون بذلك افتخار غيرهم به من حيث هو بالحقيقة عيب في اللغة . . . (٧) ثم هي مُركّبة من حروف لا يطابق بعضها حروف العربية والفارسية . . . (٨) هذا مع عدم اهتمام الناسخين لها وقلّة اكتراثهم بالتصحيح والمعارضة، (٩) حتى يضيع الاجتهاد ويفسد الكتاب في نقل له أو نقلين ويصير ما فيه لغة جديدة.

He then discusses differences in religion:

(١٠) ومنها أنهم يباينوننا بالديانة مباينة كلّية. (١١) لا يقع منّا شيء من الإقرار بما عندهم ولا منهم بشيء ممّا عندنا. (١٢) وعلى قلّة تنازعهم في أمر المذاهب بينهم بما سوى الجدال والكلام دون الإضرار بالنفس أو البدن أو الحال، (١٣) ليسوا مع من عداهم بهذه الوتيرة وإنّما يسمّونه مليج، (١٤) وهو القذر لا يستجيزون مخالطته في مناكحة ومقاربة أو مجالسة ومؤاكلة ومشاربة من جهة النجاسة، (١٥) ويستقذرون ما تصرّف على مائه وناره وعليهما مدار المعاش، (١٦) ثمّ لا مطمع في صلاح ذلك بحيلة كما يطهر النجس بالانحياز إلى حال الطهارة. (١٧) فليس بمطلق لهم قبول من ليس منهم إذا رغب فيهم أو صبا إلى دينهم. (١٨) وهذا ممّا يفسّخ كل وُصْلة ويوجب أشدّ قطيعة.

Al-Biruni makes a comparison between the ancient Greeks and the Hindus of his day:

(١٩) إنّ اليونانيين أيام الجاهلية قبل ظهور النصرانية كانوا على مثل ما عليه الهند من العقيدة؛ خاصّهم في النظر قريب من خاصّهم وعامّهم في عبادة الأصنام كعامّهم. (٢٠) ولهذا أستشهد من كلام بعضهم على بعض بسبب الاتفاق وتقارب الأمرين لا التصحيح، (٢١) فإنّ ما عدا الحقّ زائغ والكفر ملّة واحدة من أجل الانحراف عنه. (٢٢) ولكن اليونانيين فازوا بالفلاسفة الذين كانوا في ناحيتهم حتى نقّحوا لهم الأصول الخاصة دون العامّة، (٢٣) لأنّ قُصارى الخواصّ اتّباع البحث والنظر وقصارى العوامّ التهوّر واللجاج . . . (٢٤) لم يكُ للهند أمثالهم ممّن يهذّب العلوم (٢٥) فلا تكاد تجد لذلك لهم خاصّ كلام إلاّ في غاية الاضطراب وسوء النظام ومشوبًا في آخرة خرافات العوامّ من تكثير العدد وتمديد المدد. (٢٦) ومن موضوعات النِحْلة التي يستفظع أهلها فيها المخالفة، (٢٧) ولأجله يستولي التقليد

عليهم، (٢٨) وبسببه أقول فيما هو بابتي منهم أني لا أشبّه ما في كتبهم من الحساب ونوع التعاليم إلّا بصدف مخلوط بخزف أو بِدُرّ ممزوج ببَعْر.

Despite his somewhat negative introduction, al-Biruni's description of Hindu religious beliefs has much in common with Islam:

(٢٩) اعتقاد الهند في الله (سبحانه) أنه الواحد الأزلي من غير ابتداء ولا انتهاء. (٣٠) المختار في فعله القادر الحكيم الحيّ المحيي المدبّر المبقي الفرد في ملكوته عن الأضداد الأنداد، لا يشبه شيئًا ولا يشبهه شيء . . . (٣١) قال السائل في كتاب باتنجل: من هذا المعبود الذي يُنال التوفيق بعبادته؟ (٣٢) قال المجيب: هو المستغني بأزليّته ووحدانيّته عن فعل لمكافأة عليه براحة تُؤمّل وترتجى أو شدّة تُخاف وتُتّقى، والبريء عن الأفكار لتعاليه عن الأضداد المكروهة والأنداد المحبوبة، والعالم بذاته.

Vocabulary

المباينة	difference, dissimilarity
رام	want, to desire
مقتضبة	brief, concise
محوجة	deficient
فطنة	astuteness, understanding
مرُكبة	composed
ناسخ	scribe, copier
نقل	here: publication, edition
تنازع	to dispute, debate
إضرار	harm, damage
مليج	mleccha, a Hindu term for unclean outsiders
النجاسة	filth
استقْذَرَ	to consider filthy
لا مطمع في	having no desire for
صبا إلى	to yearn for
طَهّرَ	to purify

فسخ	to break off, sever
النصرانية[2]	a term for Christianity
الخاصّ	the elite of society
العامّة	the common people
استشهد	here: to cite, mention, quote
زائغ	deviant, not following the right path
ملّة	community, sect
نقّح	to correct, improve, revise
قُصارى	limit, utmost
تهوُّر	foolishness, rashness
لجاج	stubbornness
هذّب	to rectify, refine
خرافة	superstition
استفظع	to find horrible
دُرّ	pearls
بَعْر	dung
أنداد	equals, rivals
أزليّ	eternal
باتنجل	a Hindu holy book that al-Biruni translated

2 See Cultural and Contextual Clues section in Lesson One

Comprehension Exercises

A. Answer the following questions in complete Arabic sentences, based on the excerpts:

١. ما صعوبات فهم اللغة الهندية بالنسبة للناطقين بغيرها؟

___

___

٢. ما رأي البيروني في مُدوّني[3] اللغة الهندية؟

___

___

٣. كيف وصف المؤلف صراعات الشؤون الدينية بين الهنود وبعضهم؟

___

___

٤. بماذا يُسمّي الهنود أعداءهم وما صفاتهم؟

___

___

3 Scribes

٥. كيف تغلّب اليونانيون على جهلهم قبل أن تصل الديانة المسيحية إليهم؟

B. Are the following statements true in the opinion of the author? If not, why?

١. تتشابه اللغتان الهندية والعربية في الحروف والصيغ والتراكيب النحوية.

٢. في الثقافة الهندية القديمة، كانت النجاسة والقذارة من صفات الأعداء.

٣. نجح النُسّاخ الهنود في المحافظة على النصوص المكتوبة وتوضيحها للقراء.

٤. النزاعات الدينية عند أهل الهند تقتصر على الجَدل والكلام.

٥. تفوّق الفلاسفة اليونانيون على نظرائهم الهنود.

Interpreting the Text

١. هل ميّز البيروني اللغة العربية عن غيرها في هذا النص؟ لماذا؟

٢. هل يبدو البيروني متسامحًا في رأيه بالعقائد الدينية عند الهنود؟ لماذا؟

٣. كيف تطرّق البيروني لمصطلح التوحيد[4] ومعناه في هذا النص؟

4 The belief that there is only one God

٤. كيف عبَّر البيروني بالألفاظ المتضادة عن فكرته؟ وما رأيكم في هذا الأسلوب؟

____

____

٥. ما دلالات عبْقرية[5] البيروني وسِعَة اطلاعه وتطوّر فكره؟

____

____

Style and Technique

1. In line 12, al-Biruni uses the word سوى. This word you may recognize comes from the root meaning "to be equal," and is used in a number of expressions that can have different meanings that are not what one would expect from a literal reading. As used here— بما سوى —it has the meaning of "including only." Al-Biruni means to say the Hindus have religious disputes only to the level of speech, without conviction. Used with a negative, as in .. ليس سوى, it means "nothing but." Followed by a noun or pronoun, it means "other than," as in سواها "other than it." This word is related to and easily confused with سواءً, meaning "either (this or that)," or "regardless of whether (this or that)."
2. In line 14, al-Biruni makes extensive use of the Form III *masdar* (المفاعلة). Notice how many examples of this pattern you find in this one line. As this form usually denotes a reciprocal action—that is, doing something back and forth with someone else—it is especially appropriate for what al-Biruni is discussing here. Since he is making a point about how the Hindus do not mix with those

5 Genius

of lower castes, he is listing all the things they *will not* do with them. The Form III form is perfect for this because it involves mutual, usually recurring actions. Ibn Khaldun uses similar parallelism when comparing the habits of Bedouin and settled societies, describing how the members of each society interact. Being able to use the same pattern repeatedly gives a pleasant rhythm and parallelism to the text and is therefore preferred in Arabic.

3. Form X verbs (استفعل) have two general meanings: to consider something to be whatever the root meaning is, or to seek whatever the root meaning is. Al-Biruni uses two of these in lines 15 and 20: استقذر and استشهد, each invoking a different meaning of the two general meanings. If you recognize the root word قذر as meaning "filth," then the first word can be deduced to mean "to consider to be filthy." This fits well with the context, in which he is discussing how the Hindus treat lower castes. استشهد you may recognize from its familiar meaning of "to be a martyr." That meaning does not fit in this case, where al-Biruni is describing his approach to comparing the Greeks and Hindus. If you recognize the root شهد as meaning "to testify" or "bear witness," then the other meaning makes sense: to seek to bear witness, in other words "to cite as an example." Recognizing these two general meanings can help you figure out the meaning of unfamiliar words, or choose between two possibilities, as these cases demonstrate.

Using Cultural and Contextual Clues to Understand the Text

1. Al-Biruni's criticism of the Hindu religion is based on its different orientation from Islam. Like Christianity, Islam is a universal faith that holds that all people can, and should, be converted to it. Like many other Eastern religions, Hinduism makes no such claim. While both religions place great emphasis on purity and (spiritual as well as bodily) cleanliness, their different orientations mean this

is applied differently. Al-Biruni is very critical of what he sees as the aloofness of the Hindus, who separate themselves from others, rather than trying to convert them. His view, however, might well be seen by them as forcing beliefs on others.

2. Al-Biruni's unfavorable comparison of the ancient Greeks and Hindus needs to be taken with a grain of salt. Because so much of the foundational knowledge in Muslim society was inherited from ancient Greece, a major project of Muslim philosophy in the Middle Ages, if not the major project, was reconciling Greek philosophy with Islam. A lifelong effort of some of the great philosophers in this book, like al-Kindi (Chapter 3), Ibn Sina (Chapter 7), and Ibn Rushd (Chapter 9) was proving that these essentially pagan philosophers were really writing about God and that Muslim philosophy was the natural continuation of their work. Thus, in claiming that the pagan Greeks had great philosophers who corrected their ideas, he is drawing on widespread, if somewhat shaky, convictions about the soundness of the ancient Greek worldview.

Analysis and Argument

Al-Biruni's writings reveal as much about Muslim society as (probably more than) about the Hindu society that he studied. Based on what you have read, what would you conclude about his assumptions and their validity?

١. يقال إنّ الخيال[6] هو السمة المشتركة بين المبدعين، هل تقوم هذه السمة بدور في كتابات البيروني؟ اذكروا الدليل.

٢. حدّد العلماء معايير[7] خاصة لدراسة اللغة وعلومها، فهل اتّبعَ البيروني هذه المعايير عند حديثه عن اللغة الهندية؟

6 Imagination

7 Standards, criteria

٣. الدين لله والوطن للجميع[8]، شعار عربي مشهور. ناقشوا معناه في ضوء الآراء الدينية للبيروني.

٤. ما أهم السمات الفلسفية والدينية التي وردت في نص البيروني؟

Research and Presentation

Prepare a 2–3-minute presentation about the following statement:

يقول البيروني في كتابه «القانون المسعودي»: إنّ الأجسام الساقطة تنجذب نحو مركز الأرض وإنّ اختلاف قوة الجذب يرجع إلى المسافة.
أثار هذا القول للبيروني انتباه العلماء فيما بعد وقارنوا بينه وبين العالم إسحاق نيوتن صاحب قانون الجاذبية.
ابحثوا في هذا الموضوع وسجلوا نتائج البحث وناقشوها في الصفّ مع زملائكم.

You may find the following Arabic words and terms useful in your writing:

to disprove the expectations	يدحض التوقعات
by way of example	على سبيل المثال
the best example of this	خير مثال على ذلك
refute	فَنَّدَ

8 Popular Arabic saying

7

Education—Ibn Sina

الدرس السابع – ابن سينا

هو أبو علي الحسين بن عبد الله بن سينا (٣٧٠هـ/ ٩٨٠م - ٤٢٧هـ/ ١٠٣٧م) واختُصِر اسمه إلى ابن سينا، ويعرف في اللغة اللاتينية باسم .Avicenna وُلِد ابن سينا بالقرب من بلدة بخارى التي تقع الآن في أوزبكستان وتُوفيّ في همدان بإيران. كان ابن سينا عالمًا وفيلسوفًا وطبيبًا وشاعرًا. لُقِّب بالشيخ والفيلسوف الثالث بعد أرسطو والفارابي، كما لُقّب أيضا بأمير الأطباء وأرسطو الإسلام. تُوفّي ابن سينا عن عمر ناهز الستين عاما تاركًا وراءه إرثًا ثمينًا من الكتب القيمة في شتى المجالات والمواضيع. وقد نال ابن سينا تقدير العلماء والباحثين واحترامهم على مر العصور ووصفه أحدهم بقوله: إن ابن سينا ظاهرة فكرية عظيمة ربما لا نجد من يساويه في ذكائه أو نشاطه الإنتاجي.

من أشهر مؤلفاته «كتاب الشفاء» الذي يُعَدّ موسوعةً فلسفيةً علميةً نادرة، كما أنّ كتابه «القانون في الطب» من أشهر الكتب في تاريخ الطب، وقد ترجم وطبع عدّة مرات، وظلّ يُدرَّس في جامعات أوروبا حتى أواخر القرن التاسع عشر.

Prediction and Scanning

Based on the context and background given above, record your predictions as to whether you expect the author will agree with the following statements. Be prepared to discuss your predictions with classmates. Then, reading through the excerpts in the next section quickly, without the use of a dictionary, indicate whether your predictions were correct and where (in which lines) you found the answers. Again, be prepared to discuss the results with your classmates.

العبارة	التوقُّع	الدلالة
ترويض الإنسان لذاته أول خطوات إصلاح الأمة والمجتمع.		
أوصى ابن سينا بطلب العلم منذ الصغر.		
يجب على المعلم التحلّي بالأخلاق الحميدة وضبط النفس.		
يجب على المرء أن يحاسب نفسه وألا يقف دائمًا عند أخطاء الآخرين.		

From the Writings of Ibn Sina

كتاب السياسة

In *Kitaab al-siyasa,* Ibn Sina describes a comprehensive program for development of the individual, the family, and society. The term *siyasa* (سياسة) in this case means management or control of something, and is in that sense the book of achieving mastery—over oneself, one's household, and eventually one's domain. In the first excerpt below, he assets that the foundation of education and development is to have a solid understanding of one's own nature, and then to learn to control it.

(١) إنَّ أوّل ما ينبغي أن يبدأ به الإنسان من أصناف السياسة نفسه. (٢) إذ كانت نفسه أقرب الأشياء إليه وأكرمها وأولاها بعنايته. (٣) ولأنه متى أحسن سياسة نفسه لم يعيَ بما فوقها من سياسة المصر. (٤) ومن أوائل ما يلزم من رام سياسة نفسه أن يعلم أنَّ له عقلًا هو السائس ونفسًا أمَّارةً بالسوء كثيرة المعايب جمة المساوئ في طبعها وأصل خلقها هي المسوسة. (٥) وأن يعلم أنَّ كل من أراد إصلاح فاسد لزمه أن يعرف جميع فساد ذلك الفاسد معرفة مستقصاة حتى لا يغادر منه

شـيئًا، (٦) ثـم يأخـذ في إصـلاح، وإلا كان مـا يصلحـه غـير حريـز ولا وثيـق. (٧) كذلـك مـن رامَ سياسـة نفسـه ورياضتهـا وإصـلاح فاسـدها لم يجـز لـه أن يبتـدئ في ذلـك حتـى يعـرف جميـع مسـاوئ نفسـه معرفـة محيطـة.

Ibn Sina then describes the curriculum of instruction a young person should follow:

(٨) إذا اشـتدت مفاصـل الصبـي واسـتوى لسـانه وتهيّـأ للتلقـين ووعـى سـمعهُ أخـذ في تعلّـم القـرآن وصُـوّر لـه حـروف الهجـاء، (٩) ولُقّـن معـالم الديـن. (١٠) وينبغـي أن يـروي الصبـي الرجـز ثـمّ القصيـدة، فـإنّ روايـة الرجـز أسـهل وحفظـه أمكـن، لأنّ بيوتـه أقـصر ووزنـه أخـفّ. (١١) ويبـدأ مـن الشـعر بـما قيـل في فضـل الأدب ومـدح العلـم وذمّ الجهـل وعيـب السـخف (١٢) ومـا حـثّ عـلى بـرّ الوالديـن واصطنـاع المعـروف وقِـرى الضيـف وغـير ذلـك مـن مـكارم الأخـلاق.

He discusses the qualities required of a teacher:

(١٣) ينبغـي أن يكـون مُـؤدِّب الصبـي عاقـلًا ذا ديـن، بصـيرًا برياضـة الأخـلاق، حاذقًـا بتخريـج الصبيـان، وقـورًا رزينًـا، بعيـدًا مـن الخفّـة والسـخف، (١٤) قليـل التبـذل والاسترسـال بحـضرة الصبـي، غـير كـزٍّ ولا جامـد، بـل حلـوًا لبيبًـا ذا مـروءة ونظافـة ونزاهـة، قـد خـدم سَراة النـاس وعـرف مـا يتباهـون بـه مـن أخـلاق الملـوك ويتعايـرون بـه مـن أخـلاق السـفلة، وعـرف آداب المجالسـة وآداب المؤاكلـة والمحادثـة والمعـاشرة.

After obtaining the foundations of an education, the youth move on to a specialization:

(١٥) إذا فـرغ الصبـي مـن تعلّـم القـرآن وحفـظ أصـول اللغـة نظـر عنـد ذلـك إلى مـا يُراد أن تكـون صناعتـه مُوجّهـة لطريقـه. (١٦) فـإن أراد بـه الكتابـة أضـاف إلى دراسـة اللغـة دراسـة الرسـائل والخطـب ومناقـلات النـاس ومحاوراتهـم . . . (١٧) فـإذا خرجـت عـن هـذه الطبقـة إلى طبقـة أُخـرى وجـدت واحـدًا يختـار علـم الحسـاب وآخـر يختـار علـم الهندسـة وآخـر يختـار علـم الطـب. (١٨) وهكـذا تجـد سـائر الطبقـات، إذًا طبقـة طبقـة، حتـى تـدور عليهـا جميعهـا . . . (١٩) كانـت الصناعـات أوثـق وأبقـى مـن التجـارات، لأنّ التجـارة تكـون بالمـال، والمـال وشـيك الفنـاء عديـد الآلات كثـير الحوائـج. (٢٠) وصناعـات ذوي المـروءة ثلاثـة أنـواع: (٢١) نـوع مـن حيّـز العقـل وهـو صحـة الـرأي

وصواب المشورة وحسن التدبير، (٢٢) وهو صناعة الوزراء والمدبرين وأرباب السياسة والملوك. (٢٣) ونوع من حيّز الأدب، وهو الكتابة والبلاغة وعلم النجوم وعلم الطب وهو صناعة الأدباء، (٢٤) ونوع من حيّز الأيْد والشجاعة وهو صناعة الفرسان والأساورة. (٢٥) فمن رام إحدى هذه الصناعات فليفزْ بإحكامها والتقدم فيها حتى يكون من أصحابها موصوفًا بالفصاحة غير مرذول ولا مؤخَّر.

He offers more guidance on governing one's self:

(٢٦) ينبغي لمن عُني بتعرّف مناقبه ومثالبه أن يفحص عن أخلاق الناس ويتفقّد شيمهم وخلائقهم ويتبصّر مناقبهم ومثالبهم بما عنده منها، (٢٧) ويعلم أنّه مثلهم وأنهم أمثاله فإنَّ الناس أشباه، (٢٨) بل هم سواء كأسنان المشط. (٢٩) فإذا رأى المنقبة الحسنة فليعلم أنَّ فيه مثلها إما ظاهرة أو مغمورة، (٣٠) فإن كانت ظاهرة فليراعها وليواظب عليها حتى لا تبيد ولا تضمحل، وإن كانت مغمورة فليثرها وليحييها وليحافظ على استدعائها.

Vocabulary

مصر	city
رام	to want, demand
سائس	ruler, trainer
حريز	accomplished
مساوئ	disadvantages
هِجاء	spelling
لقّن	instruct, teach
رجز	*rajaz,* a kind of poetry
مدح	praise
ذم	dispraise
قرى	hospitality
حاذق	gifted, clever, brilliant
وقور	dignified
كزّ	disgusting, repugnant, unpleasant
تباهى	show off, flaunt

مؤاكلة	sharing a meal
وشيك	imminent
حاجة ج. حوائج	need
المروءة	generosity
حيّز	opportunity, field, area
مناقب	merits, advantages
مثالب	disadvantages, flaw
المشط	comb
يواظب	to do something persistently, persevere in
اضمحل	to fade away, vanish

Comprehension Exercises

A. Answer the following questions in complete Arabic sentences, based on the excerpts:

١. لماذا نصح ابن سينا بضرورة تطبيق السياسة على أنفسنا أولًا؟

____

____

٢. ما المنهج التربوي الذي وضعه ابن سينا لتعليم الصغار؟

____

____

٣. ما صفات المعلم المثالي من وجهة نظر ابن سينا؟

٤. ما التخصصات العلمية التي ذكرها ابن سينا؟

٥. بالنسبة لابن سينا، كيف يمكن معرفة إيجابياتنا وسلبياتنا مِن خلال مَن حولنا؟

B. Are the following statements true in the opinion of the author? If not, why?

١. تطبيق شعار «ابدأ بنفسك» هو الطريق لبناء دولة قوية ومجتمع متماسك.

٢. يجب أن يبدأ الشاب بتعلّم العلوم الطبيعية والفلسفة.

٣. المعلم هو أساس نجاح العملية التعليمية.

---

٤. يستطيع الشخص أن يتعلّم الكثير عن نفسه عند ملاحظة الآخرين.

---

٥. أساس قوة الشعب في سلطة الدولة العسكرية.

Interpreting the Text

١. كيف وصف ابن سينا العقل البشري وصفاته؟

---

٢. ما فائدة دراسة العلوم اللغوية والدينية في مرحلة مبكرة؟

---

٣. متى يكون الطالب مؤهلًا لاختيار تخصّصه العلمي والعملي؟

٤. ما صناعات ذوي المروءة التي ذكرها ابن سينا في النصّ؟ وما رأيكم فيها؟

٥. الناس مرايا[1] يعكس[2] بعضهم صور البعض الآخر. فسروا الجملة في ضوء قراءتكم لنص الكاتب.

Style and Technique

1. The compound Ibn Sina uses in line 30 – وإنْ – has the meaning of "even if/even though." He is advising that once someone notices something through the process of observation he describes, they should remember it and continue to work on it (expressed by the verb واظب), "even if" (وإنْ) it becomes submerged (مغمورة); that is to say, when one discovers a failing, one should remain ever mindful of it, even if they've managed to cover it up or keep it hidden. This should not be confused with the similar looking فإن at the

1 Mirrors
2 To reflect

beginning of that sentence, in which the particle "if" (إن) is being used in its normal sense.

2. In line 6 and 8, Ibn Sina uses the verb أَخَذَ collocated with the particle في. The verb normally has the familiar meaning "to take," but when it is followed by في, the meaning changes to "to start" or "to undertake" (بدأ). An exception to this meaning is the expression "أخذ في الاعتبار" which means "to take into account."
3. In line 15, Ibn Sina describes what should happen once the youth "فرغ من" learning the Qur'an. This verb, which you likely recognize as "to be empty," refers in this case to completing something absolutely. This means the youth must completely accomplish this step. Only then will one consider vocational education. Note also in that line that the verb يُراد is passive. A vocation is desired *for* him (most likely by his father or teacher).
4. The word فليثرها in line 30 refers to the verb وَثَر and its present يثر (يَثِر الشيء) means: he makes it easy and flexible.

Using Cultural and Contextual Clues to Understand the Text

1. Ibn Sina's recommendations reflect the standard educational practices of his day. In lines 8–12, the types of actions he recommends accord with how different subjects were approached. In line 8, for instance, the student is to have the letters of the alphabet shown to him (صوّر له). A teacher would demonstrate the letters until a child knew them all, only later would the pupil be allowed to start writing them. Similarly, the child is to be taught to recite (يروي) *rajaz* and poetry from memory, rather than reading or writing it. This is why Ibn Sina cautions in line 11 that the poetry chosen be that which praises high moral virtues and condemns bad behavior, because the pupil would memorize it and therefore be very influenced by the content. A young student would "learn" (تعلّم) the Qur'an—meaning memorize it, but only get a preliminary ori-

entation to (لقّن) the "outlines" (معالم) of religion. This difference reflects the priority of memorizing the exact text of the Qur'an first, and only gradually learning general principles of religion. All of these approaches are quite different from what finds in Western education today.

2. Ibn Sina's guidance in lines 26–30 about observing the good and bad behavior of others may seem strange by modern standards, where talking about another's faults is considered "gossip." He is, however, following in the tradition of *Adab*, in this case referring to the study of good behavior. Al-Jahiz's *Book of Misers* (excerpted in Chapter 2 of this book) is a prime example of this genre: literally a compendium of stories of bad behavior meant for study and edification.
3. Line 14 provides a good summation of the sources of proper behavior and taste that were expected to shape the life of a cultured person. The teacher should be familiar with the "values of kings" (أخلاق الملوك), as these were standard-setters for society, as reflected in the genre of "mirrors for princes," such as *The Unique Necklace* and *Kalila wa-Dimna* (Chapters 5 and 16 of this book, respectively). The salons or gatherings (مجالس) of notables would be the primary venues for discussion of these values, although Ibn Sina would well know they were places of wild behavior in which he often participated. Likewise, he commends study of the behavior of المؤاكلة, literally those who eat with important people, a reference to the courtly or salon-type of social gatherings.

Analysis and Argument

The principles of learning and development that Ibn Sina subscribes to are similar to those in many cultures, including in the world today. How would you evaluate his advice compared to other systems?

١. ناقشوا كيفية الالتزام بدراسة العقيدة الدينية وتعاليمها منذ الصغر وأثرها على الفرد والمجتمع.
٢. الاعتراف بالخطأ أول درجات النجاح والإصلاح؛ اذكروا أمثلة لهذا المفهوم[3] من حياتكم الشخصية.
٣. ما تقييمكم لمقولة ابن سينا إنّ الناس سواء كأسنان المشط؟ وعلام تدل؟
٤. كتب ابن سينا وصفة[4] لتحقيق سعادة الفرد والمجتمع، فما أهم شروطها ومدى فاعليتها؟

Research and Presentation

من أشهر اقتباسات[5] ابن سينا قوله:
١. المستعدّ للشيء تكفيه أضعف أسبابه.
٢. الوهم نصف الداء، والاطمئنان نصف الدواء، والصبر أول خطوات الشفاء.
٣. الوقت يُنسي الألم، ويطفئ الانتقام، بلسم الغضب ويخنق الكراهية، فيصبح الماضي كأن لم يكن.

Write a brief essay (3–4 paragraphs) on one of Ibn Sina's quotes above and whether you agree with it or not. You may find the following words and expressions useful:

priority	أوْلوية
non-essential	غير جوهري
marginal	هامشي
to some extent	إلى حدٍّ ما

3 Concept
4 Prescription
5 Quotes

8

Religion vs. Philosophy I—al-Ghazali

الدرس الثامن – الغزالي

أبو حامد محمد بن أحمد الطوسي الغزالي (٤٥٠هـ/ ١٠٥٨م – ٥٠٥هـ/ ١١١١م) أحد عظماء الفكر الإسلامي وأعلام التاريخ العربي. لُقّب الغزالي بألقاب كثيرة منها: حُجّة الإسلام وأعجوبة الزمان والشيخ الإمام البحر، وزين الدين، والعالم الأوحد وإمام أئمة الدين وصاحب التصانيف والذكاء المفرط.

وقد تضافرت عدّة عوامل كانت سببًا رئيسًا في نبوغ الغزالي وشهرته؛ كان أبرزها نشأته العلمية؛ إذ كان شغوفًا بالعلم، باحثًا عن حقائق الأمور وبواطنها، كما تمتّع بذاكرة وحافظة قوية وذكاء منقطع النظير. وعندما عمل الغزالي معلمًا في المدرسة النظامية التي أنشأها السلاجقة لتعليم مبادئ أهل السنة ذاع صيته وأصبح مقصدًا لطلاب العلم من شتى البقاع الإسلامية.

وللغزالي أكثر من ٧٠ مؤلّفًا في العلوم، والفكر الإسلامي والصوفية. أما كتابه «تهافت الفلاسفة» فقد رأى بعض النقاد بأنه نقطة تحول في مجريات التفكير في العالم الإسلامي. ويعدّ كتابه «إحياء علوم الدين» من المؤلفات الخالدة التي شملت جميع مجالات العلوم الإسلامية وناقشت أسس النظام الإسلامي والفلسفة والصوفية.

Prediction and Scanning

Based on the context and background given above, record your predictions as to whether you expect the following statements to be true. Be prepared to discuss your predictions with classmates. Then, reading through the excerpts in the next section quickly, without the use of a dictionary, indicate whether your predictions were correct and where

(in which lines) you found the answers. Again, be prepared to discuss the results with your classmates.

العبارة	التوقُّع	الدلالة
استخفّ بعض الفلاسفة بشعائر الدين وعقائده.		
يهدف الغزالي إلى إثبات خطأ فكر الفلاسفة وعدم قناعتهم بالوحي.		
استندت تعاليم الفلاسفة على تقليد الفلاسفة القدماء ومحاكاتهم مثل أرسطو وسقراط.		
العلوم الإلهية عند الفلاسفة ضعيفة ولا ترقى إلى دقة علومهم الحسابية.		

From the Writings of Al-Ghazali

تهافت الفلاسفة، مقدمة للكتاب

Al-Ghazali begins with a very strong attack against an unnamed class of philosophers, whom he accuses of heresy:

(١) قد رأيت طائفة يعتقدون في أنفسهم التميز عن الأتراب والنظراء بمزيد الفطنة والذكاء، (٢) قد رفضوا وظائف الإسلام من العبادات، واستحقروا شعائر الدين: من وظائف الصلوات، والتوقي عن المحظورات، واستهانوا بتعبدات الشرع وحدوده، (٣) ولم يقفوا عند توقيفاته وقيوده، بل خلعوا بالكلية ربقة الدين، بفنون من الظنون، يتبعون فيها رهطًا يصدون عن سبيل الله ويبغونها عوجا وهم بالآخرة هم كافرون، (٤) ولا مستند لكفرهم غير تقليد سماعي إلفي كتقليد

اليهـود والنصـارى؛ (٥) إذ جـرى عـلى غـير ديـن الإسـلام نشـؤهم وأولادهـم، وعليـه درجَ آباؤهـم وأجدادهـم، (٦) وغـيرُ بحـث نظـري، صـادر عـن التعثـر بأذيـال الشـبه، الصارفـة عـن صـوب الصـواب، والانخـداع بالخيـالات المزخرفـة كلامـع السـراب، (٧) كـما اتفـق لطوائـف مـن النظـار في البحـث عـن العقائـد والآراء، مـن أهـل البـدع والأهـواء.

Al-Ghazali attributes their erroneous ideas to their infatuation with ancient philosophers. Note the thick sarcasm in his tone:

(٨) وإنـما مصـدر كفرهـم سـماعهم أسـماء هائلـة، كسـقراط وبقـراط وأفلاطـون وأرسـطوطاليس وأمثالهـم، (٩) وإطنـاب طوائـف مـن متبعيهـم وضلالهـم في وصـف عقولهـم، وحسـن أصولهـم، ودقـة علومهـم: الهندسـة، والمنطقيـة، والطبيعيـة، والإلهيـة، واسـتبدادهم—لفرط الـذكاء والفطنة—باسـتخراج تلـك الأمـور الخفيـة، (١٠) وحكايتهـم عنهـم أنهم—مـع رزانـة عقولهـم وغـزارة فضلهم—منكـرون للشرائـع والنِّحـل، وجاحـدون لتفاصيـل الأديـان والملـل، (١١) ومعتقـدون أنهـم نواميـس مؤلفـة وحيـل مزخرفـة.

He repudiates the claims of the misguided philosophers of his day, claiming that the ancients were indeed believers in God:

(١٢) فلـما رأيـت هـذا العـرق مـن الحماقـة نابضًـا عـلى هـؤلاء الأغبيـاء، انتدبـت لتحريـر هـذا الكتـاب، (١٣) ردًّا عـلى الفلاسـفة القدمـاء، مبينًـا تهافـت عقيدتهـم وتناقـض كلمتهـم، فيـما يتعلـق بالإلهيـات، (١٤) وكاشـفًا عـن غوائـل مذهبهـم وعوراتـه، التـي هـي عـلى التحقيـق مضاحـك العقـلاء، وعـبرة عنـد الأذكيـاء، (١٥) أعنـي مـا اختصـوا بـه عـن الجماهـير والدهمـاء، مـن فنـون العقائـد والآراء، (١٦) هـذا مـن حكايـة مذهبهـم عـلى وجهـه، (١٧) ليتبـين هـؤلاء الملاحـدة تقليـدًا، اتفـاق كل مرمـوق مـن الأوائـل والأواخـر، عـلى الإيـمان بـالله واليـوم الآخـر . . . (١٨) زعـماء الفلاسـفة ورؤسـاؤهم بـراء عـما قذفـوا بـه مـن جحـد الشرائـع، وأنهـم مؤمنـون بـالله، ومصدقـون برسـله، (١٩) وأنهـم اختبطـوا في تفاصيـل بعـد هـذه الأصـول، قـد زلـوا فيهـا، فضلـوا وأضلّـوا عـن سـواء السـبيل . . .

Having conceded this, however, he shifts to his main argument, showing the inconsistency of the philosophers, using Plato and Aristotle as an example:

(٢٠) ليعلم أن الخوض في حكاية اختلاف الفلاسفة تطويل، فإن خبطهم طويل، ونزاعهم كثير، وآراءهم منتشرة، وطرقهم متباعدة متدابرة، (٢١) فلنقتصر على إظهار التناقض في رأي مقدمهم الذي هو الفيلسوف المطلق، والمعلم الأول، فإنه رتب علومهم وهذّبها بزعمهم، وحذف الحشو من آرائهم، وانتقى ما هو الأقرب إلى أصول أهوائهم، هو أرسطاليس، (٢٢) وقد رد على كل من قبله، حتى على أستاذه الملقب عندهم بأفلاطون الإلهي، (٢٣) ثم اعتذر عن مخالفته أستاذه بأن قال: أفلاطون صديق والحق صديق، ولكن الحق أصدق منه.

(٢٤) وإنما نقلنا هذه الحكاية ليعلم أنه لا تثبت ولا إتقان لمذهبهم عندهم، وأنهم يحكمون بظن وتخمين، (٢٥) من غير تحقيق ويقين، ويستدلون على صدق علومهم الإلهية بظهور العلوم الحسابية والمنطقية، ويستدرجون به ضعفاء العقول، (٢٦) ولو كانت علومهم الإلهية متقنة البراهين، نقية عن التخمين، كعلومهم الحسابية، لما اختلفوا فيها كما لم يختلفوا في الحسابية.

Vocabulary

فطنة	astuteness, understanding
توقّى (توقّي)	to avoid, avoiding
استهان	to devalue, debase
ربقة	noose (here: binding)
رَهط	group, gang
بغى	to commit outrage
عوج	deviance
إلفي	out of habit, familiarity
النصارى[1]	Christians
درج	to grow up
تعثر بأذيال	to fail, stumble
هوى ج. أهواء	whim, bias

1 See Cultural and Contextual Clues section in Lesson One.

سُقراط	Socrates
أفلاطون	Plato
أرسطاليس	Aristotle
بقراط	Hippocrates
إِطناب	exaggeration, tautology
رزانة	poise, calm
غزارة	abundance
نواميس	laws
حِيَلٌ	tricks
انتدب	to apply oneself
تهافت	incoherence
إلهيات	theology
غوائل	disasters, ruin
دهماء	masses, common folk
ملاحدة	heretics
اختبط	to fumble about
متدابرة	opposing, contrasting
هذّب	to rectify, refine
استدرج	to lure, entice

Comprehension Exercises

Answer the following questions in complete Arabic sentences, based on what the author says:

١. ما رأي الفلاسفة في أنفسهم؟

____

____

٢. كيف أثّرت أفكار الفلاسفة على معتقداتهم الدينية؟

____

____

٣. ما مصدر كفرهم؟

____

____

٤. مَن الأغبياء الذين أشار إليهم الغزالي؟

____

____

٥. ما رأي الغزالي في أرسطوطاليس؟

____

____

Interpreting the Text

١. هل كان هؤلاء الفلاسفة على دراية صحيحة بأفكار من سبقوهم؟ اذكروا الدليل.

____

____

٢. لماذا ذكر المؤلف آباء الفلاسفة وأجدادهم؟

---

٣. ما علامات الأسلوب التهكمي[2] التي ظهرت في هذا النص؟

---

٤. ماذا قدّم أرسطوطاليس لعلم الفلسفة من وجهة نظر الغزالي؟

---

٥. في رأيكم، ما هدف الكاتب في عرضه لقضية الخلاف بين أفلاطون وأرسطوطاليس؟

Style and Technique

This text is characterized by pervasive use of sarcasm and a number of words employed in idiomatic uses that may be different from what you normally associate with them. It is helpful to always bear in mind the author's purpose when judging how these are used.

2 Sarcastic

1. Al-Ghazali is mocking the attitude of the philosophers, whom he sees as so arrogant in their feelings of intellectual superiority that they discount true religion. Thus, his text is full or sarcastic references to their intelligence, which are meant as insults. Look at the expressions and phrases below and explain how these are being used ironically. A literal reading of the terms will help to show the arrogance they reflect:

Author's Intent	Literal Meaning	Phrase
		مزيد الفطنة (١)
		الأتراب (١)
		أسماء هائلة (٨)
		اختصوا عن الجماهير والدهماء (١٥)
		الفيلسوف المطلق (٢١)
		أفلاطون الإلهي (٢٢)

2. He contrasts these sarcastic statements with his actual feelings about their intellect, which he considers weak and limited. Explain how the following statements are used to denigrate the intelligence of his opponents:

ولا مستند لكفرهم غير تقليد سماعي (٤)

كتقليد اليهود والنصارى (٤)

سماعهم . . . إطناب . . . وضلال (٨-٩)

ويستدرجون به ضعفاء العقول (٢٥)

ولو كانت علومهم الإلهية متقنة البراهين (٢٦)

---

3. Another type of attack al-Ghazali uses is to accuse his opponents of an irreverent attitude toward religion. Find the phrases below in the text and explain how these are being used to level accusations that his opponents would firmly deny:

طائفة (١)

استحقروا شعائر الدين (٢)

استهانوا بالشرع وحدوده (٢)

منكرون للشرائع والنِّحل (١٠)

ومعتقدون أنهم نواميس مؤلفة وحيل مزخرفة (١١)

---

4. Finally, a portion of his attacks are outright insults of his opponents, attacking their character, intellectual weaknesses, and pre-

tensions. Below are a variety of different attacks that undermine the credibility of his opponents. Explain how each is being used.

كلامع السراب (٧)

____

____

العرق من الحماقة (١٢)

____

____

بزعمهم (٢٢)

____

____

وأنهم يحكمون بظنّ وتخمين (٢٤)

____

____

Using Cultural and Contextual Clues to Understand the Text

1. Al-Ghazali's attack is very much rooted in the religious doctrines and controversies of his day. His accusations rely on references that his audience would have readily recognized. In line 7, for example,

he equates the work of the philosophers to أهل البدع والأهواء. The word بدع, meaning "innovation" or "creation," refers to heresies. Similarly, the term أهواء has a specific context in Islamic law of arbitrary creeds that go against doctrine. Although both terms have other, secular meanings, it is clear the negative context al-Ghazali intends. The last part of line 3, beginning with يصدون, is a reference to infidels who lead people away from God, from the Qur'an (Surat al-A'raf, Ayat 45).

2. The description of Aristotle in lines 21–25 is quite intentionally calculated to show the limitations of human intellect. During the Middle Ages, Aristotle was the ultimate authority on a variety of subjects, particularly metaphysics, in both the Muslim world and Europe. The superlatives he uses for Aristotle—الفيلسوف المطلق، والمعلم الأول—as well as his achievements—رتب علومهم وهذّبها—are designed to set up a contrast and seeming contradiction with the fact that he disagreed with Aristotle whom the philosophers had deemed "divine."
3. The author also distinguishes between different types of knowledge as understood in his time. He enumerates sciences—العلوم—in line 9. These include the natural sciences (الطبيعية), engineering (الهندسة), and logic (المنطقية). Al-Ghazali was well educated in these sciences himself and in his role as coordinator of the education system in his country, supported their learning. His weak-minded opponents, however, have been misled by their study of these into thinking the ancients had magic powers (see end of line 9).

Analysis and Argument

A. Al-Ghazali addresses some of the most divisive controversies of the Middle Ages, which continue in many forms today. At the heart of the dispute is the suitability of philosophical speculation for devout Muslims. Many philosophers would refute his points, most famously Ibn Rushd (see Chapter 9 in this book). You can formulate your own position on this controversy:

١. هل يعتقد الغزالي أن الصراع المحتدم[3] هو صراع بين الدين والفلسفة، وليس بين الدين والعلم؟ وضحوا.
٢. هل يعالج الدين والفلسفة القضايا نفسها؟ لماذا؟
٣. معنى كلمة فلسفة باليونانية هو حبّ الحكمة، كيف يتفق هذا المفهوم مع ماهية[4] الفلسفة؟
٤. خلافات الرأي بين الفلاسفة القدماء تعني أن الفلسفة لا تقوم على حقائق علمية ثابتة، هل تتفقون أم تختلفون؟ ولماذا؟

B. How would al-Ghazali react to the following statements? On what basis?

١. الدين والفلسفة خطّان متوازيان لا يلتقيان.

____

____

٢. يُمكن الفصل بين التديّن والأخلاق.

____

____

٣. الفلاسفة القدماء أمثال سقراط وأفلاطون وثنيون،[5] ولذلك تحُرّم الأديان أفكارهم.

____

____

3 Raging
4 Core
5 Pagan

٤. تساعد دراسة الفلسفة على تنمية قدرة الإنسان على الفهم والنقد وإصدار الأحكام.

____

____

٥. التواضع العقلي سمة محمودة والمعرفة البشرية ليست معصومة من الخطأ.

____

____

Research and Presentation

With this chapter, you should have a clear grasp on the basic argument of al-Ghazali. As mentioned, his criticism of philosophy has been one of the most influential movements in Islamic thought. With this in mind, prepare a 2–3-minute presentation on the following topic:

أفكار الغزالي بين الأمس واليوم، وبين الشرق والغرب

Al-Ghazali himself, in describing how he will debunk his opponents, provides some useful terms for constructing an argument. Try to work these into your presentation:

revealing, exposing	كاشفًا
to infer (something) (by means of)	استدلّ (على) (بـ)
support for	مستند لـ
there is no support for____ except	لا مُسندَ لـ . . . غير
restrict [as in an argument] to	اقتصر على

9

Religion vs. Philosophy II—Ibn Rushd

الدرس التاسع – ابن رشد

كان ابن رشد (٥٢٠هـ/ ١١٢م – ٥٩٥هـ/ ١١٩٨م) واحدًا من أشهر فلاسفة الأندلس في العصور الوسطى. ويعد ابن رشد شخصية علمية متعددة التخصصات والمواهب؛ فهو فيلسوف وفقيه وطبيب وفلكي وقاضٍ وفيزيائي. يعرف ابن رشد في أوروبا باسم Averroes اللاتيني، كما يشتهر في الغرب بتعليقاته الواسعة ومؤلفاته عن الفيلسوف أرسطو، التي تُرجم الكثير منها باللاتينية والعبرية. وقد ساهمت ترجمات أعماله في اهتمام أوروبا والغرب بأرسطو وغيره من المفكرين اليونانيين.

ومن أشهر كتبه وأهمها كتاب «تهافت التهافت» وكان هذا الكتاب ردًّا مباشرًا على ما كتبه الغزالي في كتابه «تهافت الفلاسفة.»[1] وقد انتُقِد ابن رشد من عدد غير قليل من علماء المسلمين بسبب هذا الكتاب، بينما كان لهذا الكتاب عظيم الأثر على التفكير الأوروبي لفترة طويلة حتى بداية الفلسفة الحديثة والعلوم التجريبية.

Prediction and Scanning

Based on the context and background given above, record your predictions as to whether you expect the following statements to be true. Be prepared to discuss your predictions with classmates. Then, reading through the excerpts in the next section quickly, without the use of a dictionary, indicate whether your predictions were correct and where

1 See Chapter 8

(in which lines) you found the answers. Again, be prepared to discuss the results with your classmates.

الدلالة	التوقُّع	العبارة
		يعتقد ابن رشد أنّ بإمكان البشر تطوير القيم الأخلاقية والقوانين عن طريق التفكير العلماني البحت.
		الشريعة موجهة بالدرجة الأولى إلى النخبة المثقفة وليس الجماهير.
		تشير الفلسفة والمنطق إلى وجود الله ووحدانيته.
		يرى ابن رشد أنّ دراسة الفلسفة القديمة واجب شرعي.

From the Writings of Ibn Rushd

تهافت التهافت، فصل المقال

Having heard the allegation that the philosophers disregard Islamic law, Ibn Rushd responds that they in fact are among the strongest supporters of it:

(١) الشرائع ضرورية للفضائل العلمية والنظرية . . . (٢) بل القوم[2] يظهر من أمرهم أنهم أشد الناس تعظيمًا لها، وإيمانًا بها. (٣) والسبب في ذلك أنهم يرون أنها تنحو نحو تدبير الناس الذي به وجود الإنسان، بما هو إنسان وبلوغه سعادته

2 The قوم he has been discussing are the philosophers.

الخاصة به. وذلك أنها ضرورية في وجود الفضائل الخلقية للإنسان، والفضائل النظرية والصنائع العلمية. (٤) وذلك أنهم يرون أن الإنسان لا حياة له في هذه الدار إلا بالصنائع العلمية. ولا حياة له في هذه الدار ولا في الدار الآخرة إلا بالفضائل النظرية . . . (٥) وأنّ الفضائل الخلقية لا تتمكن إلا بمعرفة الله تعالى وتعظيمه بالعبادات المشروعة لهم، في ملة ملة، مثل القرابين والصلوات والأدعية . . . (٦) ويرون مع هذا أنه لا ينبغي أن يُتَعرّض بقول مثبت أو مُبطِل في مبادئها العامة، مثل: هل يجب أن يعبد الله أو لا يعبد؟ وأكثر من ذلك، هل هو موجود أم ليس بموجود.

Ibn Rushd reaffirms the division of the intellectual elite and the masses, a point on which religious conservatives had attacked the philosophers, but insists the elite remain true to their religion:

(٧) الشرائع . . . لما كانت تنحو نحو الحكمة بطريق مشترك للجميع، كانت واجبة عندهم. (٨) لأن الفلسفة إنما تنحو نحو تعريف سعادة بعض الناس العقلية، وهو من شأنه أن يتعلم الحكمة. (٩) والشرائع تقصد تعليم الجمهور عامة. (١٠) ومع هذا فلا نجد شريعة من الشرائع إلا وقد نبهت بما يخص الحكماء، وعينت بما يشترك فيه الجمهور. (١١) ولما كان الصنف الخاص من الناس[3] إنما يتم وجوده وتحصيل سعادته بمشاركة الصنف العام، كان التعليم العام ضروريًا في وجود الصنف الخاص، (١٢) وفي حياته: أما في وقت صباه ومنشئه فلا يشك أحد في ذلك، وأما عند نقلته إلى ما يخصه، فمن ضرورة فضيلته ألا يستهين بما نشأ عليه . . . (١٣) والحكماء العلماء الذين قيل فيهم إنهم ورثة الأنبياء.

He explains that Philosophy and Reason are commanded by Islam, and no threat to it:

(١٤) إن كان فعل الفلسفة ليس شيئًا أكثر من النظر في الموجودات، واعتبارها، من جهة دلالتها على الصانع، أعني من جهة ما هي مصنوعات، (١٠) فإنّ الموجودات إنما تدلّ على الصانع بمعرفة صنعتها، وأنّه كلما كانت المعرفة بصنعتها أتمّ، كانت المعرفة بالصانع أتمّ. (١٦) وكان الشرع قد ندب إلى اعتبار الموجودات، وحث على ذلك، فبيّن أنّ ما يدلّ عليه هذا الاسم إمّا واجب بالشرع وإما مندوب إليه. (١٧)

3 العلماء

فأما أنّ الشرع دعا إلى اعتبار الموجودات بالعقل . . . (١٩) وليس لقائل أن يقول إن هذا النوع من النظر في القياس العقلي بدعة، إذ لم يكن في صدر الأول. (٢٠) فإن النظر أيضًا في القياس الفقهي وأنواعه هو شيء استنبط بعد الصدر الأول، وليس يرى أنه بدعة. (٢١) فكذلك يجب أن نعتقد في النظر في القياس العقلي . . . (٢٢) بل أكثر أصحاب هذه الملة مثبتون القياس العقلي، إلا طائفة من الحشوية قليلة، وهم محجوجون بالنص.

Ibn Rushd asserts that study of the ancient philosophers is also a religious duty and strongly warns against anyone objecting to this:

(٢٣) فقد تبيّن من هذا أن النظر في كتب القدماء واجب بالشرع؛ (٢٤) إذ كان مغزاهم في كتبهم ومقصدهم هو المقصد الذي حثنا الشرع عليه، (٢٥) وأن مَن نهى عن النظر فيها مَن كان أهلًا للنظر فيها—وهو الذي جمع أمرين أحدهما ذكاء الفطرة، والثاني العدالة الشرعية والفضيلة الخلقية—فقد صدّ الناس عن الباب الذي دعا الشرع منه الناس إلى معرفة الله، (٢٦) وهو باب النظر المؤدي إلى معرفته حق المعرفة. (٢٧) وذلك غاية الجهل والبعد عن الله تعالى.

Vocabulary

فضائل	virtues
النظرية	theoretical, speculative
نحا	to lead to, to point toward
مثبت	asserting, positive
مُبطِل	canceling, negative
نبه	to call attention
منشأ	growing up, maturing
استهان	to disparage, dismiss
ندب	to deputize, entrust
حثّ	to encourage, spur
قائل	saying, one who says or tells
قياس	analogy
الصدر الأول	the earliest period, beginning (of Islam)

استنبط	to create, innovate
حشوية	literalists
محجوج	overcome by argument, easily rebutted
مغزى	intent
نهى	to forbid, prevent
فطرة	character, instinct

Comprehension Exercises

Answer the following questions in complete Arabic sentences, based on what the author says:

١. هل يؤمن الفلاسفة بالشرائع الدينية؟

____

____

٢. هل يحقّ للفيلسوف نقد مبادئ الأديان وشرائعها؟

____

____

٣. ما موقف الشريعة من البحث العقلاني والنظري؟

____

____

٤. ما تعريف الفلسفة؟

٥. ما أهمية دراسة الفلسفة؟

Interpreting the Text

١. كيف يرى الكاتب العلاقة بين الفضائل النظرية والفضائل الخلقية؟

٢. في رأيكم، لماذا تكلم ابن رشد عن الأديان بصورة عامة، ولم يقتصر كلامه على الدين الإسلامي؟

٣. كيف عرّف ابن رشد وظيفة الفلسفة (١٤)؟

٤. ابحثوا في المعجم عن الجذر «ش ر ع».

____

____

٥. هناك فرق كبير بين جهل العامة وجهل العلماء، ناقشوا هذه العبارة.

____

____

Style and Technique

1. The phrase أمرهم in line 2 and its variants أمره, أمرها, etc., is commonly used in formal writing as a way of saying "themselves," "himself," etc. In the case here, as in many instances, it need not be translated. The word أمر literally means "issue" or "matter" and is used in a large number of phrases, most often not included in the English translation:

   that which = الأمر الذي
   all about it = كل أمره
   at first = في أول الأمر

2. In line 2, Ibn Rushd uses the *tamyiiz* (تمييز) construction: أنهم أشد الناس تعظيمًا لها. He is referring to those who give most importance (عظّم) to Islamic law (الشريعة). The Form II of عظم—the familiar root for "great"—means "to treat as great, to glorify." Form II, however, will not fit into the superlative form used for Form I (أكْبَر، أجْمَل). The way this is handled is to use a Form I superlative (in this case أشدّ—most intense—but often أكثر or أقلّ) paired with the *masdar* of the desired term in the accusative case. Here, that *masdar* is تعظيمًا. The most common mistake for language learners in using

the construction is to use the adjective (which is how it would be done in English), rather than the *masdar*.

3. The conjunction إذ (lines 19, 24) has numerous meanings. It can indicate a time relationship, meaning "when" something happens, or imply sequence ("then"). It can also, as is the case here, connote a causative or supporting relationship, similar to "because," "for," or "since." In line 19, it indicates a direct causation:

   هذا النوع من النظر في القياس العقلي بدعة، إذ لم يكن موجودًا في الصدر الأول.

   "This type of analogical reasoning is innovation because it was not in the earliest period of Islam." This could also be translated as "since," "as" or "for," all used to signify the reason for the first statement.

Using Cultural and Contextual Clues to Understand the Text

1. Islamic law distinguishes between a فرض عين (individual duty), which is mandatory upon all Muslims, and a فرض كفاية (collective duty), which is something that someone in the community must perform. Prayer is a duty for all Muslims, for example, whereas conducting a burial for a deceased person need only be carried out by enough people to accomplish the task. Ibn Rushd is building on this distinction in his comments that separate out the general public (الجميع، العامة) and those capable of doing speculative reasoning, as in line 25. In this way, he is able to talk about philosophy being mandated by religious law, yet not for everybody. Al-Ghazali, by contrast, saw this as an invalid use of the concept and essentially setting up two classes of people.
2. At the center of the dispute between the philosophers and conservatives in this case is the issue of القياس or reasoning by analogy. This term has a very specific contextual implication. The principle is accepted in most schools of Islamic law as a way of applying the law to situations not mentioned in the Qur'an or Hadith but is discouraged to various degrees by different schools of law. Ibn Rushd

is talking about extending this reasoning to all areas, such as theological speculation, studying of non-Muslim religions and cultures, and so on. You can see how his argument, especially in the third excerpt, is itself an example of analogous reasoning, which he is using to demonstrate his point.

Analysis and Argument

A. Ibn Rushd's arguments are best understood in contrast to those of al-Ghazali in the previous chapter (Chapter 8). Although he claims to be refuting al-Ghazali point by point, you can deduce much from what each writer chooses to emphasize and what they do not. You can build a critical analysis of both by noting these contrasts.

١. قارنوا بين منهجي ابن رشد والغزالي ووجهة نظرهما حول الدين والفلسفة.
٢. في رأيكم، ما عواقب ظاهرة النزاع الفكري بين الفلاسفة وعلماء الدين؟
٣. يُطلِق بعضهم على ابن رشد لقب فيلسوف التنوير، وعلى الغزالي لقب الفيلسوف التائه. ما رأيكم في هذين اللقبين ومدى توافقهما مع الفكر الفلسفي والعقلي للعالمَيْن؟

B. Do you think Ibn Rushd would agree or disagree with the following statements, and why?

١. من الصعب أن تتعارض الحقيقة الفلسفية مع الحقيقة الدينية.

___

___

٢. هناك مسائل لا يجب على أي شخص متدين أن يبحث عن جوابها.

____

____

٣. للحصول على السعادة الحقيقية، لا ينبغي لنا التفكير في نشأة الكون وأحواله.

____

____

٤. نستطيع اكتساب مزيد من الخبرات من عصور ومجتمعات لا ننتمي إليها.

____

____

٥. التفكير العقلاني يجب أن يتغلب على التفكير العاطفي.

____

____

Research and Presentation

By now, you should have a solid grasp of Ibn Rushd's basic ideas. It will help if you have also read Chapter 8 on al-Ghazali, but this is not absolutely necessary. With this background, prepare a 2–3-minute argument on the following question:

العلاقة بين الدين والعلم، هل يجب أن تكون علاقة اتصال أم علاقة انفصال؟

Ibn Rushd's text offers some useful terms for building an argument. Some related terms are also included below. Incorporate these into your presentation as you structure your argument:

establishing, proving	مُثبِت
disproving, negating	مُبْطِل
by analogy	على القياس
an analogy	تمثيل
refute (an argument)	دحض

10

Impressions of Europeans—Usama ibn Munqidh

الدرس العاشر – أسامة بن منقذ

مؤيد الدولة أبو المظفر أسامة بن مرشد بن منقذ (٤٨٨هـ/ ١٠٩٥م - ٥٨٤هـ/ ١١٨٨م)، الأمير المقاتل والشاعر السياسي والمؤرخ الفذّ. كان على علاقة طيبة بأمراء المسلمين في عصره. تلقى العلم والثقافة كما كان يتلقاها أمراء هذا العصر، فدرَسَ الحديث والفقه واللغة وحفظ أبياتا كثيرة من الشعر. اعتكف في أواخر أيامه وتفرغ للبحث والتأليف والكتابة. قد يعرفه الغرب أكثر مما يعرفه الشرق، حيث تُرجِمَ أشهر كتبه، «الاعتبار»، إلى الفرنسية والألمانية منذ عدة قرون، ويُعدّ هذا الكتاب شهادة اجتماعية تاريخية نادرة عن الحروب الصليبية. ويتميز أسلوبه الوصفي في هذا الكتاب بالدقة والصدق والإبداع، كما أنه لا يخلو من روح الفكاهة.

Prediction and Scanning

Based on the context and background given above, record your predictions as to whether you expect to find the writer making the following statements. Be prepared to discuss your predictions with classmates. Then, reading through the excerpts in the next section quickly, without the use of a dictionary, indicate whether your predictions were correct and where (in which lines) you found the answers. Again, be prepared to discuss the results with your classmates.

العبارة	التوقُّع	الدلالة
يختلف العرب عن الفرنجة (المسيحيين الأوروبيين) في قناعاتهم بما يجب أن تكون عليه العلاقة بين الجنسين.		
يرى الفرنجة أنّ يسوع هو الله الصغير.		
تتشابه سلوكيات بعض الفرنجة مع المسلمين نتيجة للمعايشة.		
كان الفرنجة يساعدون أصدقاءَهم المسلمين في بعض الأوقات الصعبة.		

From the Writings of Usama ibn Munqidh

كتاب الاعتبار، الباب الأول

Usama ibn Munqidh describes gender relations among the Europeans, concluding that they have no concept of propriety:

(١) وليس عندهم شيء من النخوة والغيرة، (٢) يكون الرجل منهم يمشي هو وامرأته يلقاه رجل آخر يأخذ المرأة ويعتزل بها ويتحدث معها، (٣) والزوج واقف ناحية ينتظر فراغها من الحديث، فإذا طولت عليه خلاها مع المتحدث ومضى. (٤) ومما شاهدت من ذلك أني كنت إذا إلى نابلس أنزل في دار رجل يقال له معزّ داره عمارة المسلمين، (٥) لها طاقات تفتح إلى الطريق، يقابلها من الجانب الطريق الآخر دار لرجل إفرنجي يبيع الخمر للتجار (٦) قد فتح بيته من هذا الخمر، من أراد منها شيئًا فهي من موضع كذا وكذا، وأجرته عن ندائه النبيذ الذي في تلك القنينة، (٧) فجاء يومًا ووجد رجلًا مع امرأته في الفراش فقال له: أي شيء أدخلك عند امرأتي؟ (٨) قال: وجدت فراشًا مفروشًا نمت فيه. قال: والمرأة نائمة

معـك؟ (٩) قـال: الفـراش لهـا. كنـت أقـدر أن أمنعهـا مـن فراشـها؟ (١٠) قـال: وحـق دينـي إن عـدت فعلتهـا تخاصمـت أنـا وأنـت. (١١) فـكان هـذا نكـيره ومبلـغ غيرتـه . . . (١٢) فانظـروا إلى هـذا الاختـلاف العظيـم: مـا فيهـم الغـيرة والنخـوة وفيهـم الشـجاعة العظيمـة، ومـا تكـون الشـجاعة إلا مـن النخـوة والأنفـة مـن سـوء الأحدوثـة.

In one of his most famous anecdotes, Ibn Munqidh encapsulates the religious errors of Christianity with his recollection of an encounter with a Frank at the Dome of the Rock. How he remembers the words of the Frank reveals the fundamental difference in perception of the role of Jesus between the religions:

(١٣) ورأيـت واحـدًا منهـم جـاء إلى الأمـير معـين الديـن (رحمـه الله) وهـو في الصخـرة (١٤) فقـال: تريـد تبـصر الله صغـيرًا؟ (١٥) قـال: نعـم. فمشـى بـين أيدينـا حتـى أرانـا صـورة مريـم والمسـيح (عليـه الصـلاة والسـلام) صغـير في حجرهـا (١٦) فقـال: هـذا الله صغـير. (١٧) تعـالى الله عـما يقـول الكافـرون علـوًّا كبـيرًا.

Despite his negative opinions of Franks and Frankish manners, Ibn Munqidh believes that social contact between the groups has a positive effect:

(١٨) مـن الإفرنـج قـوم قـد تبلـدوا وعـاشروا المسـلمين فهـم أصلـح مـن القريـب العهـد ببلادهـم، (١٩) ولكنهـم شـاذ لا يقـاس عليـه. (٢٠) فمـن ذلـك أننـي نفـذت صاحبًـا إلى أنطاكيـة في شـغل، وكان بهـا الرئيـس تـادرس بـن الصفـي وبينـي وبينـه صداقـة، (٢١) وهـو نافـذ الحكـم في أنطاكيـة. (٢٢) فقـال أصحـابي يومًـا: قـد دعـاني صديـق لي مـن الإفرنـج، تجـيء معـي تـرى زيهـم؟ (٢٣) قـال: فمضيـت معـه فجئنـا إلى دار فـارس مـن الفرسـان العتـق الذيـن خرجـوا في أول خـروج الإفرنـج، (٢٤) وقـد اعتُفِـيَ مـن الديـوان والخدمـة، ولـه بأنطاكيـة ملـك يعيـش منـه، (٢٥) فأحـضر مائـدة حسـنة وطعامًـا في غايـة النظافـة والجـودة، (٢٦) ورآني متوقفًـا عـن الأكل فقـال: كل طيـب النفـس، فأنـا مـا آكل مـن طعـام الإفرنـج ولي طباخـات مصريـات (٢٧) لا آكل إلا مـن طبخهـن، ولا أُدْخِـل داري لحـم خنزيـر. (٢٨) فأكلـت وأنـا محـترز وانصرفنـا (٢٩). فأنـا بعـد مجتـازًا في السـوق وامـرأة إفرنجيـة تعلقـت بي وهـي تبربـر بلسـانهم ومـا أدري مـا تقـول. (٣٠) فاجتمـع عـليّ خلـق مـن الإفرنـج فأيقنـت مـن الهـلاك. (٣١) وإذا ذلـك الفـارس قـد أقبـل فـرآني، (٣٢) فجـاء فقـال لتلـك المـرأة: مالـك ولهـذا المسـلم؟ (٣٣) قالـت: هـذا قتـل أخـي عـرس. (٣٤) وكان هـذا عـرس فارسًـا بأفاميـة قتلـه بعـض جنـد حمـاة. (٣٥) فصـاح

عليهم وقال: هذا رجل برجاسي (أي تاجر) لا يقاتل ولا يحضر قتال. (٣٦) وصاح على أولئك المجتمعين، فتفرقوا (٢٧) وأخذ يدي ومضى، (٢٨) فكان تأثير تلك المؤاكلة خلاصي من القتل.

Vocabulary

نخوة	honor, dignity
غيرة	jealousy (here meaning protectiveness, care, ardency)
نابلس	Nablus, city in the West Bank
معزّ	Mu'izz (name of the host)
إفرنج	Franks (more generally, Europeans)
طاقة	niche in a wall that serves as a window
قنينة	flask, bottle
خاصم	to argue, quarrel
نكير	reproach, blame
أنفة	rejection, disdain
الصخرة	The Dome of the Rock in Jerusalem
عاشر	to associate closely with
شاذ	deviation, not normal
قاس على	generalize from, draw conclusions from
أنطاكية	Antioch (now in Türkiye)
نفذت صاحبًا	to send someone to accompany
نافذ	powerful, influential
زي	fashion, ways
عتيق ج. عتق	freed slave
اعتُقِيَ	set free, released from service
ملك	here: property
محترز	guardedly

تبربر	to babble
خلق	a group of people
أيقن	to be convinced of
أفامية	Apamea (in Syria)
حماة	Hama (in Syria)
برجاسي	bourgeois
مؤاكلة	sharing a meal

Comprehension Exercises

A. Answer the following questions in complete Arabic sentences, based on the excerpts:

١. ما علامات انعدام النخوة من وجهة نظر ابن منقذ؟

____

____

٢. كيف برّر الرجل وجوده في الفراش مع زوجة صاحب البيت؟

____

____

٣. ما مُعتقَد الإفرنجي في رؤية الله؟

____

____

٤. كيف طمْأَنَ الفارس ضيفه بأنّ طعامه طيّب؟

٥. كيف خلّصَ الفارس صاحبه من السيدة ومن جمهور الإفرنج؟

B. Are the following statements true in the opinion of the author? If not, why?

١. أصرّ الإفرنج على الفصل بين الرجال والنساء في المجالس.

٢. الشجاعة الحقيقية تعتمد على الأخلاق والنخوة.

٣. أظهر الإفرنج الذين عاشوا مع المسلمين وعاشروهم أخلاقًا وصفاتٍ حميدة.

٤. كان الإفرنج جبناء في الحروب.

---

٥. الإفرنج يؤمن بأنّ عيسى هو الله الصغير.

Interpreting the Text

١. ما الحدود المقبولة في العلاقة بين الرجال والنساء من وجهة نظر الكاتب؟
٢. ما ردّ الفعل الذي توقّعه ابن منقذ من صاحب البيت عندما وجد زوجته في الفراش مع رجل آخَر؟
٣. ما رأي المؤلف في شجاعة الإفرنج؟
٤. هل يبدو لك أن الكاتب يشجع علاقات الصداقة بين الإفرنج والمسلمين؟
٥. في رأيكم، لماذا اختلط الأمر[1] على المرأة الإفرنجية في السوق؟

Style and Technique

1. The phrase used after the name of the Emir Mu'in al-Din, رحمه الله, "God have mercy on him," is standard when referring to a deceased person. The phrase after the mention of Jesus, عليه الصلاة والسلام, "upon him the blessings and peace of God," is the standard صلاة for angels and prophets. Other common honorifics, or صلوات include:

---

1 Confused about

God	سبحانه وتعالى	Glorified and exalted is He
	عزّ وجلّ	Mighty and majestic
The Prophet Muhammad	صَلّى اللهُ عليهِ وسلّم	May God send blessings and peace upon him
Companions of the Prophet	رضي الله عنه	May God be pleased with him

Note that there are many variations of these phrases.

2. The phrase بـين أيدينـا (line 15), literally "in between our hands," is a metaphor meaning "in front of us." This phrase is used in several variants to convey this impression of closeness. In this case, it is plural because Usama and the Emir have more than two hands between them. When used to refer to a single person, بـين يديـه, utilizing the dual construction to indicate two hands, is used. Note that the ن of يديـن has been dropped because the word is part of an *idaafa*. This phrase is often used to refer to being in the presence of a person of importance. Ibn al-Sa'i, in Lesson 11, makes frequent use of this in his descriptions of gatherings in the presence of caliphs.
3. The word تبربـر in line 29 comes from the Greek barbarous, meaning to speak in an unintelligible tongue (the words sounding like brr... brr..., etc.) This became the root of barbarian, barbaric, and Berber. Its use here is quite negative, meaning not simply that she spoke a foreign language, but reflecting the writer's contempt for it.

Using Cultural and Contextual Clues to Understand the Text

1. The term فرنج is the rendering of the word Frank, referring to the people of France. This term was used in a general sense as a reference to anyone from Western Europe, as their presence was a relative rarity in the Middle East before the Crusades. This is similar to the use of the term روم, from Rome, as a reference to Christians from the East. Following the First Crusade in 1096, four Christian kingdoms were established in Greater Syria: Edessa (1097–1150); Antioch (1098–1287), the Kingdom of Jerusalem (1099–1291), and the County of Tripoli (1102–1289).
2. During the period Usama describes, the Dome of the Rock was under the control of the Crusader Kingdom of Jerusalem, which turned it into a church. Al-Aqsa Mosque, which is also located on the Temple Mount, became the headquarters of the Knights Templar. Usama, being only five years old when the Kingdom of Jerusalem was established, would not have remembered a time before that. The appearance of an image of Jesus and the Virgin Mary in the Dome of the Rock would thus be due to its status as a church at the time, as such an image would be forbidden in Islam, particularly in a holy site.

Analysis and Argument

Usama ibn Munqidh displays his "expertise" about a group of people with whom his audience would have had limited contact, and about whom many myths circulated. While he shows the beginnings of mutual understanding, some of his impressions are based in this limited contact. How would you answer the following questions, based on what you know now versus Ibn Munqidh's point of view?

١. هل افتقر[2] الإفرنج لصفة النخوة والأنفة؟ كيف تفسرون انطباع[3] ابن مُنقذ عنهم؟
٢. ما وجه الخلاف بين الإفرنجي وابن منقذ حول صورة عيسى وأمه مريم عليهما السلام؟
٣. هل تغيرت أخلاق الإفرنج وطباعهم نتيجة اختلاطهم بالمسلمين؟ هل توافقون ابن منقذ في رأيه بهذا الشأن؟
٤. صِفوا مشهد السوق وكيف ظهر التناقض في الرأي جليًّا[4] بين المرأة والفارس؟

Research and Presentation

Based on your understanding of Ibn Munqidh's ideas, prepare a 3–4 minute presentation of his views on the following subject:

التأثير[5] والتأثُر[6] على المسلمين: الحروب الصليبية

This argument will depend on seeing trends and signs beneath the overwhelming signs of difference. For this, verbs to show indication will be particularly useful. Try to vary up your verbs by incorporating the following:

to make clear	أوضح
to reflect	عكس
to express	أعرَبَ عن
to reveal	كشف

2 To be lacking
3 Impression
4 Obviously
5 Influence
6 Effect

11

Women in the Caliphal Court—Ibn al-Sa'i

الدرس الحادي عشر – ابن الساعي

علي بن أنجب بن عثمان بن عبد الله أبو طالب تاج الدين ابن السَّاعي (٥٩٣هـ/ ١١٩٧م - ٦٧٤هـ/ ١٢٧٥م). يعدّ واحدًا من كبار المصنفين في التاريخ. كان مولده ووفاته ببغداد التي كان شاهدًا على دمارها وسقوطها في يد المغول سنة ١٢٥٨م. عمل ابن الساعي خازنًا لكُتب المستنصرية، ومؤرخًا لمجتمع النخبة في آخر أيام الخلافة العباسية. من أشهر تصانيفه «الجامع المختصر في عنوان التاريخ وعيون السير»، وقد صنّفه في خمسة وعشرين مجلدًا، ورتّبه على مرّ السنين وجاء آخره في سنة ٦٥٦هـ. ومن مصنفاته أيضا «تاريخ الشعراء» و«أخبار الحلاج» و«أخبار قضاة بغداد» و«أخبار الوزراء» و«ذيل تاريخ بغداد» و«طبقات الفقهاء» و«غرر المحاضرة» و«أخبار المصنفين» و«مناقب الخلفاء العباسيين» وكتاب «المحب والمحبوب» و«الزهاد» و«الإيضاح عن الأحاديث الصحاح» و«إرشاد الطالب إلى معرفة المذاهب» و«شرح المقامات» للحريري، وأخيرًا كتابه الأوسع شهرة وتأثيرًا في قصور الخلفاء حينها «جهات الأئمة الخلفاء من الحرائر والإماء» المسمّى بـ «نِساء الخلفاء».

Prediction and Scanning

Based on the context and background given above, record your predictions as to whether you expect to find the following things occurring in the stories in this section. Be prepared to discuss your predictions with classmates. Then, reading through the excerpts in the next section quickly, without the use of a dictionary, indicate whether your predictions were correct and where (in which lines) you found the answers. Again, be prepared to discuss the results with your classmates.

العبارة	التوقُّع	الدلالة
امرأة تخصّصت في الأعمال الخيرية ومساعدة الناس		
امرأة مفضّلة عند الخليفة		
امرأة ذات عقل وحكمة		
امرأة حافَظَ الخليفة على بيتها تخليدًا لذكراها		

From the Writings of Ibn al-Sa'i

نساء الخلفاء، الفصل السابع والعشرون

The author describes Banafsha bint Abdullah al-Rumiyah, a consort of the twelfth-century Abbasid caliph al-Mustadi':

(١) بنفشا، بنت عبد الله الروميّة، مولاة الإمام المستضيء بأمر الله (رضي الله عنه):
(٢) كانت من خواصه وسراريّه. (٣) لها المكانة الرفيعة عنده والمنزلة العالية،
والحكم النافذ والأمر والنهي. (٤) وكانت صالحة كثيرة الخير فائضة المعروف
متفقدة للفقراء والمساكين كثيرة الصدقة والبرّ. (٥) جعلت دارها بأسفل البلد على
شاطئ دجلة مدرسة ووقفتها على الحنابلة، ووقفت عليها وقوفًا وبَنَتْ قنطرة على
نهر عيسى وعقدت جسرًا على دجلة . . . (٦) وسمعت أنها كانت في عيد الفطر
في كل سنة تُخرج زكاة الفطر صاعًا من تمر ثمّ تقول هذا ما فرضه الشرع عليَّ (٧)
وأنا لا أقنع من مثلي بهذا، (٨) فتُخرج صاعًا من الذهب العين وتأمر بتفرقته على
الفقراء، وأعتقت خلقًا من الموالي الجواري والمماليك.

Ibn al-Sa'i describes the caliph al-Mutawakkil's relationship with the enslaved woman Mahbuba:

(٩) محبوبة جارية المتوكّل كانت مُولّدة شاعرة مغنّية متقدمة في الحالتين على طبقتها. (١٠) وكانت حسنة الوجه والغناء، (١١) أهداها عبيد الله بن طاهر للمتوكّل على الله لما وُلّيّ الخلافة في جملة أربعمائة جارية قيان وسواذج فتقدمتهن جميعا عنده . . . (١٢) علي بن الجهم قال: كنت يومًا بحضرة المتوكّل وهو يشرب ونحن بين يديه إذ دفع إلى محبوبة تفاحة مغلفة بغالية فقبّلتها وانصرفت عن حضرته ثمّ خرجت جارية لها ومعها رقعة فدفعتها إلى المتوكّل فقرأها وضحك ثم رمى إلينا فقرأناها . . . (١٣) فما بقي والله أحد إلاّ استظرفها واستملح الأبيات.

At a time when the Abbasid Caliphate was weakened, the caliph al-Mu'tadid attempted to increase his influence over the largely independent Tulunid state in Egypt by marrying the granddaughter of the emir Ahmad ibn Tulun, Qatr al-Nada:

(١٤) تزوّجها الإمام المعتضد بالله وهي عند أبيها بمصر (١٥) ووصلت إلى بغداد . . . وزُفّت إليه وكان معها من الجهاز ما لا يكاد أن يوجد مثله في خزائن ملوك الأرض، وكانت من أعقل النساء وأرأسهن . . . (١٦) المعتضد قال لها يومًا: بما تشكرين الله إذ جعل أمير المؤمنين زوجك؟ فقالت: بما يشكر به أمير المؤمنين إذ جعل أحمد بن طولون من رعيته . . . (١٧) قطر الندى بقيت عند الإمام المعتضد بالله إلى أن توفيت . . . (١٨) ودُفِنت داخل قصر الخلافة.

The last effective Abbasid caliph before the Mongol invasion, al-Nasir li-Din Allah, attempted to reassert power over the Seljuq Turks through his marriage to the daughter of the Seljuq sultan, Seljuqi Khatun:

(١٩) خطبها الإمام الناصر لدين الله—قدّس الله روحه—فزُوّجت منه، (٢٠) وأنفذ إليها من جاء بها ودخل بها وأعطاها من الجواهر الثمينة وتحف الخلفاء والملوك ما لا تُعرف قيمته. (٢١) وصادفت منه قبولًا عظيمًا فأقامت عنده مدّة يسيرة في أرغد عيش وأصفاه، ثمّ عاجلها ريب المنون، (٢٢) فاستُلبت من غضارتها ونعيمها ولحقت بالغابرين. (٢٣) ووجد الناصر لدين الله من الحزن عليها والأسف على

فراقها ما منعه من الأكل والشرب أيامًا. (٢٤) وتُركت دارها بجميع ما فيها من الأقمشة والأثاث على حالها سنين عديدة لا تُفتح ولا يؤخذ منها شيء.

Vocabulary

مولاة	lady, consort
سُرِّيَّة ج. سراري	concubine
بِرّ	charity, goodness
دجلة	the Tigris River
وقّف على	to create a waqf (religious endowment) for
الحنابلة	the Hanbalis (school of religious law)
قنطرة	stone bridge, viaduct
نهر عيسى	a canal connecting the Tigris and Euphrates
صاع	an old unit of measure for solid items
تفرق	to distribute
جارية	enslaved woman
أهدى	to give as a gift
قيان	female singers
رقعة	piece of cloth or paper
وُلي	to be appointed
بين يديه	in his presence (lit. between his hands)
استظرف	to consider (something or someone) witty or charming
استملح	to consider (something or someone) beautiful
بيت ج. أبيات	line(s) of poetry

زُفّت	to be married, to be moved from her family's house to her husband's house in a wedding procession
أرأس	firm
رعية	subjects, citizens
قدّس الله روحه	may God sanctify his soul
أنفذ إلى	to send someone or something
يسيرة	ease
أرغد	most carefree
أصفى	most serene
ريب المنون	trick of fate
استلب	to steal, wrest away from
غضارة	prosperity, luxury
غابر	mortal, perishable, stale
فراق	farewell, separation
أقمشة	cloths, textiles

Comprehension Exercises

A. Answer the following questions in complete Arabic sentences, based on the excerpts:

١. مَنْ بنفشا؟

____

____

٢. كيف وصلت محبوبة إلى ديوان الخليفة المتوكّل؟

____

____

٣. من زوج قطر الندى؟ وكيف كانت مراسم الزواج؟

____

____

٤. ماذا أهدى الخليفة الناصر زوجته الجديدة؟

____

____

٥. كيف حَزِن الخليفة الناصر على زوجته؟

____

____

B. Are the following statements true in the opinion of the author? If not, why?

١. لم يكن لبنفشا مكانة مميزة في قصر الخليفة.

____

____

٢. أَوْلَت[1] بنفشا للفقراء اهتمامًا كبيرًا.

____

____

٣. كانت قطر الندى من الفقراء عند زواجها من الخليفة.

____

____

٤. كان الإمام الناصر لدين الله كريمًا سخيًّا مع زوجته.

____

____

٥. تُوفيت زوجة الإمام الناصر نتيجة التعذيب[2] في سجون الخليفة.

____

____

1 Paid great attention = أولت اهتمامًا كبيرًا
2 Torture

Interpreting the Text

١. المرأة قوة تغيّر في المجتمع. كيف تتوافق هذه المقولة مع شخصية بنفشا؟

____

____

٢. ما المهارات التي ساعدت محبوبة على التقرُّب من الخليفة المتوكّل؟

____

____

٣. ما دلالات الترف والثراء التي ذكرها الكاتب عند حديثه عن قطر الندى؟

____

____

٤. أين دُفِنت قطر الندى بعد وفاتها؟ وعلامَ يدل ذلك؟

____

____

٥. ما المِحَن[3] التي أصابت زوجة الإمام الناصر لدين الله؟

____

____

---

3 Ordeals

Style and Technique

1. Ibn al-Sa'i uses traditional blessings when mentioning the names of caliphs, similar to those used when mention the names of the prophets or companions. After the name of the caliph al-Mustadi' bi-Amr Allah, he uses the traditional رضي الله عنه (may God be pleased with him). After the name of al-Nasir li-Din Allah, he adds قدّس الله روحه (may God sanctify his soul). A similar expression that may be used is قدّس الله سرّه (God sanctify his secret). The "secret" in this case also refers to the soul but reflects the belief that the soul is a secret matter between the person and God.
2. Line 10 features the use of the "false *idaafa*," a stylistic device that uses an adjective in combination with a noun. While technically an *idaafa* must be made up of two or more nouns, this phrase is accomplishing the same meaning using an adjective for its first term. The phrase حسنة الوجه translates as the similar English phrase "fair of face." The adjective will agree with the subject in gender and the following noun is always in the definite. Examples of this construction include كثير الكلام or قليل الأدب.
3. ما لا تُعرف قيمته in line 20 might be confusing to the reader because the word ما لا could be read as meaning "money or funds" which would seem to make sense in the context. In this case, however, ما لا is a compound of two parts: ما + لا: the particle ما is the definite conjunctive pronoun having the meaning of الّذي (اسم موصول بمعنى الّذي), while لا is a negation particle. Together, it carries the meaning of "that which does not." Other popular expressions using ما لا include ما لا نهاية (endless); ما لا عين رأت (what no eye has ever seen); and ما لا طاقة لنا به (that which we do not have the power to bear). Line 23 (ما منعه عن الأكل): ما here is also a definite conjunctive pronoun meaning الذي.

Using Grammar and Structure Clues to Understand the Text

1. The Form X verb form (استفعل) often means to consider something or someone to be whatever the basic meaning of the root is. In line 13, two of these occur. استظرف from the root ظرف, which means to be charming or witty. The Form X, استظرف, therefore, is to consider someone witty or charming. Similarly, the root of استملح is ملح, which means to be beautiful. The Form X, therefore, is to consider something beautiful. Both describe the audience's reaction to Mahbuba.
2. The parallel structure in line 16 uses two clauses beginning with بما to convey the meaning of "as much as," with the two things being equated. In this case, Qatr al-Nada's joy at having the caliph as her husband is equated to his joy at having a relationship with her father, Ahmed ibn Tulun. As in many structures, the English equivalent does not introduce the second clause with any words (a comma would be the indication that the second half of the comparison is beginning). The Arabic here uses بما to introduce both parts. This conjunction can also mean "including" and "since."
3. This text includes several verbs in passive voice(المبني للمجهول). For example, in line 11 we find the verb وُلِّيَ (he was assigned a position). It is clear this refers to the caliph, as it is the only verb conjugated for "he." Try to identify the other passive verbs in the text, as well as their objects (نائب الفاعل) and discuss the possible reasons why the author chooses to use the passive.

Analysis and Argument

Below are some famous sayings about women. Discuss your opinion of these statements and how you think the author would react:

١. تُفضّل المرأة أن تكون جميلة أكثر من أن تكون ذكية، لأنها تعلم أن الرجل يرى بعينيه أكثر ما يفكر بعقله.
٢. النساء مِثْلُ الصحافة؛ أفضل وسيلة لنقل الأخبار.
٣. وراء كل رجل عظيم امرأة تقول له: لستَ عظيمًا.
٤. عندما يصمت الرجل فاعلم أنّه يفكّر وعندما تصمت المرأة فاعلم أنها تدبّر مكيدة[4].
٥. قلب المرأة لؤلؤة[5] تحتاج إلى صيّاد ماهر.

Research and Presentation

Based on your understanding of Ibn al-Sa'i's text, prepare a 3–4-minute argument on the following question:

لو عاصر ابن الساعي عالمنا الآن، كيف سيُصنّف زوجات الزعماء وأبرز النساء الرائدات في السياسة؟

Your argument should include some specific examples from today's world that would either fit well with or go against the values Ibn al-Sa'i seems to promote. To facilitate this, some verbs expressing the idea of things agreeing with certain ideas or values will be useful:

to comport with	اتفق مع
to reflect	عَكَسَ
appropriate	ملائم
to conform to	انسجم مع

4 Plot
5 Pearl

12

Travel Literature—Ibn Battuta

الدرس الثاني عشر - ابن بطوطة

مُحَمَّدُ بْنُ عَبْدِ اللهِ بْنُ مُحَمَّد اللَّوَاتِي الطَّنْجِي المعروف بابْنِ بطوطة (٧٠٣هـ/ ١٣٠٤م - ٧٧٩هـ/ ١٣٧٧م). وُلد ونشأ في مدينة طنجة بالمغرب. وكانت عائلته تقدّس العلم عامة والعلوم الشرعية بصفة خاصة، وكان معظم رجال العائلة يعمل في سلك القضاء. قرّر ابن بطوطة في أوائل العشرينيات من عمره الذهاب إلى مكة لأداء فريضة الحج، ولكن رحلته استمرّت ٢٩ عامًا، زار فيها نحو أربع وأربعين دولة من الدول الإسلامية وغير الإسلامية، وقطع خلالها أكثر من ٧٥ ألف ميل، أي ما يعادل ١٢١ ألف كيلومتر، وهي مسافة لم يقطعها أي رحالة غيره حتى ظهور عصر النقل البخاري بعد ٤٥٠ سنة. ونالت رحلاته تقديرًا كبيرًا نظرًا لقيمتها التاريخية والجغرافية؛ فقد التقى فيها بعدد كبير من الحكّام والوزراء والشخصيات المهمة، واستحقّ ابن بطوطة عن جدارة لقب أمير الرحالة المسلمين. أما كتابه «تحفة الأنظار في غرائب الأمصار وعجائب الأسفار» أو ما يعرف اختصارا بـ«رحلات ابن بطوطة»، فَيُعدّ وثيقة ومصدرًا علميًّا لا غنى عنه لتلك الحقبة التاريخية.

Prediction and Scanning

Based on the context and background given above, record your predictions as to whether you expect the following observations to be true. Be prepared to discuss your predictions with classmates. Then, reading through the excerpts in the next section quickly, without the use of a dictionary, indicate whether your predictions were correct and where (in which lines) you found the answers. Again, be prepared to discuss the results with your classmates.

الدلالة	التوقُّع	العبارة
		عاش المسلمون في الصين في حالة من القهر وأُجبِروا على إخفاء دينهم.
		كان الحرير في الصين رخيصًا جدًّا، بينما القطن غالي الثمن.
		كان الفنانون الصينيون ماهرين بشكل خاص في التصوير الواقعي للناس.
		دخل ابن بطوطة أكبر كنيسة مسيحية في العالم وصلّى بجانب المسيحيين.

From the Writings of Ibn Battuta

رحلات ابن بطوطة

Among his many journeys, Ibn Battuta's trip to China is perhaps best known. Despite its brief duration, it marks the far eastern extent of his travels and contains a record of his astonishment at the marvels of Chinese civilization. Ibn Battuta describes the religious habits of people of China:

(١) أهلُ الصين كفّار يعبدون الأصنام ويحرقون موتاهم كما تفعل الهنود. (٢) وكفّار الصين يأكلون لحوم الخنازير والكلاب ويبيعونها في أسواقهم.

Ibn Battuta's notes on the conditions of Muslims in China:

(٣) في كلّ مدينة من مدن الصين مدينة للمسلمين ينفردون بسكناهم، ولهم فيها المساجد لإقامة الجمعات وسواها. (٤) وهم معظمون محترمون.

The wealth of China, especially its silk industry:

(٥) وهــم أهــلُ رفاهيــة وســعة عيــش إلاّ أنهــم لا يحتفلــون في مطعــم ولا ملبــس. (٦) وتــرى التاجــر الكبــير منهــم الــذي لا تحــصى أموالــه كثــرة، وعليــه جبــة قطــن خشــنة. (٧) وجميــعُ أهــل الصــين إنّــما يحتفلــون في أواني الذهــب والفضّــة . . . (٩) والحريــر عندهــم كثــيرٌ جــدًّا لأنّ الــدود تتعلّــق بالثــمار وتــأكلُ منهــا، فــلا تحتــاج إلى كثــير مؤنــة، (١٠) ولذلــك كثــر، وهــو لبــاس الفقــراء والمســاكين بهــا، (١١) ولــولا التجــار لمــا كانــت لــه قيمــة، (١٢) ويبــاع الثــوب الواحــد مــن القطــن عندهــم بالأثــواب الكثــيرة مــن الحريــر.

Ibn Battuta's admiration for the artistic talents of the Chinese:

(١٣) وأهــلُ الصــين أعظــمُ الأمــم إحكامًــا للصناعــات وأشــدّهم إتقانًــا فيهــا؛ (١٤) وذلــك مشــهورٌ مــن حالهــم، قــد وصَفــه النــاس في تصانيفهــم فأطنبــوا فيــه، (١٥) وأمّــا التصويــرُ فــلا يُجاريهــم أحــدٌ في إحكامــه مــن الــروم ولا مــن ســواهم، (١٦) فــإن لهــم فيــه اقتــدارًا عظيــمًا.

Ibn Battuta relates an amusing anecdote as evidence of the artistic skill of the Chinese:

(١٧) ومــن عجيــب مــا شــاهدت لهــم مــن ذلــك أني مــا دخلــتُ قــطّ مدينــة مــن مدنهــم ثــمّ عــدتُ إليهــا إلاّ ورأيــتُ صــورتي وصــور أصحــابي منقوشــةً في الحيطــان والكواغــد، موضوعــةً في الأســواق. (١٨) ولقــد دخلــتُ إلى مدينــة الســلطان فمــررتُ عــلى ســوق النقّاشــين ووَصَلــتُ إلى قــصر الســلطان مــع أصحــابي، (١٩) ونحــنُ عــلى زي العراقيــين، (٢٠) فلــمّا عــدت مــن القــصر عشــيًّا مــررتُ بالســوق المذكــورة، فرأيــتُ صــورتي وصــور أصحــابي منقوشــة في كاغــد قــد ألصقــوه بالحائــط، (٢١) فجعــل كلّ واحــد منّــا ينظــرُ إلى صــورة صاحبــه لا تخطــئ شــيئًا مــن شــبهه.

Ibn Battuta was welcomed into many non-Muslim countries, among them the Byzantine Empire, the leading Christian power of his day. Here, he describes his visit to the Hagia Sofia in present-day Istanbul, once the largest church in the world:

(٢٢) إنّما نذكر خارجَها، وأما داخلها فلم أُشاهده، (٢٣) وهي تسمّى عندهم آيا صُوفيا . . . (٢٤) ويُذكر أنّها من بناء آصف بن برخياء، وهو ابن خالة سليمان، عليه السلام، (٢٥) وهي من أعظم كنائس الروم، وعليها سور يُطيف بها، فكأنّها مدينة، وأبوابها ثلاثة عشر بابًا، (٢٦) ولها حرم هو نحو ميل، عليه بابٌ كبير، ولا يمنع أحد من دخوله، وقد دخلته مع والد الملك . . . (٢٧) وعلى باب الكنيسة سقائف يجلسُ بها خدّامُها الذين يقمّون طرقَها ويوقدون سُرُجَها، ويغلقون أبوابها، (٢٨) ولا يدعون أحدًا يدخلها حتى يسجد للصليب الأعظم عندهم، الذي يزعمون أنّه بقيّة من الخشبة التي صُلبَ عليها شبيهُ عيسى، عليه السلام، (٢٩) وهو على باب الكنيسة مجعول في جعبة ذهب طولُها نحو عشرة أذرع، وقد عرضوا عليها جعبة ذهب مثلها حتى صارت صليبًا.

Vocabulary

يَنفَرد	to be unique
سِوى	except
رفاهية	luxury
يحتفلون	to celebrate, be interested in
تُحْصى	to be counted, be calculated
خَشِنة	ragged, rough
مَؤنة	supply
تَعلّق بـ	to hang on
ثِمار	fruits
أطْنب	to exaggerate
تصويرٌ	illustration, painting
قَطّ	never, in no circumstance
كاغد ج. كواغد	sheet(s) of paper
عشيًّا	in the evening
ألصق	to stick, affix
تُخطئ	to mistake
آيا صُوفيا	Hagia Sofia, (lit "Holy Wisdom" in Greek) Cathedral

آصف بن برخياء	Asaph son of Berechiah, legendary builder of Hagia Sofia
يُطيف	to encircle, surround
حرَم	a sacred territory or space
سقائف	booths, sheds
يقُمّ	to sweep
يُوقد	to enkindle, light
سُرُج	lamp, light
يزعُم	to claim, allege
شبيهُ عيسى	one who resembles Jesus (a reference to the Muslim belief that Jesus himself was not crucified)
مجعول	had put
جَعبة	case, frame
ذراع (أذرُع)	cubit(s)—a unit of measurement about the length of an arm

Comprehension Exercises

Answer the following questions in complete Arabic sentences, according to the author's opinions:

١. كيف وصف ابن بطوطة ديانة أهل الصين؟

____

____

٢. ماذا قال ابن بطوطة عن مسلمي الصين؟

____

____

٣. ما قيمة الحرير بالنسبة لقيمة القطن في الصين؟

____

____

٤. ماذا يلبس الفقراء في الصين؟

____

____

٥. ماذا رأى ابن بطوطة في السوق؟

____

____

٦. تعدُّ آيا صوفيا تحفة معمارية، وضّحوا ذلك.

____

____

Interpreting the Text

١. كيف تختلف عادات ومعتقدات أهل الصين عن تعاليم الإسلام؟

---

٢. كيف كانت الأحوال المعيشية للمسلمين في الصين؟

---

٣. لماذا كان الحرير رخيصًا ووفيرًا في الصين؟

---

٤. ما أبرز نقاط الخلاف بين عقائد ابن بطوطة وعقائد المسيحيين في هذا النص؟

---

٥. كيف وصف ابن بطوطة إتقان أهل الصين للصناعات المختلفة؟ وكيف قارَنَ بينهم وبين غيرهم في هذا المجال؟

---

٦. ما مظاهر تقدّم الشعوب في فن البناء والعمارة قديمًا؟

____

____

Style and Technique

1. In discussing the silk industry, in line 11, Ibn Battuta notes: لــولا التجــار لمــا كانــت لــه قيمــة. The first term, لــولا, a compound of the counterfactual "if" and "not," means "if not for" whatever follows it, in this case, "the merchants." This construction is common in classical writing and can be made using a following pronoun suffix (such as لــولاه, "if not for him"). The second part of the sentence, the "then" clause, is introduced by لـ, here stating that "it (silk) would have no value." As with other uses of لــو, the result clause is in the perfect tense, although the result is clearly hypothetical, and has not taken place.
2. In describing the habits of the Chinese, Ibn Battuta makes several uses of the verb احتفــل بـــ (see lines 5–9). This verb is most commonly used to mean "celebrate," as in: نحتفــل بعيــد الاســتقلال. A second use of the verb, with the same following preposition (بـــ) is to mean "concern oneself with." That is the meaning intended here: لا يحتفلــون في مطعــم ولا ملبــس (line 5) = They do not concern themselves with food or clothing. يحتفلــون في أواني الذهــب والفضّــة (line 7) = They concern themselves with gold and silver vessels.
3. In line 17, Ibn Battuta notes that مــا دخلــتُ قــطّ مدينــة مــن مدنهــم ("I never entered any of their cities") without returning later to find a picture of himself. The word قَــطُّ here is not related to the verb "to cut" قَــطَّ or the word for a male cat قِــطّ, but rather is used to add an emphatic "ever" to a statement, or, as in this case of a negative assertion, "never." As is the case here, it is typically used with negative sentences.

4. مـا can be a tricky word, as it has many usages, particularly in classical writing. Note the use of مـا twice in line 17. Additionally, both instances are followed by past tense verbs. One of these, however, means "what" and the other is a negating particle. ما شـهدتُ, here to be translated "what I saw," is described as "amazing" .(مـن عجيـب) The next instance, مـا دخلـتُ, means "I did not enter." The following قـطّ (see above) further renders this "I never entered." This sentence provides a good example of how context and surrounding idioms indicate the correct reading of the two phrases.
5. In line 22 of his description of the Hagia Sofia church, as in many other places in his text, Ibn Battuta uses the construction . . . أمّـا فـ . . . . This very common construct, sometimes called the "topic-comment" sentence, is much more prevalent in Arabic than its equivalent in English. The first term, أمّـا means "as for" and introduces a topic or thing. The second term, the particle فـ, as it does in many constructions, introduces the result, or information clause of a two-part construction. فـ would not normally be translated in English, but in similar statements, its function is typically carried by a comma:

   أمّا. . .فـ = as for . . . , . . .

   The function of this construct is to highlight and isolate for consideration what comes between أمّـا and فـ. Observe Ibn Battuta's usage in line 22:

   أما داخلها فلم أُشاهده "as for the inside, I did not see it"

   Here, Ibn Battuta, before describing the exterior of the marvelous Hagia Sofia church in great detail, makes a point of emphasizing that he did not go inside, for clearly implied religious reasons. By using this construct, he manages to shift the topic from his description of the outside of the church, drawing a strong conceptual boundary between describing the outside of a building and entering an active place of worship.

Using Cultural and Contextual Clues to Understand the Text

1. At the time of Ibn Battuta's visit, China was under the control of the Yuan (Mongol) Dynasty (1271–1368). Despite the devastation that the Mongols had caused in the Arab world, by the time of Ibn Battuta's visit, the Mongol Dynasty had brought stability to China, while encouraging the entry of foreigners to the country. The dynasty would collapse shortly after Ibn Battuta's visit, but he had the good fortune to arrive when conditions for a foreign, particularly Muslim, visitor were at their most favorable. In fact, the Mongol khan, Kublai, had appointed Sayyid Ajall Shams al-Din Omar al-Bukhari, a Muslim from the Central Asian city of Bukhara, as governor of the province of Yunnan in China.
2. Constantinople (modern-day Istanbul, Türkiye) had once been for Christendom what Baghdad was for the Muslim world. Planned and dedicated by a powerful emperor as the new capital of the largest empire of its day, it was for centuries the largest city in the world and the most renowned center of the arts, commerce, and religion. Named by Emperor Constantine after himself when he chose it as the new capital of the Roman Empire, Constantinople would remain the center of the Eastern Orthodox Church and the Byzantine Empire long after the fall of Rome. The great Hagia Sofia was the world's largest cathedral for nearly a thousand years. By the time of Ibn Battuta's visit, Constantinople's golden years were behind it. The Byzantine Empire had been gradually reduced by the expanding territory of the Seljuq (and later Ottoman) Turks until little remained outside of Constantinople. Constantinople had also been sacked in the 1200s and its great library destroyed, but in this case, it had been European Crusader forces, not Mongols who inflicted the damage. Having enjoyed something of a renewal in the period between that inglorious takeover and the final Ottoman conquest in 1453, Constantinople in Ibn Battuta's time expe-

rienced a period of stability and good relations with its neighbors. It was as a direct result of these relations that Ibn Battuta would make his first journey outside the realm of Islam into the once great center of Christendom.

Analysis and Argument

Discuss the following questions based on the evidence in these excerpts and your knowledge of the historical events.

١. ما تصوركم لمفهوم التعايش بين الأديان؟ وما مدى تحقّقه في عالمنا المعاصر؟
٢. يستعين الاقتصاديون بقانون العرض والطلب[1] في تفسير أحوال السوق والمال والأعمال، فهل هناك أمثلة لهذا القانون في النص؟
٣. هل يوجد في وصف ابن بطوطة لأحوال أهل الصين ما يدّل على تسامحهم الديني وقبول الآخر؟
٤. هل اختلفت الفنون في بلاد الصين مع غيرها أم تشابهت؟ اذكروا أمثلة توضّح رأيكم.

Research and Presentation

Travel literature was one of the most popular genres of the Islamic Golden Age. Ibn Battuta stands as the leading example, but not the only one, of a cultural ambassador (at times officially, and at times as a private citizen). Prepare a 2–3-minute presentation to answer the following question:

للسفر إيجابيات كثيرة، فهو وسيلة للترفيه واستكشاف أماكن جديدة ومعرفة شعوب وثقافات مختلفة وغيرها من الأمور، فما هي سلبيات السفر؟

1 Supply and demand

In discussing social phenomena like this, some of the following expressions can be useful:

(positive or harmful) effect	أثر (إيجابي أو مؤذ)
to lead to	أدّى إلى
unintended consequence	نتيجة غير مرغوبة
intangible	غير ملموس

13

History—Ibn Khaldun

الدرس الثالث عشر - ابن خلدون

هو عبد الرَّحمن بن مُحَمَّد بن خَلْدُون أبو زَيْد وَلِيّ الدِّين الحَضْرَمِيّ المعروف بابن خَلْدُون (٧٣٢هـ/ ١٣٣٢م - ٨٠٨هـ/ ١٤٠٦م). كان ابن خلدون أحد أهم مفكري العرب في العصور الوسطى. ولد في تونس في القرن الرابع عشر الميلادي وكانت أسرته أسرةَ علم وأدب وثقافة، فقد حفظ ابن خلدون القرآن الكريم في طفولته، وكان أبوه هو معلمه وناصحه.

ويعدّ ابن خلدون واحدًا من أهم العلماء الذين تتباهى بهم الحضارة الإسلامية، فهو مؤسس علم الاجتماع وأول من قدّم هذا العلم مفصّلًا على أسسه الحديثة، وقد اهتدى إلى نظريات متميزة فيه حول قوانين العمران ونظرية العصبية، وبناء الدول وأطوار أعمارها وتدهورها. وقد سبقت آراؤه ونظرياته ما توصل إليه بعدها بعدة قرون عدد من مشاهير العلماء الغربيين. وقيل إنّ ابن خلدون قد اعتزل الحياة بعد تجارب مليئة بالنكبات والحزن على وفاة أبويه وعدد من معلميه بوباء الطاعون الذي انتشر في جميع أنحاء العالم في القرن الثامن الهجري وتفرغ أربع سنوات للبحث والدراسة لكتابة مؤلفه الخالد، أو ما عُرف بمقدمة ابن خلدون.

وتميّز ابن خلدون برحابة الأفق وسعة الاطلاع على ما كتبه مَن سبقوه عن البشرية وأحوالها، كما تميّز بقدرة نادرة على عرض الآراء ونقدها، مع إنصاف أصحاب الآراء المخالفة لرأيه. وقد كان لخبرته الواسعة في الحياة السياسية والشئون الإدارية إلى جانب أسفاره المتعددة أثر بالغ في موضوعية مؤلفاته عن التاريخ وعلم الاجتماع.

Prediction and Scanning

Based on the context and background given above, record your predictions as to whether you expect the author to agree with the following statements. Be prepared to discuss your predictions with classmates. Then, reading through the excerpts in the next section quickly, without the use of a dictionary, indicate whether your predictions were correct and where (in which lines) you found the answers. Again, be prepared to discuss the results with your classmates.

العبارة	التوقُّع	الدلالة
البدو هم أصل الحضارات.		
العَصَبية هي المصدر الرئيس للصراع والانقسام داخل القبائل البدوية.		
أهل البدو أكثر شجاعة من أهل الحضر.		
لكل جيل صفاتٌ وطباعٌ متباينة.		

From the Writings of Ibn Khaldun

المقدمة، الباب الثاني، الفصول الثالث والثامن والحادي عشر

Essential to Ibn Khaldun's theory of history is the division between the urban and Bedouin peoples:

(١) قد ذكرنا أن البدو هم المقتصرون على الضروري في أحوالهم العاجزون عما فوقه، وأن الحضر المعتنون بحاجات الترف والكمال في أحوالهم وعوائدهم، (٢) ولا شك أن الضروري أقدم من الحاجي والكمالي وسابق عليه، لأن الضروري أصل والكمالي فرع ناشئ عنه، (٣) فالبدو أصل المدن والحضر، وسابق عليهما، لأن أول مطالب الإنسان الضروري، ولا ينتهي إلى الكمال والترف إلا إذا كان الضروري حاصلًا، فخشونة البداوة قبل رقة الحضارة. (٤) ولهذا نجد التمدن غاية للبدوي

يجـري إليهـا وينتهـي بسـعيه إلى مقترحـه منهـا. (٥) ومتـى حصـل عـلى الريـاش الـذي يحصـل لـه بـه أحـوال الـترف وعوائـده عـاج إلى الدّعـة . . .

Ibn Khaldun's key concept is *'asabiyya,* translated as "group feeling" or cohesion:

(٦) . . . العصبيـة إنـما تكـون مـن الالتحـام بالنسـب أو مـا في معنـاه. (٧) وذلـك أن صلـة الرحـم طبيعـي في البشر إلا في الأقـل، (٨) ومـن صلتهـا النعـرة عـلى ذوي القربـى وأهـل الأرحـام (٩) أن ينالهـم ضيـم أو تصيبهـم هلكـة، فـإن القريـب يجـد في نفسـه غضاضـة مـن ظلـم قريبـه أو العـداء عليـه (١٠) ويـودّ لـو يحـول بينـه وبـين مـا يصلـه مـن المعاطـب والمهالـك نزعـة طبيعيـة في البـشر.

This leads to his theory of the natural life cycle of dynasties:

(١١) إن عمـر الدولـة لا يعـدو في الغالـب ثلاثـة أجيـال، (١٢) لأن الجيـل الأول لم يزالـوا عـلى خلـق البـداوة وخشـونتها وتوحشـها مـن شـظف العيـش والبسـالة والافـتراس والاشـتراك في المجـد، (١٣) فـلا تـزال بذلـك سَـوْرةُ العصبيـة محفوظـةً فيهـم، فحدُّهـم مرهـفٌ وجانبهـم مرهـوبٌ والنـاس لهـم مغلوبـون (١٤) والجيـل الثـاني تحـول حالهـم بالملـك والتَّرفُّـهِ مـن البـداوة إلى الحضـارة، ومـن الشَّـظف إلى الـترف والخِصـب، ومـن الاشـتراك في المجـد إلى انفـراد الواحـد بـه وكسـل الباقـين عـن السـعي فيـه، ومـن عـز الاسـتطالة إلى ذل الاسـتكانة فتنكسر سَـوْرةُ العصبيـة بعـض الـشيء . . . (١٥) وأمـا الجيل الثالـث فينسـون عهـد البـداوة والخشـونة كأن لم تكـن، ويفقـدون حـلاوة العـز والعصبيـة بـما هـم فيـه مـن ملكـة القهـر، (١٦) ويبلـغ فيهـم الـترف غايتـه بـما تَبَنَّقـوه مـن النعيـم وغضـارة العيـش فيصـيرون عيـالًا عـلى الدولـة ومـن جملـة النسـاء والولـدان المحتاجـين للمدافعـة عنهـم، وتسـقط العصبيـة بالجملـة وينسـون الحمايـة والمدافعـة والمطالبـة، (١٧) ويُلبّسـون عـلى النـاس في الشـارة والـزّي وركـوب الخيـل وحسـن الثقافـة يمَوّهـون بهـا. (١٨) وهـم في الأكثـر أجبـن مـن النسـوان عـلى ظهورهـا، (١٩) فـإذا جـاء المطالـب لهـم لم يقاومـوا مدافعتـه، (٢٠) فيحتـاج صاحـب الدولـة حينئـذ إلى الاسـتظهار بسـواهم مـن أهـل النجـدة ويسـتكثر بالمـوالي، (٢١) ويصطنـع مـن يغنـي عـن الدولـة بعـض الغنـاء حتـى يتـأذن الله بانقراضهـا، (٢٢) فتذهـب الدولـة بـما حملـت. (٢٣) فهـذه كـما تـراه ثلاثـة أجيـال فيهـا يكـون هـرم الدولـة وتخلفهـا (٢٤) ولهـذا كان انقـراض الحسـب في الجيـل الرابـع. كـما مـر في أن المجـد والحسـب إنـما هـو أربعـة آبـاء (٢٥) وقـد أتينـاك فيـه ببرهـان طبيعـي كافٍ ظاهـر مبنيّ عـلى مـا مهَّدنـاه قبـل مـن المقدّمـات فتأمّلـه، (٢٦) فلـن

تعـدو وجـه الحـق إن كنـتَ مـن أهـل الإنصـاف. وهـذه الأجيـال الثلاثـة عمرهـا مائـة وعـشرون سـنة عـلى مـا مـر . . .

Vocabulary

مقتصرون على	limited to, restricted to
معتنون بـ	concerned with
الكمال	here: luxury
خشونة	a tough, rugged lifestyle
الدعة	tenderness
عاج إلى	turns to
التحام	cohesion
نعرة	pride (usually in race or group)
في الأقل	rarely, in the least
غضاضة	deficiency, stain
ضيم	wrong, harm
الهلكة	loss, ruin
شظف	hardship
بسالة	courage
افتراس	predation, ravening
مرهف	here: sharp
استطالة	arrogance, overbearing
استكانة	passivity, submission
غضارة	prosperity, luxury
استظهار بـ	appeal for assistance from
نجدة	auxiliaries
بانقراضها	extinction, dying out
ظاهر	apparent, visible

Comprehension Exercises

A. Answer the following questions in complete Arabic sentences, based on what the author says:

١. ما الفرق بين البدو والحضر؟

٢. ما العصبية؟ وما مظاهرها؟

٣. ٣. كم جيلًا تستمرّ الدولة عادةً؟

٤. ما التغييرات التي تطرأ على الجيل الثاني؟ وماذا يحدث للعصبية حينئذ؟

٥. كيف صوّر ابن خلدون الجيل الثالث وما يحدث للدولة بعدها؟

B. Ibn Khaldun's argument is based on a contrast between the urban and Bedouin peoples. The use of contrasting nouns and adjectives throughout reinforces the sharp distinction between the two that he wishes to establish. Using your understanding of the words below, place these in the proper category in Ibn Khaldun's view in the box below. In the bottom section, add words of your own that Ibn Khaldun does not use, but which fit this contrast.

الترّف – الخشونة – غضاضة – الاستكانة – الدعة – العصبية – شظف – الافتراس – الوحش – البسالة	
البدو	الحضر

Interpreting the Text

١. ما مدى التوافق بين قول ابن خلدون بأنّ البدو أصل المدن والحضر ورأيه في الفرق بين هذين المتضادَيْن[1]؟

____

____

٢. ما الدور الذي تؤديه العصبية في النفس البشرية ومعتقداتها؟

____

____

٣. ناقشوا بإيجاز كيفية تطوّر الأجيال من وجهة نظر ابن خلدون.

____

____

٤. لماذا يلجأ[2] صاحب الدولة لاستبدال الجيل الثالث بالموالي وغيرهم للدفاع عن دولته؟

____

____

1 Opposites
2 To resort to

٥. كيف صوّر ابن خلدون نهايات الدول واضمحلالها[3]؟

Style and Technique

In this as in other Classical texts, words and phrases may differ substantially from modern usage. A quick, literal reading could give a mistaken impression of the author's meaning. Some examples in this text are discussed below:

1. In line 13, the word سَوْرة is not the same as the more familiar سُورة, referring to a chapter of the Qur'an. In an unvoweled text, these two would look the same. The term used here, with the diphthong "aw" in place of the long vowel "uu" means "strength," "force," or "intensity." It is often used in an *idaafa*—as here—in the same way as words like قلة or عدم. Here, Ibn Khaldun refers to the second generation of conquering Bedouin as still having سورة العصبية among them, indicating there is still a power, or intensity of *'asabiyya* operative, although it diminishes with each passing generation.
2. In line 23, at the end of his description of the decline of the state, Ibn Khaldun asserts فتذهب الدولة بما حَملت referring to the final demise of the state. Two familiar verbs, each with many possible nuances, are being used for a particular effect. A literal reading—"it goes with what it carries"—might not sound so tragic, especially for a Bedouin group, but what the author has in mind is much more gloomy. The verb ذهب in this context means to be lost in vain. The second verb, حمل, while familiar in its meaning of "carry" has many different uses that can convey different attitudes toward the subject. Among the meanings are to be pregnant, to misunderstand,

3 Decay

to attack, to convert and to convince. The context here, however, indicates the meaning of "to embody, to hold in itself," as it refers to what is lost when the state collapses. This reinforces the sense of loss, as not only the state but everything it stands for is gone.

Using Grammar and Structure Clues to Understand the Text

1. Ibn Khaldun juxtaposes antonyms (التضاد) to highlight his meaning. For example, in line 3: "فخشونة البداوة قبل رقة الحضارة" places the toughness (خشونة) of the Bedouin in direct contrast with the delicateness (رقة) of urban dwellers. In line 15, the phrase "من عز الاستطالة إلى ذل الاستكانة" sets up a contrast between overbearing (استطالة) and submissiveness (استكانة). This technique supports his overall goal of establishing a sharp contrast between the two societies, which underlies his whole message.
2. At the same time, he also uses synonyms (المترادفات) in order to strengthen and clarify his meaning. For example, in line 8: "ذوي القربى وأهل الأرحام" repeats the mention of kinship, but in doing so strengthens the idea of a bond between people. In the phrase that follows in line 9: "أن ينالهم ضيم أو تصيبهم هلكة" the image of suffering a loss is expressed twice, but repeating the picture with two different words—هلكة ،ضيم—doubles the emotional impact, similar to saying "rack and ruin" in English.
3. In line 17, we see an example of a "one-word sentence" in Arabic. While the English translation would require at least three words, the nature of Arabic allows for verb, subject, and direct object to be expressed in a single word:

تبنّقوه:
تبنّق – verb
وا – past tense conjugation indicating the subject "they"
وه – direct object "it"

The most popular Arabic structure that may include this form is the verbal descriptive sentence, like: "شـاهدت فيلـما لا أحبّـه" where لا أحبـه is a complete sentence, or "قـرأ صديقـي قصـة أعجبتْـه كثـيرًا" in which أعجبتـه contains subject, object and verb.

Analysis and Argument

A. Ibn Khaldun's ideas are certainly controversial and not accepted by all. In this section, you will prepare responses of three or four sentences in Arabic to the following propositions, stating your own opinions. In class, you can use these as the basis for a debate:

١. الحياة المتمدنة لا تؤدي بالضرورة إلى إضعاف الشعب. في بعض الأماكن، تكون حياة المدينة قاسية ونجد عصبية قوية بين السكان.

٢. نظريات ابن خلدون متعلقة بمجتمعات معينة فقط مثل المجتمعات الشرقية. ولذلك فهي غير مناسبة للغرب ومجتمعاته المتنوّعة.

٣. أفكار ابن خلدون مناسبة للمجتمعات القديمة، ولكن في العالم الحديث، الوطن يحلّ محل القبيلة ويشعر الشعب بعصبية وطنية قوية مثل العصبية القديمة. لذلك، تستطيع الدولة الحديثة أن تستمرّ طويلًا.

٤. في رأيك، أين نشهد العصبية اليوم؟ هل ما زالت كما كانت في عصر ابن خلدون؟

٥. أصبحت القوة الاقتصادية والتكنولوجية الآن أهم من العصبية في تعزيز الدولة وبنائها. ومن المستبعد تمامًا أن تنهار الدولة المتقدمة بسبب جماعات بدائية مثل البدو أو غيرهم.

B. Do you feel that Ibn Khaldun would agree with the following statements? Why or why not?

١. الازدهار الاقتصادي هو أفضل وسيلة لضمان أمن الدولة على المدى الطويل.

____

____

٢. من المهم أن تتذكّر الأمة تاريخها وتُكرّم مؤسسيها.

____

____

٣. وجود جيش قوي مؤلّف من مواطنين وطنيين أمر أساسي لاستقرار الدولة.

____

____

٤. العنصرية من أخطر القضايا التي تهدّد أمن الدولة.

____

____

٥. من الممكن أن تتحول البلاد الفقيرة إلى دول أكثر استقرارًا وقوةً من البلاد الغنية.

____

____

Research and Presentation

You are by now familiar with the essential ideas of Ibn Khaldun. Prepare a 3–4-minute presentation on the following:

ناقشوا حدثًا من التاريخ يدعم أفكار ابن خلدون أو يدحض أفكاره.

Your presentation should use a parallel of what Ibn Khaldun would have predicted would happen at each stage, and what actually did occur. Be sure to then summarize by showing what this proves or disproves. Incorporate some of the terms below in preparing your argument:

argument, evidence (for)	حُجّة
clear evidence	دليل قاطع
underlying cause (of)	سبب كامن (وراء)
immediate cause	سبب مباشر
thorny issue	قضية شائكة

14

Popular Storytelling—*The Arabian Nights*

الدرس الرابع عشر – ألف ليلة وليلة

ظهرت الطبعة الأولى من كتاب «ألف ليلة وليلة» باللغة الإنجليزية في الربع الأول من القرن الثامن الميلادي، وقد اختلفت الآراء حول أصل الكتاب وبداية ظهوره. ويتصدر كتاب «ألف ليلة وليلة» مركزًا رفيع المستوى في الأدب الشعبي العربي والغربي، وقد اسهم هذا الكتاب قي تشكيل جزء مهم من الموروث الثقافي العربي.

ويتضمن الكتاب باقة من الحكايات التي يناهز عددها المائتين، وقد مزجت هذه الحكايات الواقع بالأساطير وتناولت قصصًا من التاريخ والعادات والتقاليد وأخبار الملوك وعامة الناس واللصوص والجن وروايات على ألسنة الحيوانات والطيور، ولعل أشهر قصص كتاب «ألف ليلة وليلة»: علاء الدين والمصباح السحري، وعلي بابا والأربعون لصًّا، ورحلات السندباد البحري، التي يعرفها الشرق والغرب على حد سواء. وقد اختلف العلماء والنقاد حول مؤلف هذا الكتاب، فمنهم من رأى أن مؤلفه شخص واحد، ورجّح آخرون وجود أكثر من مؤلف لهذا الكتاب نظرًا للتنوع الضخم في أحداثه اجتماعيًّا وجغرافيًّا ولغويًّا.

Prediction and Scanning

Based on the context and background given above, record your predictions as to whether you expect to find the following in the story. Be prepared to discuss your predictions with classmates. Then, reading through the excerpts in the next section quickly, without the use of a dictionary, indicate whether your predictions were correct and where

(in which lines) you found the answers. Again, be prepared to discuss the results with your classmates.

الدلالة	التوقُّع	العبارة
		الملوك بشكل عام مستبدون وظالمون ومكروهون من شعوبهم.
		الخيانة وعدم الإخلاص أبرز صفات زوجات الملوك في هذه القصة.
		الملك في القصة ينتقم من الأبرياء على ذنوب لم يرتكبوها.
		شهرزاد، بطلة القصة، ترفض في البداية طلب والدها.

From *The Arabian Nights*

ألف ليلة وليلة، حكاية شهرزاد والملك شهريار

The story begins long ago with two kings:

(١) كان فيما مضى من قديم الزمان وسالف العصر والأوان ملك من ملوك ساسان بجزائر الهند والصين، صاحب جند وأعوان وخدم وحشم، (٢) له ولدان أحدهما كبير والآخر صغير، وكانا فارسين بطلين، (٣) وكان الكبير أفرس من الصغير وقد مَلَكَ البلاد وحكم بالعدل بين العباد وأحبه أهل بلاده ومملكته، (٤) وكان اسمه الملك شهريار، وكان أخوه الصغير اسمه الملك شاه زمان، وكان ملك سمرقند العجم.

King Shah Zaman, the younger, sets out on a journey to visit his brother:

(٥) وقصده أن يزوره حاكمًا في بلاده وخرج طالبًا بلاد أخيه، (٦) فلما كان في نصف الليل تذكر حاجة نسيها في قصره، (٧) فرجع ودخل قصره فوجد زوجته راقدة في فراشه معانقة عبد . . . (٨) ثم أنه سلّ سيفه وضرب الاثنين في الفراش . . . (٩) وسار إلى أن وصل إلى مدينة أخيه ففرح أخوه بقدومه . . . (١٠) وجلس معه يتحدث بانشراح فتذكر الملك شاه زمان ما كان من أمر زوجته.

In the palace of King Shahryar, Shah Zaman discovers something shocking:

(١١) وكان في قصر الملك شبابيك تطل على بستان أخيه، فنظر وإذا بباب القصر قد فتح وخرج منه عشرون جارية وعشرون عبدًا، (١٢) وامرأة أخيه تمشي بينهم وهي في غاية الحسن والجمال، (١٣) حتى وصلوا إلى فسقية وخلعوا ثيابهم وجلسوا من بعضهم . . . (١٤) ولم يزالوا في بوس وعناق ونحو ذلك حتى ولّى النهار . . . (١٥) وبعد هذا جاء أخوه من السفر . . . فأعاد عليه جميع ما رآه.

King Shahryar becomes mad with rage and exacts a most brutal revenge:

(١٦) ثم أنه رمى عنق زوجته وكذلك أعناق الجواري والعبيد، (١٧) وصار الملك كل يوم يأخذ بنتًا بكرًا يزيل بكارتها ويقتلها من ليلتها. (١٨) ولم يزل على ذلك مدة ثلاث سنوات، فضجّت الناس وهربت ببناتها، ولم يبق في المدينة بنت تتحمل الوطء. (١٩) ثم أن الملك أمر الوزير أن يأتيه ببنت على جري عادته، فخرج الوزير وفَتّش فلم يجد بنتًا، (٢٠) فتوجّه إلى منزله وهو غضبان مقهور خائف على نفسه من الملك. (٢١) وكان الوزير له بنتان ذواتا حسن وجمال وبهاء، الكبيرة اسمها شهرزاد والصغيرة اسمها دنيازاد. (٢٢) وكانت الكبيرة قد قرأت الكتب والتواريخ . . . المتعلقة بالأمم السالفة والملوك الخالية والشعراء، (٢٣) فقالت لأبيها: ما لي أراك متغيرًا حامل الهم والأحزان . . . وقد قال بعضهم في المعنى شِعرًا . . . (٢٤) فلما سمع الوزير من ابنته هذا الكلام حكى لها ما جرى له من الأول إلى الآخر مع الملك. (٢٥) فقالت له بالله يا أبتِ زوّجني هذا الملك، فإما أن أعيش وإما أن أكون فداء لبنات المسلمين وسببًا لخلاصهن من بين يديه. (٢٦) فقال لها: بالله عليكِ لا تخاطري بنفسك أبدًا، فقالت له: لا بد من ذلك.

Shahrazad sets out to save the women of the kingdom, and in doing so, begins the "Thousand and One Nights Entertainment":

(٢٧) فجهّزها وطلع إلى الملك شهريار، وكانت قد أوصت أختها الصغيرة وقالت لها: إذا توجهت إلى الملك أرسلت أطلبك، (٢٩) فإذا جئت عندي ورأيتِ الملك قضى حاجته مني، فقولي يا أختي حدّثينا حديثًا غريبًا نقطع به السهر، (٣٠) وأنا أُحدّثُ حديثًا يكون فيه الخلاص إن شاء الله.

Vocabulary

ساسان	Sassan (ancient Persia)
عون ج. أعوان	servant, bodyguard
حشم	entourage, servants
سمرقند	Samarkand (city in Uzbekistan)
عجم	non-Arab (usually Persian)
معانقة	embrace
سل	unsheathe (a sword)
انشراح	joy, delight
جارية	enslaved woman
فسقية	fountain, well
بوس	kissing
أعاد	repeat, retell
بكر/ بكارة	virgin/virginity
ضجّ	make noise, cry out
الوطء	sexual penetration
مقهور	defeated, saddened
أحزان	low spirits, sorrows
جرى	happened
فداء	redemption, sacrifice
تخاطري	to risk, hazard
أوصت	to confide, entrust
سهر	stay up at night

Comprehension Exercises

A. Answer the following questions in complete Arabic sentences:

١. مَن ملكُ ساسان؟ ومَن أولاده؟

____

____

٢. ماذا رأى الملك شاه الزمان في قصره؟ وماذا رأى في بستان قصر أخيه؟

____

____

٣. كيف عاقب الملك حاشيته بعد اكتشافه خيانة زوجته؟

____

____

٤. لماذا أرادت شهرزاد الزواج من الملك؟

____

____

٥. ماذا طلبت شهرزاد من أختها؟

B. Find Arabic phrases in the text that have the following meanings in English:

1. seeking:

2. of the utmost (highest):

3. persisted in:

4. loaded with cares:

5. pass the night:

C. Find Arabic synonyms or equivalents in the text for the following words and phrases:

١. سابِق:

____

٢. مَهْزوم:

____

٣. رَوْعَة:

____

٤. أَحْضَرَ إلى:

____

٥. إِنْقاذ:

____

Interpreting the Text

١. قارنوا بين الملك شهريار وشقيقه.

____

____

٢. في رأيكم، لماذا قرر شاه الزمان إخبار شقيقه بما رآه في الحديقة؟

____

____

٣. كيف أثّر حادث زوجة شهريار في أهل المدينة؟

____

____

٤. ما رأيكم في شخصية شهرزاد؟

____

____

٥. ماذا كانت نصيحة الوزير لابنته؟ وهل تتفقون مع هذه النصيحة؟

____

____

Style and Technique

1. In line 1, the long opening is typical of classical texts making reference to an ancient, imagined past, similar to the familiar "once upon a time." These particular phrases would be quite familiar to an Arabic-speaking audience. The expressions make use of the "false *idaafa*" construction, that is, an *idaafa* made with an adjective as its first term. This is a stylistic technique, much like the English "fair of

face," or "advanced in years." Note, for example: قديم الزمان (literally: "old of ages") and سالف العصر ("bygone of era").

2. This story makes extensive use of the *haal* construction, which tells us what was happening as something else occurred. The *haal* is often introduced with و, as in "دخل الغرفة وهو يبتسم." The و can be omitted and the verb replaced with an active participle in the accusative, such as "دخل الغرفة باسمًا" which means the same as the previous example. In line 5, there are two such instances. What is the meaning of:

   يزوره حاكمًا في بلاده: ______________________________

   خرج طالبًا بلاد أخيه: ______________________________

3. The stories of *The Arabian Nights,* with their frequent references to sex, employ a number of euphemisms. In line 29, for example, as Shahrazad is explaining what is to happen during her wedding night with the king, she says: ورأيت الملك قضى حاجته مني

   What is the literal meaning of this phrase?

   ____

Using Cultural and Contextual Clues to Understand the Text

1. The gender relations portrayed in *The Arabian Nights* can be shocking for modern standards. The tropes displayed here reflect traditional Arab values in which the chastity of the women determined the honor of one's household. Infidelity on the scale depicted in this story would shame the head of the household as a weak leader and an ineffective moral guide.
2. *The Arabian Nights* were popular entertainment for an adult audience, not the children's tales that they have been adapted into in

modern times. In this regard, both Shahryar and his brother are buffoonish characters, meant to look foolish as mighty kings who don't even know what is going on in their own homes. This is particularly evident in the way that Shah Zaman comes to his older brother seeking advice for his wife's unfaithfulness, only to find that his brother's domestic situation is even worse. The blindness of Shahryar is a theme that continues throughout the stories, as he doesn't realize that Shahrazad is effectively deceiving him by telling stories to forestall her own death.

3. The format of a "frame story," in which other tales are embedded—here, the story of Shahrazad and King Shahryar—is a common trope in Middle Eastern storytelling. As oral storytelling had traditionally been a primary form of entertainment in Arab culture, the ability of a storyteller to hold an audience's attention over an extended period of time, while still delivering emotional payoffs, was a mark of skill. Audiences for the Arabian Nights series would experience numerous exciting and amusing stories, but still have their attention held by the overarching story of Shahrazad and her attempts to tame the murderous king. Shahrazad, the epitome of the master storyteller, or *hakawatiyya,* displays her skill by always keeping the king in suspense—even when she ends one story, she has introduced the hook for the next one.

Writing Exercises

A. Translate the following sentences into Arabic, using vocabulary from this reading. Hints in parentheses indicate which lines to look at for similar structures:

    1. She left her home, seeking a new life. (5)

    ____

2. The royal palace overlooks the sea. (11)

____

3. They didn't stop walking until they reached the city. (14)

____

4. The people grumbled because of the new laws. (18)

____

5. Don't ever risk yourself. (26)

____

B. Rearrange the words below into coherent sentences:

١. أوطانهم - العلم - خرجوا - طالبين - من

____

____

٢. فرح - بعد - برجوع - الملك - سفره - الشعب

____

____

٣. على - بلاده - وزيره - بالمحافظة - الملك - أوصى

____

____

٤. ما - الهمّ - أراك - حامل - لي(؟)

____

____

٥. كل - الشيوخ - على - الملك - الوزير - أعاد - ما سمعه - من

____

____

Discussion Questions

١. هل تؤيدون فكرة إخبار الآخرين بالحقائق حتى لو كانت صادِمة؟ لماذا؟
٢. هل كانت طريقة انتقام الملك شهريار لخيانة زوجته مناسبة لعصره فقط أم قد نرى مثلها هذه الأيام؟
٣. كيف يمكن للإنسان أن يكظم غيظه[1] في حالة الغضب؟
٤. ما أعلى درجات الخيانة من وجهة نظركم؟
٥. هل أنْصفَ[2] هذا النص المرأة أم صوّرها بطريقة غير عادلة؟

1 To repress anger
2 To treat with justice

Research and Presentation

The Arabian Nights presents a picture of a fantasy world, yet many of its assumptions are grounded in the historical context in which it was written. Based on what you can infer from the text, prepare a 2–3-minute presentation on the following question:

روايات ألف ليلة وليلة ودورها في ترسيخ[3] الصورة النمطية للشرق في أذهان الغرب

In making this presentation, some of the following terms may help to explain your reasoning process:

to infer	استنتج
to assume	افترض
to conclude from	اسْتَدَلّ من

3 Setting up

15

Fantasy and Adventure—

Sindbad the Sailor

الدرس الخامس عشر – السندباد البحري

تنتسبُ حكايات السندباد البحري إلى عهد الخليفة العباسي، هارون الرشيد (١٧٠هـ/ ٧٨٦م – ١٩٣هـ/ ٨٠٩م). وقد اهتم خلفاء العصر العباسي بالتجارة وبتسهيل سُبلها للتجار والبحارة؛ فقاموا ببناء الأساطيل لحماية السواحل من غارات اللصوص والقراصنة، كما حفروا الآبار وأنشأوا المنابر في الثغور وأصبحت عواصم الخلافة وأهم مدنها مثل بغداد ودمشق مركزًا استراتيجيًّا للقوافل وشريانًا أساسيًّا ا يربط بين الشرق والغرب والشمال والجنوب.

وقد ألهمت حكايات البحر وما تحمله الرحلات البحرية من مغامرة وخيال وتشويق رواة الأدب ومؤلفي الأساطير؛ فقاموا في كتاباتهم بنسج وابتداع شخصيات أسطورية امتزج فيها الواقع بالخيال.

وتُعدّ شخصية السندباد البحري ورحلاته واحدة من أشهر الأمثلة على هذا النوع من الأدب. وقد اختلف المؤرخون حول شخصية السندباد البحري هل وإن كانت شخصية تاريخية واقعية أم من وحي الخيال.

وقد غابت حكايات السندباد عن الترجمات العربية لقصص «ألف ليلة وليلة» وبدأت في الظهور مع التراجم الفرنسية للقصص في عام ١٧١١.

Prediction and Scanning

Based on the context and background given above, record your predictions as to whether you expect to find the following in the story. Be prepared to discuss your predictions with classmates. Then, reading through the excerpts in the next section quickly, without the use of a dictionary, indicate whether your predictions were correct and where (in which lines) you found the answers. Again, be prepared to discuss the results with your classmates.

العبارة	التوقُّع	الدلالة
تغيّرت أحوال معيشة السندباد من الغنى إلى الفقر.		
أرض الجزيرة لم تكن في الأصل أرضًا.		
في وقت الخطر، يرفض قائد السفينة ترك أي شخص وراءه يموت.		
وجد سندباد نفسه أسير ملكٍ يسيء معاملته.		

From the *Tales of Sindbad*

الرحلة الأولى للسندباد البحري

Sindbad describes how he became a merchant sailor:

(١) . . .كان لي أبٌ تاجر، وكان من أكابر الناس والتجار، وكان عنده مالٌ كثير ونَوالٌ جزيل، وقد مات وأنا ولد صغير، وخَلّف لي مالًا وعقارًا وضِياعًا. (٢) فلما كَبِرتُ وضعت يدي على الجميع وقد أكلت أكلًا مليحًا وشربت شربًا مليحًا، وعاشرت الشباب وتجملت بلبس الثياب ومشيت مع الخِلّان والأصحاب. (٣) واعتقدتُ أن ذلك يدوم لي وينفعني، ولم أزل على هذه الحالة مدة من الزمان، (٤) ثم أني رجعت إلى عقلي وأَفَقْت من غفلتي فوجدت مالي قد مالَ وحالي قد حالَ، وقد ذهب جميع ما كان معي . . . (٥) ثم إني قمت وجمعت ما كان عندي من أثاث وملبوس وبعتُه، ثم بعت عقاري وجميع ما تملك يدي فجَمَعت ثلاثة آلاف درهم، (٦) وقد

خطر ببالي السفر إلى بلاد الناس . . . (٧) فقمت واشتريت لي بضاعة ومتاعًا وأسبابًا وشيئًا من أغراض السفر، (٨) وقد سمحت لي نفسي بالسفر في البحر فنزَلت المركب وانحدرت إلى مدينة البصرة مع جماعة من التجار. (٩) وسِرنا في البحر مدة أيام وليال، وقد مررنا بجزيرة بعد جزيرة، ومن بحر إلى بحر ومن بر إلى بر. (١٠) وفي كل مكان مررنا به نبيع ونشتري ونُقايض بالبضائع فيه.

Sindbad's first adventure on the strange island:

(١١) وقد انطلقنا في سَيْر البحر إلى أن وصلنا إلى جزيرة كأنها روضة من رياض الجنة، (١٢) فأرسى بنا صاحب المركب على تلك الجزيرة ورمى مراسيلها وشد للسقالة، (١٣) فنزل جميع من كان في المركب في تلك الجزيرة وعملوا لهم كوانين وأوقدوا فيها النار، (١٤) واختلفت أشغالهم؛ فمنهم من صار يطبخ ومنهم من صار يغسل ومنهم من صار يتفرج. (١٥) وكنت أنا من جملة المتفرجين في جوانب الجزيرة، (١٦) وقد اجتمع الركاب على أكل وشرب ولهو ولعب. (١٧) فبينما نحن على تلك الحالة وإذا بصاحب المركب واقف على جانبها وصاح بأعلى صوته: يا ركاب السلامة أسرعوا واطلعوا إلى المركب وبادروا إلى الطلوع واتركوا أسبابكم واهربوا . . . (١٨) فإن هذه الجزيرة التي أنتم عليها ما هي جزيرة وإنما هي سمكة كبيرة رست في وسط البحر فبني عليها الرمل فصارت مثل الجزيرة وقد نبت عليها الأشجار من قديم الزمان، (١٩) فلما أوقدتم عليه النار أحسّت بالسخونة فتحركت، وفي هذا الوقت تنزل بكم في البحر فتغرقون جميعًا، فاطلبوا النجاة لأنفسكم قبل الهلاك.

Sindbad recounts his escape from near death:

(٢٠) فمنهم من لحق المركب ومنهم من لم يلحقها، (٢١) وقد تحركت تلك الجزيرة ونزلت إلى قرار البحر بجميع ما كان عليها، وانطبق عليها البحر العجاج المتلاطم بالأمواج. (٢٢) وكنت أنا من جملة من غرق، ولكن الله تعالى أنقذني ونجاني من الغرق ورزقني بقصعة خشب كبيرة من القصع التي كانوا يغسلون فيها، (٢٣) فمسكتها بيدي وركبتها من حلاوة الروح . . . (٢٤) وقد نشر الريس قلاع المركب وسافر بالذين طلع بهم في المركب ولم يلتفت لمن غرق منهم. (٢٥) ومازلت أنظر إلى تلك المركب حتى خُفيت عن عيني، (٢٦) وأيقنتُ الهلاك ودخل عليّ الليل وأنا على هذه الحالة. فمكثتُ على ما أنا فيه يومًا وليلة، (٢٧) وقد ساعدني الريح والأمواج إلى أن رست بي تحت جزيرة عالية وفيها أشجار مطلّة على البحر.

Far from home and his comrades, Sindbad encounters the inhabitants of the island, who take him to their king:

(٢٨) وصلنا إلى مدينة الملك المهرجان وقد دخلوا عليه وأعلموه بقصتي، (٢٩) فطلبني، فأدخلوني عليه وأوقفوني بين يديه، فسلمت عليه فردَّ عليّ السلام ورحّب بي، وحيّاني بإكرام وسألني عن حالي، فأخبرته بجميع ما حصل لي وبكل ما رأيته من المبتدأ إلى المنتهى. (٣٠) فعند ذلك تعجب مما وقع لي وما جرى لي، فعند ذلك قال لي: يا ولدي والله لقد حصل لك مزيد السلامة (٣١) لولا طول عمرك ما نجوت من هذه الشدائد، ولكن الحمد لله على السلامة. ثم إنه أحسن إلي وأكرمني وقربني إليه وصار يؤانسني بالكلام والملاطفة، (٣٢) وجعلني عنده عاملًا على مينا البحر وكاتبًا على كل مركب عبرت إلى البر. وصرت واقفًا عنده لأقضي له مصالحه، وهو يحسن إلي وينفعني من كل جانب. (٣٣) وقد كساني كسوة مليحة فاخرة، وصرت مقدمًا عنده في الشفاعات وقضاء مصالح الناس. (٣٤) ولم أزل عنده مدة طويلة وأنا كلما أشق على جانب البحر أسأل التجار والمسافرين والبحريين عن ناحية مدينة بغداد، لعل أحدًا يخبرني عنها فأروح معه إليها وأعود إلى بلادي، فلم يعرفها أحد.

Never giving up hope of returning home, Sindbad experiences another of his many lucky encounters:

(٣٥) ورأيت في ذلك البحر سمكة طولها مائتا ذراع، ورأيت أيضًا سمكًا وجهه مثل وجه البوم، ورأيت في تلك السّفْرة كثيرًا من العجائب والغرائب مما لو حكيته لطال شرحه . . . (٣٦) وقفت يومًا من الأيام على جانب البحر وفي يدي عكاز على جري عاداتي، (٣٧) وإذا بمركب قد أقبلت وفيها تجار كثيرة. فلما وصلت إلى مينا المدينة وفرضتها طوى الريس قلوعها وأرساها على البر ومد السقالة وأطلع البحرية جميع ما كان في تلك المركب إلى البر . . . (٣٨) فقلت لصاحب المركب: هل بقي في مركبك شيء؟ (٣٩) فقال: نعم يا سيدي، معي بضائع في بطن المركب ولكن صاحبها غرق . . . (٤٠) وصارت بضائعه معنا فغرضنا أننا نبيعها ونأخذ ثمنها لأجل أن نوصله إلى أهله في مدينة بغداد دار السلام. (٤١) فقلت للريس: ما يكون اسم ذلك الرجل صاحب البضائع؟ (٤٢) فقال: اسمه السندباد البحري وقد غرق منا في البحر. (٤٣) فلما سمعت كلامه حققت النظر فيه فعرفته وصرخت عليه صرخة عظيمة وقلت: يا ريس أعلم أني صاحب البضائع التي ذكرتها وأنا السندباد البحري!

From poverty and desperation, Sindbad explains how he acquired his great wealth:

(٤٤) دخلت عند الملك وشكرته على فضله وإحسانه، (٤٥) ثم استأذنته في السفر إلى بلادي وأهلي، فودعني وأعطاني شيئًا كثيرًا عند سفري من متاع تلك المدينة. (٤٦) فودعته ونزلت المركب وسافرنا بإذن الله تعالى . . . (٤٧) فرحت بسلامتي وعودتي إلى بلادي. (٤٨) وبعد ذلك توجهت إلى مدينة بغداد دار السلام ومعي من الحمول والمتاع والأسباب شيء كثير له قيمة عظيمة . . . (٤٩) ثم أني اشتريت لي خدمًا وحشمًا ومماليكَ وسراريَ وعبيدًا حتى صار عندي شيء كثير، واشتريت لي دورًا وأماكن وعقارًا أكثر من الأول.

Vocabulary

نوال	favor, blessings
عاشر	to associate closely with
ضيعة ج. ضِياع	estate, domain
مليح	pleasant, delicious (lit: salty)
خليل ج. خِلّان	loyal friend
نفع	to profit, benefit
غفلة	negligence
خطر ببال	to occur to one's mind
أغراض	belongings, necessities
أسباب	here: small items for trading
انحدر	to go down to
بَر	land, ground (as opposed to بحر)
روضة ج. رياض	garden
سقالة	scaffold, gangplank
كوانين	cooking pot, a stove using firewood
طلوع	to embark, come up
هلاك	annihilation, destruction
قرار	here: the bottom

متلاطم	clashing, crashing
قصعة	tub, large bowl
حلاوة روح	survival instinct
ريس	(naval rank, captain) officer, first mate
التفت	to turn toward, pay attention to
رسا/ أرسى	to come to rest\to make anchor
كسوة	a type of garment
شفاعة	mediation, advocacy
ذراع	a unit of measure, a cubit
بومة ج. بوم	owl
عكاز	staff, rod
استأذن	to seek permission
ودّع	to bid farewell

Comprehension Exercises

A. Answer the following questions in complete Arabic sentences. Hints are given in parentheses for lines in the text in which to find the information:

١. كيف كانت حياة التاجر وولده؟ (١-٣)

____

____

٢. كيف تصرّف[1] ابن التاجر (السندباد) في أمواله؟ وماذا قرّر أن يفعل بعدها؟ (٥-٨)

____

____

٣. أين وصل السندباد عند سفره؟ (٨-١٢)

____

____

٤. ما أصل الجزيرة التي رسي عليها المركب؟ وماذا حدث لها؟ (١٨-٢٢)

____

____

٥. ماذا قال الملك للسندباد عند وصوله إلى المدينة؟ (٢٩-٣٢)

____

____

B. Find Arabic phrases in the text that have the following meanings in English:

1. He left me money (1st paragraph):

____

1 Conducted

2. I thought it would continue like that (1st paragraph):

____

3. We buy, sell, and trade (1st paragraph):

____

4. He shouted in his loudest voice (2nd paragraph):

____

5. He did not pay attention to those who drowned (3rd paragraph):

____

6. You survived these adversities (4th paragraph):

____

C. Find Arabic synonyms or equivalents in the text for the following words and phrases:

١. حدائق:

____

٢. أشعل:

____

٣. لم ينظر أو يهتم:

---

٤. الصعوبات والمحن:

---

٥. ألبسني:

---

٦. هدفنا:

Interpreting the Text

١. ما مظاهر التّرف[2] التي عاش فيها السندباد؟ (١–٣)

---

٢. صِفوا[3] حياة الركاب على الجزيرة التي نزلوا فيها؟ (١٢–١٧)

---

2 Appearances of luxury
3 To describe

٣. كيف نجا سندباد من الغرق؟ (٢٢-٢٤)

---

٤. هل تعامل ريس المركب بحكمةٍ عند غرقه؟ لماذا؟ (٢٤-٢٦)

---

٥. ما الحوار الذي دار بين السندباد وصاحب المركب؟ وماذا كانت المفاجأة التي اكتشفها السندباد؟ (٣٨-٤٤)

Style and Technique

1. The phrases in line 4 فوجدت مالي قد مال وحالي قد حال are examples of juxtaposing homonyms (الجناس), considered one of the speech beautifiers (المحسنات اللفظية) in Classical rhetoric (البلاغة). These are instances of words that sound alike but are different in meaning. In this case, the verb مال means "to depart" or "to decline," while the more familiar noun مال means "money" or "wealth." Similarly, the verb حال in this case means "to change," while the familiar noun حال means "condition" or "situation." The poetic quality of placing these homonyms beside each other is further amplified by the similarity of the two pairs of words: حال and مال being only one letter removed from each other. The result is a much more poetic and memorable composition than merely فقدتُ أموالي وتغير

وضعـي المـادي. This is an example of an effect that is lost when the sentence is translated.

2. Lines 14, 20: مِنهُـم مَـن this structure has the meaning of "[there were] among them [those] who . . ." the word مَـن in this case carrying the same meaning as الـذي. It is used frequently in this story to indicate "some did . . . and some did . . ." but has a more poetic sound than merely saying بعـض البحريـين.
3. This text makes extensive use of the particles ف (then, so, for) and قـد (in the past tense: had done something) to facilitate the pacing of the storytelling. As you likely know, these particles are usually not necessary, but they convey a sense of relation between events. ف indicates an action that follows immediately after another, or because of the preceding action. In a narrative, it gives a sense of rapid action or events leading in a sequence to something. In this case, Sindbad is conveying the sense of his decision to go to sea leading directly to adventures that follow one after another. When used in the past, قـد has the effect of distancing one past action from more recent past actions, or indicating something was done completely. Here Sindbad is setting the scene by telling us things had been completed in order to put him in the situation that starts his adventures (he had a rich father, he inherited a lot of money, he wasted it all). These particles can add nuance to the time frame of a narrative, giving it more dimensions than simple past, present, and future.

Using Grammar and Structure Clues to Understand the Text

1. The particle و can be used to introduce a *haal* construction, indicating what the condition was when something happened. In this case, the و should not be read as "and" but is closer to "while." Often, you have to use context to determine which use is intended. In the following excerpt from line 1, where Sindbad is speaking of

his father, determine which uses of و are simple "and" conjunctions and which are introducing a *haal* construction:

وقد مات وأنا ولد صغير وخلّف لي مالًا وعقارًا وضياعًا.

2. In line 11, Sindbad arrives at جزيرة كأنها روضة. The particle كـ is a familiar one meaning "like" or "as," meaning the island was like a beautiful garden. It has a pleasing poetic quality when phrased this way, but if you wanted to make the meaning more clear and precise without the aesthetics, how else could you phrase this sentence?
3. In line 31, in the sentence لولا طول عمرك ما نجوت من هذه الشدائد, the phrase لولا means "if not for." This construction requires a condition (if something were not true) and a result (then). The particle ف is often used to introduce the "then" clause, but not in this case. The hypothetical result begins with the word ما, which has several meanings, but here means "not." There is also an implied message here, when the king speaks of Sindbad's long life, that a long life has been destined or ordained for him. Putting this together, what is the sentence saying?
4. The verb صار, like its synonym أصبح, has the familiar meaning "to become." As it is used at several points in this excerpt, such as line 31 صار يؤانسني بالكلام both can be used to mean "began," or "took to" doing something. This has the effect of describing how the action unfolded. How does the use of this construction enhance the narration of the relationship between the king and Sindbad?

Writing Exercises

A. Translate the following sentences into Arabic, using vocabulary from this reading. Hints in parentheses indicate which lines to look at for similar structures:

1. Once we were seated and gathered in the living room, my friends began to have fun. (15)

____

2. I hoped he would soon come back to his senses and wake up from his negligence. (4)

____

3. “Get out of there!” Nora’s mother shouted. (17)

____

4. The children thought the summer would last forever. (3)

____

5. God saved me from drowning. (22)

____

B. Rearrange the words below into coherent sentences:

١. بالسفر – في – سمحت – الصيف – أصدقائي – لي – والدتي – مع

____

____

٢. في – مررنا – نلتقط – كل – الصوّر – مكان – به – كنّا

---

٣. جزيرة – وفيها – البحر – هذه – مطلّة – على – هادئة – أشجار

---

٤. أعرف – معي – كيف – كثيرة – ولا – أبيعها – بضائع(!)

---

٥. بشفاء – فرحنا – من – مرضه – جدّي

Discussion Questions

١. ناقشوا هذه العبارة في ضوء قصة السندباد: دوام الحال من المحال.[4]
٢. الجزيرة كانت في الأصل سمكة كبيرة. بيّنوا[5] كيف يمكن للإنسان أن ينخدع[6] في الأشياء من حوله؟

4 Nothing is forever.
5 To explain
6 To be deceived by

٣. خمنوا المعاني والاستعمالات الأخرى لمصطلح «حلاوة روح» في اللغة؟
٤. كيف تميّز[7] صاحب المركب بأمانته[8]؟
٥. ما أكثر الأشياء قيمةً في نظركم؟

Research and Presentation

استمعوا من الإنترنت إلى الأغنية الفلكلورية «مالي مال وحالي حال» وحاولوا ترجمة كلماتها إلى الإنجليزية.

7 Distinguished
8 His trust

16

Moral Literature—Ibn al-Muqaffaʿ *Kalila wa-Dimna*

الدرس السادس عشر – ابن المقفع كليلة ودمنة

أبـو مُحمّـد عبـد الله بـن المقفـع (١٠٦هـ/ ٧٢٤م - ١٤٢هـ/ ٧٥٩م) مفكّـر وكاتـب فـارسي الأصـل. تميـزت كتاباتـه وأسـلوبه باليـسر والوضـوح والبعـد عـن الألفـاظ الغريبـة والمعـاني المبهمـة، فهـو صاحـب أسـلوب السـهل الممتنـع؛ ذلـك الأسـلوب البعيـد كل البعـد عـن التكلـف والصنعـة، ولكـن مـن الصعـب محاكاتـه[1] ومضاهاتـه.

يعـدُّ كتـاب ابـن المقفـع «كليلـة ودمنـة» مـن أكثـر كتـب الـتراث شـهرة وأوسـعها انتشـارًا، وهـو واحـد مـن أفضـل كتـب الأدب التـي تحـرّرت مـن قيـود الحـدود الزمنيـة والحِقَـب التاريخيـة والأصنـاف البشريـة والمراحـل العمريـة. وقـد اسـتخلص الـرواة والمؤرخـون أن أصـل هـذا الكتـاب يعـود للفيلسـوف الهنـدي بيدبـا، وكان الهـدف مـن الكتـاب إصـلاح الأخـلاق في السياسـة والاجتـماع وتهذيـب النفـوس، وقـد وَرَدَت نصائحـه عـلى ألسـنة الحيوانـات والطيـور.

نُقِـل الكتـاب إلى الأدب الفـارسي عندمـا قـام برزويـه بترجمتـه إلى اللغـة الفهلويـة، وهـي الفارسـية الآن. وأخـيرًا وصـل إلى الأدب العـربيّ حينـما قـام ابـن المقفـع بترجمتـه في القـرن الثـاني الهجـري وإبّـان العـصر العبـاسي. وقـد ألمـح ابـن المقفـع بـين سـطوره إلى كثـير مـن آرائـه السياسـية وأفـكاره الفلسـفية. وتُعـدّ النسـخة العربيـة الأهـم بـين الترجمـات الأخـرى والأكثـر جـودة، ويصنـف النقـاد العـرب القدامـى كتـاب كليلـة ودمنـة في المرتبـة الأولى مـن كتـب العـرب الخالـدة ومـن التحـف العربيـة النـادرة.

1 Imitation

Prediction and Scanning

Based on the context and background given above, record your predictions as to whether you expect to find the following in the story. Be prepared to discuss your predictions with classmates. Then, reading through the excerpts in the next section quickly, without the use of a dictionary, indicate whether your predictions were correct and where (in which lines) you found the answers. Again, be prepared to discuss the results with your classmates.

العبارة	التوقُّع	الدلالة
يجب الحفاظ على الأشياء الثمينة ذات القيمة الغالية.		
بطل القصة قرد، وكان ملكًا سابقا نفاهُ شعبه خارج البلاد.		
الصداقة بين القرد والسلحفاة أفسدها جشع القرد وحبّه للمال.		
النسخة العربية من كتاب «كليلة ودمنة» لها قيمة مميّزة عن نظائرها.		

From the Writings of Ibn al-Muqaffa'

كليلة ودمنة، القرد والغيلم

As is the pattern in the tales of *Kalila wa-Dimna,* the wise king directs his philosopher-advisor to instruct the assembly on a particular point of wisdom using a fictional story:

(١) قال الملك للفيلسوف: اضرب لي مَثَلَ الرجل الذي يطلب حاجته حتى إذا ظَفِر بها أضاعها. (٢) قال الفيلسوف: إنّ إصابة الحاجة أهون من الاحتفاظ بها، (٣) ومن ظفر بأمر ولم يحسن الاحتفاظ به أصابه ما أصاب الغَيْلم الذي ضيّع القرد بعد أن استمكن منه.

The philosopher begins by telling the background of how the monkey and the tortoise came to meet:

(٤) زعموا أنّ جماعة من القِرَدة كان لها ملك . . . فطال عمره حتى بلغ الهَرَم، (٥) فوثب عليه قرد شابٌّ من أهل بيته . . . فنفوا القرد الهَرِم وملّكوا الشاب. (٦) فانطلق هاربًا، فلحق بساحل البحر، فانتهى إلى شجرة من شجر التين نابتة على شاطئ البحر . . . (٧) وفيه غيلم، وهو السلحفاة الذكر . . . فخرج الغيلم إلى القرد فتصافحا وتصادقا وأَلِف كل واحد منهما صاحبه.

He then sets up the dilemma at the heart of the story:

(٨) [الغيلم] أتى منزله فوجد زوجته عليلة منهوكة سيئة الحال. (٩) فقال لها: يا أختِ، كيف الحال؟ (١٠) فلم تجبه. فقال: إني أراك منهوكة. فلم تجبه. (١١) فأعاد المسألة فأجابت عنها جارة لها وقالت له: ما أشدَّ حال زوجتك! (١٢) أما مرضها فشديد، وأما الدواء فأشدُّ . . . (١٣) وليس له دواءٌ إلاّ قلب قرد. (١٤) قال الغيلم في نفسه: هذا أمرٌ عسيرٌ. من أين أقدر على قلب قرد إلاّ قلب صديقي؟ (١٥) أَفَغادِرٌ بصديقي أم مُهْلِك زوجتي؟

The tortoise then sets out to accomplish the necessary task:

(١٦) أتى القرد فحيّاه، وقال: ما حبسك عني يا أخي كل هذا الحبس؟ (١٧) . . . قال الغيلم: إنّ مما بطّأني عنك مع شوقي إليك الحياء منك والاحتشام، لقلّة مكافأتي إياك بحسن بلائك ومعروفك إليّ . . . (١٨) ولكن أحببت أن تزورني في منزلي، فإنه في جزيرة كثيرة الشجر طيبة الفواكه، فأسعفني بطلبي. (١٩) واركب ظهري لننطلق إلى منزلي. (٢٠) فرغب القرد في الفواكه، وتابع الغيلم وركب ظهره، (٢١) فسبح به الغيلم حتى إذا لَجَّج به في البحر. (٢٢) عرض في نفسه قُبح ما يريده . . . (٢٣) ثم قال [القرد] للغيلم: ما يحبسك؟ وما لي أراك كأنك مهموم؟ (٢٤) قال: يُهِمُّني أنك تأتي منزلي فلا توافق فيه كل الذي أحبه لك، فإنّ زوجتي عليلة. (٢٥) قال القرد:

لا تهتمّ. فإنّ الهمّ لا يُغني شيئًا. والتمس لزوجتك الأدوية والأطباء . . . (٢٦) قال الغيلم: زعمت الأطباء أنه لا دواء لها إلاّ قلب قرد.

The clever monkey devises a way of escape:

(٢٧) ثمّ قال للغيلم: يا خليلي . . . لو كنتُ علمت بهذا كنتُ قد جئت بقلبي معي. (٢٨) قال الغيلم: أين قلبُك؟ (٢٩) قال: خلّفته في مكاني الذي كنتُ فيه. (٣٠) قال: وما حَمَلك على ذلك؟ (٣١) قال: سُنَّة فينا معشر القرود، إذا خرجنا إلى زيارة أخ أو صديق نُخلِّف قلوبنا لتزول الظِّنّة عنّا. فإن شئت أتيتك به سريعًا. (٣٢) ففرح الغيلم بطيب نفس القرد، وانقلب به راجعًا حتى بلغ الساحل. (٣٣) وثَب القرد إلى الشجرة فصعدها وأقام الغيلم ساعة ينتظره.

The philosopher wraps up the story with an understanding between the monkey and the tortoise:

(٣٤) ناداه الغيلم: يا خليلي، عجّل، خذ قلبك وانزل! . . . (٣٥) [قال القرد:] ولكنك احْتَلْتَ لي وخدعتني بقولك فكافأتك بمثل ذلك. واستدركت تفريطي وما كنت ضيّعت من نفسي. (٣٦) قال الغيلم: أنتَ الصادق البارّ، وذو العقل يُقِلّ الكلام ويبالغ في العمل، ويعترف بالزلّة (٣٧) ويتثبت في الأمور قبل الإقدام عليها . . . (٣٨) فهذا مثل الذي يطلب أمرًا حتى إذا استمكن منه أضاعه.

Vocabulary

ظفر	to gain possession of
أهون	easier
غَيْلَم	male tortoise
استمكن	take possession, mastery over
زعم	to claim, say
هَرَم	old, decrepit
وَثَب	to leap (the first mention: to attack, challenge)
ملّك	to make a king
تصافح	to shake hands, greet

تصادق	to become friends
أَلِف	to become acquainted
عليل	ailing
منهوك	exhausted, weakened
عسير	difficult
مهلك	death, demise, withering away
حبس	holding back, detention (absence)
بطّأ	to be delayed
احتشام	bashfulness, embarrassment
بلاء	good behavior, noble action
أغنى	to enrich, avail
لجّج	to reach the depths of the sea
التَمَس	to seek urgently
خلّف	to leave behind
معشر	group, troop
عجّل	hurry
استدرك	to set right
تفريط	negligence
بارّ	honest, truthful
زلّة	mistake
تثبت	to make certain of
إقدام	undertaking

Comprehension Exercises

A. Answer the following questions in complete Arabic sentences. Hints are given in parentheses for lines in the text in which to find the information:

١. لماذا روى الفيلسوف هذه القصة؟ (١–٣)

٢. لماذا هرب القرد إلى الشجرة؟ (٤–٧)

٣. ماذا وجد الغيلم عند رجوعه إلى بيته؟ (٨–١٠)

٤. ما الدواء الوحيد لزوجة الغيلم حسب كلام الجارة؟ (١١–١٢)

٥. ماذا كان الهدف الحقيقي وراء دعوة الغيلم للقرد؟ (١٦–١٩)

٦. كيف هرب القرد من الغيلم؟ (٢٧-٣١)

B. Find Arabic phrases in the text that have the following meanings in English:

1. It is said that (4):

2. He lived long (4):

3. Reflected on (22):

4. Long time no see (23):

5. A wise person (36):

6. Admits his mistake (36):

C. Find Arabic synonyms or equivalents in the text for the following words and phrases:

١. حصل على (١):

٢. أسهل (٢):

٣. مريضة (٨):

٤. ٤. صعب (١٤):

٥. قبيلة (٣١):

Interpreting the Text

١. لماذا اختار القرود قردًا شابًّا ليكون ملكهم الجديد؟

٢. كيف فاضَلَ[2] الغيلم بين زوجته وصديقه؟

____

____

٣. ماذا قرّر الغيلم وكيف نفّذ قراره؟

____

____

٤. كيف شَعرَ القرد بنية[3] الغيلم؟ وبماذا نصحه؟

____

____

٥. مَن كان أكثر ذكاءً وحنكة:[4] الغيلم أم القرد؟ ولماذا؟

____

____

Style and Technique

1. Many of the unfamiliar words in this text can be figured out by using the roots and patterns. For example, several instances of Form II verbs (فعّـل) are used. This form generally means to cause some-

2 To compare two things to see which is better
3 Intention
4 Skill, experience

one or something to do or be whatever the Form I means. بطّأ you may recognize as related to the word for slow. In this form, it means to slow down, or to delay (that is, to make slow). خلف means to follow, lag behind or be behind. خلّف, then, is to leave something behind (to make it be behind). ملّك, similarly, being related to the familiar word for king, means to make one a king, which is what the monkeys do with the young monkey.

2. A particular challenge in Arabic is الأضْداد, words that have two opposite meanings. (English has these as well; the word "oversight," for example could mean carefully watching over something or failing to do so). In line 17, the tortoise uses the word بلاء which can mean both a misfortune or a commendable action. The context makes it clear which meaning the tortoise intends.
3. The verb أغنى in line 25, like many Arabic verbs, has a range of meanings. The Form I form of this root can mean to be rich or to have no need of something. Form II (غنّى) has a very different meaning, "to sing." The form here is Form IV (أغنى) which can mean "to enrich," "suffice," or "profit." In this case, prepositions, which are often clues to meaning, do not help. The expression used here, however, is a common one meaning "to be of no benefit." The context, in which the monkey begins by saying "لا تهتم," supports this meaning.
4. Similarly, the verb أتى in line 31 has many different meanings. "To come," as it is used in line 16, is probably the most familiar. The intended meaning can be determined by the prepositions that accompany the verb. In this case, where the monkey is saying "I will bring," the receiver of the thing is the direct object and the thing brought takes the preposition ب. Here, the direct object is "you" and the indirect object is "it" (the heart). That, combined with the conditional إذا شئت "if you wish," produces "if you wish, I will bring it to you." أتى can also mean "to guide to," with the person being guided indicated by ب and the place by إلى. With على, the verb can mean "to eliminate" or "to mention," so context is needed.

Using Cultural Clues to Understand the Text

1. The abridged version of the story presented above reflects the storyline in most popular renditions of it, including the many adapted for children. Ibn Muqaffaʿ's full text includes much longer internal monologues from the characters on their ethical dilemmas and strategies, including an extended struggle by the tortoise to choose his wife or his friend. In the full version, the wife has faked her illness and invented the convenient cure as a means of breaking up the friendship between her husband and the monkey, of which she was jealous. This aspect of the story is typically left out in popular versions because it introduces too many conflicting ethical dilemmas. The full story, with all its ethical questions, reflects the serious, educational nature of the *Kalila wa-Dimna* stories and the complex nature of choices faced by leaders that the stories are meant to teach.
2. The tortoise's deception is based on expectations of good behavior (*adab*), which are part of the overall instruction of the elite with which the audience of *Kalila wa-Dimna* would be quite familiar. He is claiming his absence is due to shame at not being able to provide the hospitality that the monkey has by letting the tortoise visit his tree. He is playing on both expectations of hospitality—a bedrock Arab virtue—and social standing, by saying a visit to his island would relieve the tortoise's shame.
3. The monkey's story, as implausible as it is, likewise relies on traditional values to persuade the tortoise. Just as hospitality is an essential component of *adab*, jealousy and envy are taboo. A guest receiving hospitality must balance appreciation with avoiding being envious of the host's abundance, especially the qualities of his spouse. Conversely, one should not judge if the host has less than the guest. Here, the monkey is claiming that it is custom (سُنَّة) to leave one's heart at home so as not to judge one way or the other.

The essential point is that neither one is sincere and both have deception in mind.

Writing Exercises

A. Translate the following sentences into Arabic, using vocabulary from this reading. Hints in parentheses indicate which lines to look at for similar structures:

1. You can get what you want, but can you keep it? (2)

    ____

2. This storm is so strong! (11)

    ____

3. They say there is no hope now except prayer. (26)

    ____

4. The important thing is to confess your mistake. (25, 36)

    ____

5. He doesn't say much, but he works hard. (36)

    ____

B. Rearrange the words below into coherent sentences:

١. حتى - يطلب - إذا - حاجته - ظفر - كالذي - بها - أضاعها - لا - تكن

____

____

٢. التسعين - جدي - عمر - حتى - بلغ - السنة - طال

____

____

٣. كنتُ - لو - بهذا - لساعدتك - قد - عَلِمتُ

____

____

٤. العرب - الشراب - سُنَن - إكرام - الطعام - له - من - الضيف - وتقديم

____

____

٥. دائمًا - الصادق - بزلَّته - يعترف - الشخص

____

____

Discussion Questions

١. هل هناك أوجه تشابه بين ما فعله القرد الشاب وما يحدث في عصرنا من انقلابات عسكرية في بعض البلدان؟ دلّلوا على رأيكم بالأمثلة.
٢. ما أبرز صور العلاقات الإنسانية والاجتماعية المتشابكة بين البشر في هذا النص؟
٣. ما تقييمكم[5] لشخصية الغيلم؟
٤. لو كان لكَم صديقٌ عزيزٌ، هل يمكن أن تغدروا[6] به يومًا ما إذا اضطررتم؟ علّلوا إجابتكم.
٥. ما الحكم والمواعظ المستفادة من هذه القصة؟

Research and Presentation

This moral fable presents a number of difficult ethical choices and some harshly pragmatic views on human nature. Based on your discussion of the issues in the exercises above, prepare a 3–4-minute presentation on the following question:

هل يُمَيِّز الإنسان بين الخير والشر وبين الصواب والخطأ بالفِطرة[7] أم أنّه يكتسب الحسّ[8] الأخلاقي تدريجيًّا مع الوقت بالتعلُّم والممارسة؟

Some terms or expressions may be helpful in constructing this argument:

the end justifies the means	الغاية تبرّر الوسيلة
relativism	النسبوية
integrity	النزاهة
idealism	المثالية

5 Evaluation
6 To betray, play false
7 Instinct
8 Sense

17

The *Maqamat*—al-Hariri

الدرس السابع عشر – الحريري

أبو محمد القاسم بن علي بن محمد بن عثمان الحريري البصري (٤٤٦هـ/ ١٠٥٤م - ٥١٦هـ/ ١١٢٢م) من أكبر أدباء العرب، وصاحب كتاب مقامات الحريري. وقد حظيت مقاماته من الشهرة والانتشار ما لم يحظَ به كتابٌ آخر من كتب الأدب العربيّ، وما لبثَ الحريري أنْ ينتهي من تأليفها حتى جاءه الورّاقون والكُتّاب في بغداد يطلبون تدوينها، كما تسابق العلماء لقراءتها. وقيل إن الحريري دوّن بخطّ يده سبعمائة نسخة في سنة ٥١٤هـ وحدها، وقد ذاع صيت مقاماته حتى وصلت إلى الأندلس، وحينها وفَدَ فريق من علمائها لقراءة المقامات عليه، ثم رجعوا إلى بلادهم فتلقاها عنهم العلماء والأدباء، وتناولوها بالرواية وبالشرح والتحليل.

المقامات فن من فنون الكتابة العربية ظهر في العصر العباسي علي يد بديع الزمان الهمذاني، ثم تَبِعَه الحريري، وهو نوع من القصص القصيرة قائم على الحركات التمثيلية، ويدور الحوار فيها بين شخصين، البطل والراوي، ويلتزم مؤلفها بالصنعة الأدبية التي تعتمد على السجع والبديع. وتهدف المقامات إلى الترفيه والتثقيف والنصح والإرشاد.

Prediction and Scanning

Based on the context and background given above, record your predictions as to whether you expect to find the following in the story. Be prepared to discuss your predictions with classmates. Then, reading through the excerpts in the next section quickly, without the use of a dictionary, indicate whether your predictions were correct and where (in which lines) you found the answers. Again, be prepared to discuss the results with your classmates.

العبارة	التوقُّع	الدلالة
كان الشيخ في القصة فقيرًا ويلبس ملابس قديمة.		
جذب الشيخ اهتمام الحضور بخطابه وقصّته.		
لم يتعاطف الناس كثيرًا مع الشيخ وقصّته.		
كشف المؤلف في النهاية عن الهوية الحقيقية للشيخ.		

From *The Maqamat of Abu Zayd al-Saruji*

مقامات أبي زيد السروجي، المقامة الثالثة والثلاثون

The narrator, al-Harith, describes his visit to the city of Tbilisi (تفليس), in Georgia:

(١) فاتَّفَقَ حين دخلتُ تفليس أن صلَّيتُ مع زُمرة مفاليس. (٢) فلما قضينا الصلاة وأزمعنا الانفلات، برز شيخ باديَ اللَّقوة، بالي الكِسوة والقوة. (٣) فقال: عزمتُ على من خُلق من طينة الحرّية وتفوَّق دَرّ العصبية إلاّ ما تكلَّف لي لُبْثة، (٤) واستمع منّي نَفْثة ثم له الخيار من بعدُ وبيده البَذل والرّدّ. (٥) فعقد له القوم الحُبَى.

The afflicted man begins to relate his tale of woe:

(٩) فلما آنس حُسن إنصاتهم ورزانة حَصاتِهم، قال: يا أُولي الأبصار الرامقة والبصائر الرائقة! (١٠) أما يُغني عن الخبر العيان ويُنْبئ عن النار الدخان؛ شيب

لائــح، و وهــن فــادح، و داء واضــح، و الباطــن ففاضــح (١١) لقــد كنــتُ والله مِمَّــن مَلَــكَ ومــال، وولي وآل، ووصــل وِصــال. (١٢) فلــم تَــزَل الجوائــح تُسْــحِت، والنوائــب تَنْحِــتُ، حتــى الوكــرُ قَفْــرٌ والكــفُّ صِفْــرٌ والشِّــعارُ ضُرّ والعَيــش مــرّ . . . (١٣) ولم أقُــم هــذا المقــام الشــائن وأكشــف لكــم الدَّفائِــن إلاّ بعدمــا شَــقيت ولُقيــتُ وشِــبْتُ ممّــا لَقيــت. (١٤) فليتنــي لم أكــن بقيــت. ثــم تَــأوَّه تــأوُّه الأســيف . . .

As common in the *maqamat*, the character then goes into verse to express himself:

(١٥) أَشكو إلى الرّحمنِ سبحانه / تقلُّب الدهر وعِدوانَه
(١٦) وحادثاتٍ قَرَعَتْ مَرْوَتي / وقَوَّضتْ مَجدي وبُنيانه
...
(١٧) وأمْحَلَتْ رَبْعي حتى جَلَتْ / من ربْعِيَ المَمْحلِ جِرذَانَه
...
(١٨) وَازْوَرَّ من كان له زائرًا / وعافَ عافي العُرفِ عِرفانَه
(١٩) فهَلْ فَتىً يحزُنُه ما يرى / من ضُرّ شيخٍ دَهرُهُ خانَه
(٢٠) فَيفْرُجَ الهمَّ الذي هَمَّهُ / ويصلح الشأنَ الذي شانَه

From this moving scene, the narrator then reveals the secret of the story:

(٢١) فازْدَهــى القــوم بذكائــه ودهائِــه واخْتَلَبَهــم بحســن أدائِــه مــع دائِــهِ حتــى جَمَعــوا لــه خبايــا الخُبَــن وخفايــا الثُّبَــن. (٢٢) وقالــوا لــه: يــا هــذا إنّــك حُمْــتَ عــلى ركِيَّــة بَكِيَّــة وتعرضْــتَ لخلِيَّــةٍ خَليّــة، (٢٣) فَخُــذْ هــذه الصُّبابَــة وهَبْهَــا لا خَطــأ ولا إصابــة. (٢٤) فَنَــزّلَ قُلَّهــم مَنزلــة الكُثْــرِ ووصــل قَبُولــه بالشــكر. (٢٥) ثــمّ تــولّى يجــرُّ شِــقَّهُ وينهَــبُ بالخَبْــط طُرْقَــهُ . . . فصُــوِّرَ لي أنّــه مُحيــلٌ لِحلْيَتِــهِ، مُتصنّــعٌ في مِشْــيتِهِ. (٢٦) فَنَهَضْــتُ أنهــجُ منهاجَــه وأَقْفــو أدراجَــه وهــو يلْحَظُنــي شــزْرًا ويُوسِــعُني هَجْــرًا حتــى إذا خــلا الطريــق وأمكــن التحقيــق. (٢٧) نَظَــرَ إليّ نَظَــرَ مــن هَــشَّ وبَــشَّ . . . ثــم ضحِــك مَلِيًّــا وتمثَّــل لي بــشرًا سَــويًّا. (٢٩) فــإذا هــو شــيخنا السروجــي لا قَلَبَــةَ بجســمه ولا شُــبْهَةَ في وَسْــمه. (٣٠) ففرحــتُ بلُقْيَتِــه، وكَــذِب لَقْوَتِــه.

Abu Zayd al-Saruji concludes with a poem:

(٣١) ظهرتُ بِرَثٍّ لِكيْما يُقالَ / فقيرٌ يُزَجّي الزمانَ المُزَجّى
(٣٢) وأظْهَرْتُ للناسِ أنْ قَدْ فُلِجْتُ / فكَمْ نالَ قلبي به ما تَرَجّى
(٣٣) ولولا الرثاثةُ لم يُرْث لي / ولولا التفالجُ لم ألْقَ فُلْجا

Vocabulary

زُمرة	group
مفلس ج. مفاليس	bankrupt, penniless
أزمع	make ready, determine to
بادٍ	plainly, obviously
لقوة	palsy
بالٍ	worn out
طينة	clay
درّ	milk
نفث	spit, expectoration (here, a metaphor for his speech)
عقد الحُبى	to sit by drawing up the legs under one's garment
آنس	to notice
رزانة	tranquility
رامق	perceptive, seeing
رائق	bright, clear
عِيان	eye witnessing
يُنبئ	foretell, give warning of
وصل	here: to associate with
صال	assault
جائحة ج. جوائح	catastrophe
وكر	nest
نوائب	ups and downs
كف	palm of the hand
صفر	became empty, void

شائن	bad state, disrepute
دفائن	hidden
شقي	to be miserable
تأوّه	moan
تقلّب الدهر	the fickleness, fortunes of time
قرع	to hammer, strike
مروة	pebble, rock
ربع	quarter (here, dwelling)
جلو	to strip clear
فتى	young man
ازدهى	to be roused
اختلب	to captivate
خبايا	hidden things (treasures)
ركية	a well
خلية خلية	empty cell
صبابة	pittance, small amount
نزّل	to receive hospitably
خبط	to stumble
محيل	faking, making a trick
نهج	to follow, pursue
شزرًا	looking askance, suspiciously
هشّ وبشّ	friendly, amiable
سوي	(here) straight, unimpaired
قلبة	sickness, ailment
السروجي	Abu Zayd al-Saruji, the main character in the *Maqamat*
رثّ	to be raggedy, disheveled
زجّى	here: to forbear
فلج	to have palsy, paralysis
ترجّى	to hope

Comprehension Exercises

A. Answer the following questions in complete Arabic sentences. Hints are given in parentheses for lines in the text in which to find the information:

١. أين كان الراوي[1] عندما رأى الشيخ؟ (١-٣)

____

____

٢. ماذا أراد الشيخ؟ (٣-٤)

____

____

٣. كيف كان حال الشيخ قبل مرضه؟ (١١-١٢)

____

____

٤. ما ردّة فعل[2] الجمهور على خطبة الشيخ؟ (٢١-٢٣)

____

____

1 Narrator
2 Reaction

٥. ماذا كان رأي الراوي في هذا الشيخ في البداية؟ (٢٥)

B. Find Arabic phrases in the text that have the following meanings in English:

1. I appeal to, call on (3):

2. It's up to him (how to respond) (4):

3. I was wealthy and powerful (11):

4. I lost everything (12):

5. To make much of (24):

6. How often (32):

C. Find Arabic synonyms or equivalents in the text for the following words and phrases:

١. جمهور(١):

____

٢. أطلب من (٣):

____

٣. شَرِب (٣):

____

٤. كنت أتمنّى (١٤):

____

٥. توجّع (١٤):

____

٦. فئران (١٧):

____

٧. هيئته ومظهره (٢٩):

____

Interpreting the Text

١. ما أبرز ملامح شخصية الراوي في هذه القصة؟

---

٢. كيف لفَتَ الشيخ انتباه الجمهور بعد الصلاة؟

---

٣. لماذا تصنّع[3] الشيخ المرض والعجز من وجهة نظركم؟

---

٤. كيف انطلت[4] حيلة الشيخ على مَن سمعوه؟

---

3 To pretend
4 Was deceived

٥. بماذا برّرَ[5] الشيخ خدعته وكذبه على الناس؟

____

____

Style and Technique

1. Al-Hariri's text can be very challenging even for advanced readers of Arabic. To understand the story and appreciate its poetic qualities, however, one need not translate every word. Al-Hariri's rather verbose anti-hero, Abu Zayd al-Saruji, uses a good deal of repetition in his ornate speech and one can grasp his main ideas from the key words in his sentences. In following his story, therefore, it is essential to note where he stops repeating and transitions to a new point. In his extended poetic appeal in lines 15–20, for example, his verbs and possessive endings indicate that he is talking about himself and, from a sampling of the words, it is clear he is lamenting his misfortunes. In line 19, however, he begins with "هل فتى," indicating he is now talking about a young man, and thus not himself. From the familiar words that follow (حزن، ضرّ، شيخ) one can see he is now switching to the payoff of his sad speech: asking the young people in the audience to have pity on him, a supposedly stricken old man.
2. From a brief scan of al-Hariri's text, one can see that he values rhyme in his prose. This means that often he uses words from different roots with shared consonants. In line 11, for example, the word وصل is familiar from the root which has "to arrive" and "to be related" among its meanings. In this context, it is related to وَصْل (relation), referring to the fact that he had close relatives and associates. The rest of the phrase, صال, maintains the rhyme, but comes

5 Justified

from a different root, the meaning "to assault, attack." These two pair well, indicating he had loved ones and opponents—a man with strong social presence. The rhyme and shared consonants contrasting with the opposing meanings.

3. Similarly, one must use the structural context to determine the intended meanings of words. When Abu Zayd begins addressing the crowd, in line 10, he says أمـا يُغنـي عـن الخـبر العيـان. The verb أغنـى has many meanings, including "to be rich, to be enriched," "to benefit from," but also "to protect against." Likewise, الخـبر can mean "information," but also "rumor." These meanings are nearly opposite in their implications, so context must help clarify. The phrase العيـان refers to "eye-witnessing," and Abu Zayd's speech up to this point has been flattering the audience for their clear vision and discernment. Structurally, the two sentences in line 10 have a parallel structure and share the same preposition, عـن. The second sentence, يُنْبـئ عـن النـار الدخـان, says that smoke anticipates fire. This structure helps us interpret what is meant by the first part of the line: eye witnessing being the subject. Putting together the possible meanings, Abu Zayd is most likely saying something equivalent to "seeing is believing," describing his audience as the type that separate out the truth from the erroneous information, or as the English expression would say "sift the wheat from the chaff." This fits best with the flattery he is using on his audience (which he intends to cheat, of course). He does not switch to talking about himself until after this.

4. Due to the poetic nature of al-Hariri's writing, he tends to use similar sounding words in close proximity, which can be confusing. In these cases, recognizing the structure of his constructions will help identify what is meant. In line 14, for example, the words تَـأَوَّهَ تَـأَوُّهِ look identical. This is because the verb and *masdar* form of Form V (تفعّـل) look the same without voweling. Recognizing the sentence as an example of the cognate accusative (المفعـول المطلـق) clarifies which word is meant in each case. As discussed in Chapter 18, this

structure uses a verb and its related *masdar* to describe the way an action is performed:

دَرسَ الكتاب دراسةً مكثفة.
ضحكَ ضحكةَ المجنونِ.

In both cases, the noun tells how the verb was performed ("an intense studying," "the laugh of a crazy person"). While this would sound very awkward in English, it has poetic eloquence in Arabic. In this case, al-Hariri tells us that the old man "moaned" (تـأوَّه) "the moan of the stricken" (تـأوُّهِ الأسـيفِ). The *masdar* تـأوُّه, being in an *idaafa,* carries no ال thus making it look like the verb.

Using Cultural Clues to Understand the Text

1. The *maqama* genre is considered to have begun with al-Hariri's predecessor, Badi' al-Zaman al-Hamdani (969–1007). His stories also involve a poetic rogue, Abu al-Fath al-Iskandari. A *maqama* is literally "a sitting" and reflects that these stories were meant to simulate an oral storytelling session, thus their emphasis on their poetic quality. The mix of rhymed prose (سـجع) and poetry became hallmarks of the genre. The *maqama* genre was revived in the early twentieth century by Egyptian author Muhammad al-Muwaylihi with his 1907 Hadith 'Isa ibn Hisham, which uses the same narrator as al-Hamadani's *maqamat.* Some literary scholars have cited the *maqamat* as an influence on the development of the modern Arabic novel, as an alternative to viewing the novel as an entirely European import.
2. Traditionally, Arab culture has placed great value on poetic skill. Even scientific or philosophical texts will include lines of poetry to elaborate on their points. The rogue Abu Zayd is given wide latitude for his dishonesty and mischief by the narrator (and by extension, the author and reader) due to his poetic skill. In this sto-

ry, although caught in a deception by the narrator, he essentially absolves himself by displaying his skill at verse. Although he has cheated the crowd, he has also given them the gift of his poetry. In this sense, he is differentiated from the uncouth misers in al-Jahiz's *The Misers* (Chapter 2 of this book), for example.

Writing Exercises

A. Translate the following sentences into Arabic, using vocabulary from this reading. Hints in parentheses indicate which lines to look at for similar structures:

1. After I completed my work, I decided to leave. (2)

   ____

2. It's up to you what to do about this problem. (4)

   ____

3. I was one of those who didn't believe him. (11)

   ____

4. I felt that his concern for her was fake. (25)

   ____

5. How many times have we heard the same story? (32

   ____

B. Rearrange the words below into coherent sentences:

١. الحقيقة - بحثتُ - عندما - هذه - برزت - في - لي - مثل - المسألة - واضحة

____

____

٢. الملوك - رُحّبَ - ترحيب - زيارتهم - بِـ

____

____

٣. خاصة - إلى - يحتاج - الخطابة - موهبة - فنّ

____

____

٤. مصطنعًا - أنّ - كان - تصوّرت - ذكائه

____

____

٥. رأيته - فرحًا - تهلّلْتُ - عندما

____

____

Discussion Questions

١. ما تقييمكم لشخصية الراوي والشيخ في هذه القصة؟ وهل نالت إعجابكم أم لا؟
٢. ما أهم المؤثرات[6] التي تساعد في تشكيل الرأي العام؟
٣. كيف نحمي أنفسنا ومجتمعاتنا من المظاهر الخادعة والأشخاص المحتالين[7]؟
٤. معادلة المظهر والجوْهر، كيف نفسرها وما مدى أهميتها في حياتنا؟
٥. يُعْرف السجع بأنه تشابه فواصل الكلام على الحديث نفسه والنغمة نفسها تقريبًا، حاولوا مضاهاة[8] السجع في هذه المقامة بمفردات وكلمات تعرفونها.

Research and Presentation

Al-Hariri presents a challenging set of values and beliefs on trust, charity, cunning, and poetic skill. The popularity of these tales, and the many other collections like it, suggest that his views were popular and accepted, at least as entertainment. Based on your understanding of the attitudes in this story, prepare a 3–4-minute presentation on the following topic:

يقول الكاتب الأمريكي الساخر مارك توين: خداعُ الناس أسهل من إقناعهم أنهم قد خُدِعوا.
ناقشوا هذه المقولة ومدى توافقها مع أفكاركم وقناعاتكم[9].

Some terms of moral comparison may be helpful in constructing this argument:

standards of behavior	مقياس السلوك
the public good	الصالح العام
social custom	العُرف الاجتماعي

6 Effects
7 Fraudulent, deceitful
8 Imitation, simulation
9 Beliefs, convictions

18

Philosophical Novel—Ibn Tufayl

Hayy ibn Yaqdhan

الدرس الثامن عشر – ابن طفيل

حي بن يقظان

هو الفيلسوف المفكر القاضي الطبيب الشاعر الأندلسي ابن طفيل (٤٩٨هـ/ ١١٠٥م - ٥٨١هـ/ ١١٨٥م). ترك إرثًا علميًّا وآثارًا خالدة في مجالات متنوّعة، منها الرياضيات والطب والأدب والفلك والفلسفة ويعرفه الغرب باسم Abubacer.

قصته المشهورة «حي بن يقظان» واحدة من أهم كلاسيكيات الأدب العربي القديم، وهي رواية ذات أبعاد فلسفية عميقة ترمز للإنسان وعلاقته بالكون والدين. وتحكي قصة إنسان يُدعى حي بن يقظان وجد نفسه وهو ما زال طفلًا ساكنًا لأرضٍ لا أناس فيها، فاتخذ من الحيوان أنيسًا، ومن الطبيعة مأوًى، وبعد مرور الأيام وعندما نضج جسده وعقله، عكف على التّأمُّل في الكون وشؤونه، وهو الأمر الذي هداه إلى حتمية وجود خالق لهذا الكون. شارك في تأليف هذه القصة عدد من فلاسفة العرب والمسلمين، كان أولهم ابن سينا وتلاه السهروردي ثمّ ابن طفيل وأخيرًا ابن النفيس، ولكن القصة ارتبطت عند أكثرهم بابن طفيل، وقد حاول فيها التقريب بين المعرفة العقلية والمعرفة الدينية في إطار فلسفي، وقد تُرْجِمَت هذه القصة إلى لغات كثيرة ونالت شهرة عالمية واسعة.

Prediction and Scanning

Based on the context and background given above, record your predictions as to whether you expect to find the following in the story. Be prepared to discuss your predictions with classmates. Then, reading through the excerpts in the next section quickly, without the use of a dictionary, indicate whether your predictions were correct and where (in which lines) you found the answers. Again, be prepared to discuss the results with your classmates.

العبارة	التوقُّع	الدلالة
نشأ الطفل وتربّى بين الحيوانات في الغابة.		
تعلّمَ حيّ علم التشريح من كتاب وجده في الجزيرة.		
أدركَ البطل وجود الله من خلال معجزة سماوية.		
على الرغم من نشأته بعيدًا عن الحضارة الإنسانية، أصبح حيّ فقيهًا في العلم.		

From the Writings of Ibn Tufayl

حي بن يقظان

To set up his thought experiment, Ibn Tufayl imagines an infant dropped on an isolated island:

(١) ذكر سلفنا الصالح—رضي الله عنهم—أن جزيرة من جزائر الهند التي تحت خطّ الاستواء، (٢) وهي الجزيرة التي يتولّد بها الإنسان من غير أمّ ولا أبّ وبها شجر يُثْمر نساء . . . (٣) تلك الجزيرة أعدل بقاع الأرض هواءً . . . (٤) فلما اشتدّ الجوع بذلك الطفل بكى واستغاث، وعالج الحركة، فوقع صوته في أذن ظبية فُقِد طلاها . . . (٥) فلما سمعت الصوت ظنّتْهُ ولدها . . . وحَنّت الظبية وحَنَت عليه . . . (٦)

وما زالت تتعهده وتربيه وتدفع عنه الأذى . . . (٧) إنّ الظبية التي تكفلت به وافقت خصبًا ومرعى أثيثًا، فكثُر لحمها ودرّ لبنها، حتى قامت بغذاء ذلك الطفل أحسن قيام. (٨) وكانت معه لا تبعد عنه إلا لضرورة الرعي. وأَلِف الطفل تلك الظبية حتى كان بحيث إذا هي أبطأت عنه اشتدّ بكاؤه فطارت إليه.

The child, Hayy ibn Yaqdhan, begins to learn the natural sciences through inductive reasoning. In this example, he examines the body of the deer that had been taking care of him:

(٩) وكان قد شاهد . . . في الأشباح الميتة من الوحوش وسواها أنّ جميع أعضائها مصمتة لا تجويف فيها إلا القِحْف والصدر والبطن، (١٠) فوقع في نفسه أن العضو الذي بتلك الصفة لن يعدو أحد هذه المواضع الثلاثة. (١١) وكان يغلب على ظنه غلبة قوية أنه إنما هو في الموضع المتوسط من هذه المواضع الثلاثة؛ (١٢) إذ استقر في نفسه أن جميع الأعضاء محتاجة إليه وأن الواجب بحسب ذلك أن يكون مسكنه في الوسط . . . (١٣)—إذ كان قد شاهد الدماء متى سالت وخرجت انعقدت وجُمدت ولم يكن هذا إلا دمًا كسائر الدماء—(١٤) [وقال:] أنا أرى أن هذا الدم موجود في سائر الأعضاء لا يختص به عضو دون آخر.

From his observations, Hayy develops more abstract theories and classifications:

(١٥) ثم إنّه بعد ذلك أخذ في مآخذ أُخر من النظر فتصفَّح جميع الأجسام التي في عالم الكون والفساد، (١٦) من الحيوانات على اختلاف أنواعها، والنبات والمعادن وأصناف الحجارة والتراب والماء والبخار والثلج والبرد والدخان واللهيب والجمر، (١٧) فرأى لها أوصافًا كثيرة وأفعالًا مختلفة وحركات متفقة ومضادة، (١٨) وأمعن النظر في ذلك وتثبَّت فرأى أنها تتفق ببعض الصفات وتختلف ببعض وأنها من الجهة التي تتفق بها واحدة ومن الجهة التي تختلف فيها متغايرة ومتكثرة، (١٩) فكان تارة ينظر خصائص الأشياء وما يتفرد به بعضه عن بعض، (٢٠) فتكثر عنده كثيرةً تخرج عن الحصر وينتشر له الوجود انتشارًا لا يضبط. (٢١) وكانت تتكثر عنده أيضًا ذاته، كان ينظر إلى اختلاف أعضائه وأن كل واحد منها منفرد بفعل وصفة تخصه، (٢٢) وكان ينظر إلى كل عضو منها فيرى أنه يحتمل القسمة إلى أجزاء كثيرة جدًا، (٢٣) فيحكم على ذاته بالكثرة، وكذلك على ذات كل شيء.

From natural sciences, Hayy progresses logically to spiritual matters, reflecting the author's belief that such insights can be derived by pure reason:

(٢٤) فعلم بالضرورة أن كل حدث لا بد له من محدث، فارتسم في نفسه بهذا الاعتبار فاعل للصورة ارتسامًا على العموم دون تفصيل . . . (٢٥) فلما لاح له من أمر هذا الفاعل ما لاح على الإجمال دون تفصيل حدث له شوق حثيث إلى معرفته على التفصيل . . . (٢٦) فإذن لا بد للعالم من فاعل ليس بجسم، وإذا لم يكن جسمًا فليس إلى إدراكه لشيء من الحواس سبيل، لأن الحواس الخمس لا تُدرك إلا الأجسام، أو ما يلحق الأجسام . . . (٢٧) وإذا كان فاعلًا للعالم فهو لا محالة قادر عليه وعالم به. . . (٢٨) وقد تبرهن أن قدرته غير متناهية وأن جميع الأجسام وما يتصل بها أو يتعلق بها ولو ببعض التعلق هو متناهٍ منقطع. (٢٩) فإذن العالم كله بما في السماوات والأرض والكواكب وما بينها وما فوقها وما تحتها فعله وخلقه ومتأخر عليه بالذات وإن كانت غير متأخرة عليها بالزمان.

Eventually, after Hayy has deduced all the principles for proper living and devoted himself to communion with God, a stranger arrives on his island. This visitor, Absal, teaches Hayy how to speak relatively quickly, and then proceeds to learn from Hayy great truths of religion:

(٣٠) فجعل أبسال يسأله عن شأنه ومن أين صار إلى تلك الجزيرة، (٣١) فأعلمه حي بن يقظان أنّه لا يدري لنفسه ابتداءً ولا أبًا ولا أمًّا أكثر من الظبية التي ربتّه، (٣٢) ووصف له شأنه كله وكيف ترقى بالمعرفة حتى انتهى إلى درجة الوصول. (٣٣) لما سمع أبسال منه وصف تلك الحقائق والذوات المفارقة لعالم الحس العارفة بذات الحق—عز وجل—ووصف ذلك الحق—تعالى وجلّ—بأوصافه الحسنى (٣٤) ووصف له ما أمكنه وصفه مما شاهده عند الوصول من لذّات الواصلين وآلام المحجوبين، (٣٥) لم يشك أبسال في أن جميع الأشياء التي وردت في شريعته من أمر الله—عز وجل—وملائكته وكتبه ورسله واليوم الآخر وجنته وناره هي أمثلة هذه التي شاهدها حي بن يقظان، (٣٦) فانفتح بصر قلبه وانقدحت نار خاطره وتطابق عنده المعقول والمنقول . . .

Vocabulary

سلفنا	our predecessors
خطُّ الاستواء	the equator
ظبية	deer
استغاث	to call for help
طلا	a deer's offspring
حنّ	to feel sympathy, affection for
تعهد	here: to care for
أذى	harm
أثيث	abundantly growing
أَلِف	to become used to, familiar with
أبطأ	to delay, slow down
مصمتة	solid, uniform
تجويف	cavity, hollowness
قِحْف	skull
انعقدت	to clot, coagulate
تصفَّح	to examine
برهن	to prove, demonstrate
معدن ج. معادن	minerals
بخار	vapor
لهيب	flame
أمعن	to apply oneself to, to focus on
متأخر على	subsequent to
لاح	to be evident, appear
الوصول	here: arriving at an intimate knowledge of God
ملاك ج. ملائكة	angel
واصلين	those who have arrived (at the knowledge of God)
انقدح	to spark a fire
محجوب ج. محجوبون	those hidden or veiled (here, from the knowledge of God)

المعقول	that which is reasoned
المنقول	that which is passed on (i.e., traditions)

Comprehension Exercises

A. Answer the following questions in complete Arabic sentences. Hints are given in parentheses for lines in the text in which to find the information:

١. ما الصورة التي كانت عليها الجزيرة؟ (١–٣)

____

____

٢. كيف بدأت العلاقة بين الظبية وحيّ؟ (٤–٦)

____

____

٣. كيف تعلّم حي علم تشريح الجسم وأعضائه؟ (٩–١٠)

____

____

٤. ما الملاحظات التي دفعته إلى الاعتقاد بوجود الله؟ (٢٤–٢٥)

____

____

٥. علامَ استدلّ أبسال بعد حديثه مع حي؟ (٣٥-٣٦)

____

____

B. Find Arabic phrases in the text that have the following meanings in English:

1. And other things (9):

____

2. Would not be other than (more than) (10):

____

3. Took another point of view (15):

____

4. What is unique to each (19):

____

5. Pictured in his mind (24):

____

6. Agrees with (36):

____

C. Find Arabic synonyms or equivalents in the text for the following words and phrases:

١. أجدادنا:

____

٢. مناخ معتدل:

____

٣. تسيطر على تفكيره:

____

٤. إنّه مشترك بين الجميع:

____

٥. غير ملموس:

____

٦. أصبح واعيًا:

____

Interpreting the Text

١. ما احتياجات الإنسان الأساسية في طفولته؟ (٤-٦)

____

____

٢. ماذا كانت أهمية اكتشاف تجاويف الجسم وخصائصه؟ (٩-١٣)

____

____

٣. كيف انتقل حيّ من فهم الأشياء الملموسة إلى المفاهيم المجردة؟

____

____

٤. ما النتائج التي توصّل إليها حيّ حول صفات الكون وعناصره؟ (١٥-٢٠)

____

____

٥. هل اعتقد الكاتب بوجود تعارض[10] بين المعرفة الدينية والمعرفة المادية؟ (٣٥-٣٦)

____

____

10 Conflict

Style and Technique

1. Line 10 includes an example of the cognate accusative (المفعول المطلق): يغلب على ظنه غلبة قوية. While this would sound awkward if translated literally in English, it is considered a stylistic device in Arabic. The *masdar* غلبة of the verb يغلب is added to an adjective to show how the action took place; in this case قويةً. Similar examples are: درسته دراسةً مكثفةً or ساعدني مساعدةً كبيرةً. The cognate accusative will usually be indefinite and accusative. The *taa marbuta* in this case makes the accusative endings less obvious, but they are normally a clue to the construction. English discourages repeating the same or similar words in close proximity, but due to the poetic nature of Arabic, the repetition of the same root enhances the tonal quality of the statement.
2. In a text dealing so heavily with learning, Ibn Tufayl uses a large number of expressions to describe Hayy's process of coming to know something. These are chosen to reflect the way he acquires knowledge. You can also use this to vary your expressions from simply saying تعلّم. The process begins in line 9 with what he observed: شاهد. In line 10, he uses the phrase يغلب على ظنه to indicate that a conclusion is becoming overwhelmingly clear based on his repeated observation. In the next line, this causes a derivative idea to استقر في نفسه. In other words, an inference based on the observation is "settling in his consciousness," meaning it is becoming more probable and reasonable.
3. The verb وقع في in line 10 in this case has the meaning "to come to mind" or "to understand." The verb وقع when collocated with the preposition في can carry many different meanings. The context is essential for determining the correct meaning. For example:

fell in love	وقع في الحب
fell into trouble	وقع في ورطة
got caught by the police	وقع في أيدي الشرطة

was deceived — وقع في فخّ
insulted the man — وقع في الرجل
happened that day — وقع في هذا اليوم

Using Cultural and Contextual Clues to Understand the Text

1. Much of Ibn Tufayl's narrative deals with issues that were major philosophical disputes in his time, but whose significance may be lost on us. Beginning in line 26, and throughout his speculations on the creator, Hayy emphasizes that the creator cannot have a body (ليس بجسم). The rationalists, of whom Ibn Tufayl was an ardent supporter, clashed with religious traditionalists on a number of issues. One of these was the anthropomorphisms in the Qur'an—that is, statements referring to human characteristics, such as body parts, for God. Rationalists denied the literal meaning of these and insisted they were metaphors. Here, Hayy concludes through pure reason that an eternal creator could not have a body, and therefore, body parts.
2. One of the most bitter controversies—considered a heresy by many—involved the eternity of the created world, a phenomenon in which rationalists believed but many religious traditionalists did not. In line 29, Hayy concludes that the creation comes after (متأخّر على) the creator "in essence if not in time" (بالذات وإن كانت غير متأخرة عليها بالزمان), the standard rationalist explanation of the relation of an eternal God to an eternal creation.
3. Similarly, the relationship between knowledge that could be apprehended by reason (المعقول) and that which was divinely revealed and passed down (المنقول) was a major point of disagreement between the two sides. The rationalist camp, to which Ibn Tufayl belonged, asserted that even the deepest spiritual truths could be derived from logic, and therefore, there should be no limits on intellectual activity. The conclusion that Absal makes in line 36 is a

reference to this controversy and invokes those two terms that had well-known implications.

Writing Exercises

A. Translate the following sentences into Arabic, using vocabulary from this reading. Hints in parentheses indicate which lines to look at for similar structures:

1. The problems we face are common to all people. (14)

 ____

2. I began to look at this question from a different point of view. (15)

 ____

3. Our senses are not able to perceive some forms of matter. (26)

 ____

4. We are not able to prove the existence of life on other planets. (29)

 ____

5. I was amazed at the level his knowledge had reached. (32)

 ____

B. Rearrange the words below into coherent sentences:

١. من – مُحدِث – له – بالضرورة – حدث – لا بد – كل

____

____

٢. بقاع – الجزيرة – هواءً – أعدل – الأرض – هذه

____

____

٣. اشتد – عندما – ابتعدت – عنه – أمه – بالبكاء

____

____

٤. بالمعرفة – هذه – كيف – ترَقّى – الدرجة – إلى – حتى – انتهى(!)

____

____

٥. وصْفِهِ – له – وَصفَ – أمكنه – ما

____

____

Discussion Questions

١. هل تتفقون مع رؤية الكاتب في مطابقته[11] بين المعرفة المادية والمعرفة الدينية؟ ولماذا؟
٢. هل شخصية حيّ في القصة تُمثّل إنسانًا عاديًا أم عبقريًّا[12]؟ وضحوا إجابتكم بالأمثلة.
٣. كيف يكتسب الإنسان المعرفة والخبرة في الحياة؟
٤. ما سلبيات وإيجابيات العُزلة[13] الاجتماعية من وجهة نظركم؟
٥. هل الكون من حولنا يلهمنا[14] بأسئلة أم بأجوبة؟ كيف؟

Research and Presentation

Prepare a 3–4-minute presentation about the following question:

هل أَلهَمَت قصة «حي بن يقظان» لابن طفيل أدباء الغرب؟
اكتبوا رأيكم مقارنين بين حيّ بطَل[15] هذه القصة وماوكلي بطل رواية «كتاب الأدغال» وطرزان بطل رواية «طرزان القردة».

Some of Ibn Tufayl's own rhetorical devices will be helpful to you:

according to that, because of that	بحسب ذلك
to be in harmony, agreement	طابَقَ ______ و______
it must be true that	لا بد أنّه صحيح

11 Correspondence
12 Genius
13 Isolation
14 Inspire
15 Hero, protagonist

19

Satire—Abu al-'Alaa' al-Ma'arri

الدرس التاسع عشر – أبو العلاء المعري

أبو العلاء المعري (٣٦٣هـ/ ٩٧٣م – ٤٤٩هـ/ ١٠٥٧م) شاعرٌ فَذٌّ[1] وفيلسوفٌ وأديبٌ عربيٌّ مِنَ العصرِ العبَّاسي، اشتُهِرَ بآرائِه وفلسفتِه المثيرةِ للجدلِ في زمنه. وُلد وتُوفي بمعرّة النعمان بمحافظة إدلب في سوريا ومنها جاء لقبه المعري. فَقَدَ المعري بصره نتيجة إصابته بمرض الجدري وهو في سن الرابعة، وكان لا يعرف من الألوان إلا اللون الأحمر؛ وقد ذكر المعري سبب ذلك بأنّهُ ارتداه في أثناء علاجه من هذا المرض. ولكن هذه المحنة لم تثنيه عن طلب العلم، ودراسة فنون اللغة والأدب والقراءة والحديث. ويُذكر أن المعري كانَ نباتيًّا، وكانَ يَدعمُ حقوقَ الحيوانِ ويُحرِّمُ إيذاءه، وكانَ يَلبسُ الثِّياب الخشنة، وذُكر عنه أنه انتقد بعض العقائدَ الدينِية صراحةً حتى وصل الأمر إلى حدِّ تَكفيرِه. وقد اعتزل الناس فترة طويلة من الزمن وظلَّ حبيسًا في بيتِه حتى وفاتِه ولذلك أُطلق عليه لقب «رَهين المحبَسيْن»، أي محبس العَمى ومحبس الدار. وقد أَوْصى أن يُكتَبَ على قبرِه عِبارة «هذا جَناهُ أبي عليَّ، وما جَنيْتُ على أَحَد.» ويَقصدُ أنَّ أباه بزَواجِه من أمِّه كان سببًا في وجوده في هذه الدُّنيا. وذكرت بعض المصادر أنّ نحو ثمانين شاعرًا وقفوا على قبره يوم وفاته يرثونه بقصائدهم.

Prediction and Scanning

Based on the context and background given above, record your predictions as to whether you expect to find the following in the story. Be prepared to discuss your predictions with classmates. Then, reading through the excerpts in the next section quickly, without the use of a

1 Distinguished

dictionary, indicate whether your predictions were correct and where (in which lines) you found the answers. Again, be prepared to discuss the results with your classmates.

العبارة	التوقُّع	الدلالة
الكاتب يحاول التقرب من الله وطلب المغفرة.		
يحاول الكاتب جاهدًا معرفة الطريق إلى الجنة.		
عندما قابل الكاتب الشيطان وجده في حالة مزرية.		
الكاتب يمدح فنون الأدب وصناعته.		

From the Writings of Abu al-ʿAlaaʾ al-Maʿarri

رسالة الغفران، المجلد الأول

Al-Maʿarri has been challenged by a noted grammarian, Ibn al-Qarih, for his lack of piety. In his satirical response, al-Maʿarri has Ibn al-Qarih narrate his attempts to enter Heaven. First, Ibn al-Qarih appeals to Ridwan, the angel who guards the gates of Heaven:

(١) لما نهضتُ أنتفض من الرَّيم، وحضرتُ حرصات القيامة . . . (٢) ولقيني الملك
الحفيظ بما زَبِر لي من فعل الخير، فوجدتُ حَسَناتي قليلة كالنُّفَأِ في العام الأرمل . . .
(٣) إلا أن التوبة في آخرها كأنها مصباح أبيلٍ رفع لسالك السبيل. (٤) فلما أقمت في
الموقف زُهاء شهر أو شهرين، وخِفْتُ في العَرق من الغرق، زيَّنَت لي النفس الكاذبة
أنْ أنظِم أبياتًا في رضوان، خازن الجنان . . . (٥) ثمّ ضانكتُ الناس حتى وقفتُ منه
بحيث يسمع ويرى، فما حفل بي، ولا أظنّه أَبِهَ لما أقول. (٦) فغبرتُ بُرهة، نحو
عشرة أيام من أيام الفانية، ثم عملت أبياتًا [جديدة] . . . (٨) دعوتُ بأعلى صوتي:

يـا رضـوان، يـا أمـين الجبـار الأعظـم عـلى الفراديـس، ألم تسـمع ندائـي بـك واسـتغاثتي إليـك؟ (٩) فقـال: لقـد سـمعتُك تذكـر رضـوان ومـا علمـتُ مـا مَقصِـدُك، فـما الـذي تطلـب أيهـا المسـكين؟ (١٠) فأقـول: أنـا رجـل لا صـبر لي عـلى اللّـواب، أي العطـش، وقـد اسـتطلتُ مـدة الحسـاب، ومعـي صَـكٌّ بالتوبـة، وهـي للذنـوب كلهـا ماحيـة . . . (١١) فقـال: إنـك لغبـين الـرأي! أتأمـل أن آذن لـك بغـير إذن مـن ربّ العـزة؟

Ibn al-Qarih will make a desperate search around the gates of Heaven for anyone who can help him. After being turned down by everyone, he tries to defend a man accused of grammar mistakes from a Heavenly mob, then runs into trouble himself:

(١٢) وإذا جماعـةٌ مـن هـذا الجنـس كلُّهـم يلومونـه عـلى تأويلـه. (١٣) فقلـت: يـا قـوم، إن هـذه أمـورٌ هينـةٌ، فـلا تعنتـوا هـذا الشـيخ . . . إنـه مـا سـفك لكـم دمًـا، ولا احتجـن عنكـم مـالًا، فتفرَّقـوا عنـه. (١٤) وشـغلتُ بخطابهـم والنظـر في حَويرهـم، فسـقط منّـي الكتـاب الـذي فيـه ذكـر التوبـة، ورجعـتُ أطلبـه فـما وجدتـه. (١٥) فأظهـرتُ الوَلَـه والجـزع، فقـال أمـير المؤمنـين: لا عليـك، ألـك شـاهدٌ بالتوبـة؟ (١٦) فقلـت: نعـم، قـاضي حلـب وعُدولُهـا. (١٧) فقـال: بمـن يُعـرف ذلـك الرجـل؟ فأقـول: بعبـد المنعـم بـن عبـد الكريـم قـاضي حلـب، حرسـها الله، في أيـام شـبل الدولـة. (١٨) فأقـام هاتفًـا يهتـف في الموقـف: يـا عبـد المنعـم بـن عبـد الكريـم قـاضي حلـب في زمـان شـبل الدولـة، هـل معـك علـمٌ مـن توبـة عـلي بـن منصـور الحلبـي الأديـب؟ (١٩) فلـم يُجبـه أحـد.

Eventually, Ibn al-Qarih will go to visit Hell, and be surprised by what he finds there also:

(٢٠) فيطلّـع فـيرى إبليـس، لعنـه الله، وهـو يضطـرب في الأغـلال والسلاسـل، ومَقامـع الحديـد تأخـذه مـن أيـدي الزّبانيـة. (٢١) فيقـول: الحمـد لله الـذي أمكـن منـك يـا عـدوّ الله وعـدوَّ أوليائـه! (٢٢) لقـد أهلكـتَ مـن بنـي آدم طوائـفَ لا يعلـم عددَهـا إلاّ الله. (٢٣) فيقـول: مـن الرجـل؟ (٢٤) فيقـول: أنـا فُـلان بـن فُـلانٍ، مـن أهـل حلـب، كانـت صناعتـي الأدب، أتقـرب بـه إلى الملـوك. (٢٥) فيقـول: بئـس الصناعـة! إنهـا تهَـبُ غُفّـةً مـن العيـش، لا يتَّسـع بهـا العيـال، وإنهـا لمَزَلّـةٍ بالقَـدَم وكـم أهلكـتُ مثلـك! (٢٦) فهنيئًـا لـك إذ نجـوتَ . . . (٢٧) ولكـن أسـألك عـن خـبرٍ تخبرنيـه؛ إنّ الخمـر حُرّمـت عليكـم في الدنيـا وأُحلّـت لكـم في الآخـرة، فهـل يفعـل أهـل الجنّـة بالولـدان المخلَّديـن فعـل أهـل القَريـات؟ (٢٨) فيقـول: عليـك البَهْلـة! أمـا شَـغَلَك مـا أنـت فيـه؟ (٢٩) أمـا سـمعت

قوله تعالى «ولهُم فيها أزواجٌ مُطهَّرةٌ وهُم فيها خالِدون»[2]؟ (٣٠) فيقول: وإنّ في الجنّة لأشْرِبة كثيرة غير الخمر . . .

Vocabulary

رَيم	here: grave
حرص ج. حرصات	plains, empty land
مَلَك	angel
حسنة ج. حسنات	good deed
التوبة	repentance
زُهاء	approximately
بيت ج. أبيات	line of poetry
رِضوان خازن الجنان	Ridwan, the guardian of the gates of Heaven
ضانك	here: to push through, squeeze by
أَبِه	to take notice of
بُرهة	a moment, a short time
استغاثة	call for help
مسكين	unfortunate, poor (person)
لا صبر لي على	I cannot bear (something)
صكّ	document, deed
ماحية	eraser
ربّ العزة	The Lord of Might (i.e., God)
تأويل	interpretation, explanation
ترقّق	have pity
لا عليك	don't worry yourself
شبل الدولة	ruler of Aleppo (1029–38)
غلال	shackles, fetters
فُلان	so-and-so, unnamed person

2 Qur'an 2:25

لا يتسع لـ	does not accommodate, suffice (for)
أهل القريات	a reference to the people of Sodom and Gomorrah
حرّم	to forbid
أحلّ	to permit
بهلة	cursed
مطهر	pure, immaculate

Comprehension Exercises

A. Answer the following questions in complete Arabic sentences, based on the story:

١. هل كان ابن القارح على قيد الحياة[3] في بداية هذه القصة؟

____

____

٢. لِمَن كتب ابن القارح أبيات الشعر؟ ولماذا؟

____

____

3 على قيد الحياة = alive

٣. أي نوع من الرسائل كان يحمل ابن القارح؟

____

____

٤. لماذا حمد ابن القارح الله عندما رأى الشيطان في الجحيم؟

____

____

٥. ماذا طَلَب الشيطان من ابن القارح؟

____

____

B. Are the following statements true? If not, why?

١. سَمح رضوان لابن القارح بدخول الجنة.

____

____

٢. فَقَدَ ابن القارح رسالة مهمة.

____

____

٣. زعم إبليس أنّ شرب الخمر مباح في الجنة.

____

____

٤. مَدَحَ[4] الشيطان حِرفة[5] ابن القارح.

____

____

٥. وجد ابن القارح شهودًا لرسالة التوبة.

____

____

Style and Technique

1. In line 2, the narrator evaluates his good deeds by describing them as: النُّفَـأ في العـام الأَرْمَـل. The word نُفـأ means fragments of scattered plants, and العـام الأرمـل means the year with little rain, goods, or benefits. You will recognize the root as the same as the word for "widow." Such a year would have very few plants growing, and thus the metaphor is one of humility.
2. In line 15, the Commander of the Faithful tells Ibn al-Qarih "لا عليـك," literally meaning "nothing to you." By this, he means "don't worry about it," or "it's no big deal." The expression is like the Egyptian colloquial معلـش.

4 To praise
5 Profession

3. 3. The word فُلان (line 24) is used in Arabic as a filler for an actual name, equivalent to the English expression "so and so." It is typically used as an example, when there is no actual person to refer to, the way a blank is often used. One might find this in a template for a letter, for example. Here it is used as a substitute for an actual name, which often happens when the actual name is unimportant for the discussion at hand. Here, we have Ibn al-Qarih proudly announcing himself and his position, but it is rendered as if he is an unimportant placeholder who could be replaced by anyone.
4. In line 25, Satan ridicules Ibn al-Qarih's profession by telling him "إنها تهبُ غُفةً من العيش" meaning that it is barely enough to sustain life.

Using Cultural and Context Clues to Understand the Text

1. Because the author's target, Ibn al-Qarih, was a proud grammarian who often corrected others' language use, al-Ma'arri mocks his style by using a lot of obscure words. Many of the terms used in Ibn al-Qarih's supposed narration are chosen simply because they are rare and will sound like someone trying to show off their vocabulary.
2. Similarly, since al-Ma'arri is trying to mock Ibn al-Qarih's attitude of religious superiority and very doctrinaire stance, the visions of Heaven and Hell presented here are intentionally absurd. Al-Ma'arri was a skeptic who believed that the divine was beyond human understanding and the symbols used in the sacred texts were, at most, metaphors. Figures like Ibn al-Qarih who claimed to have exact knowledge of spiritual matters they could relate in earthly terms were targets of ridicule. This explains the very earthly visions of Heaven, with its jostling crowds and lost letters.
3. In line 8, Ibn al-Qarih appeals to Ridwan, the angel tasked with guarding Heaven. Although this character does not appear in the

Qur'an or early Islamic writings, he became important in later traditions, playing a role similar to Saint Peter in Christian folklore.

Writing Exercises

A. Using vocabulary from the text, express the following in Arabic:

1. My good deeds are few, but my repentance is sincere. [6](2–3)

____

2. He was not able to push his way to the front of the crowd. (5)

____

3. No one heard my call for help. (8)

____

4. If we do not have pity on the unfortunate, who will have pity on us? (9, 13)

____

5. The current budget[7] is not sufficient for the needs of the community (25)

____

6 مخلص
7 ميزانية

B. Rearrange the words in coherent sentences, using the text for clues:

١. الشيخ – يقبل – معظم – تأويل – هذا – العلماء – لا

---

٢. أنظِم – زيّنت – الكاذبة – النفس – أنْ – أبياتًا – لي

---

٣. على – شخصًا – صبر – له – لا – الانتظار – كان

---

٤. يدها – سَقَطَ – ولم – من – تجده – الكتاب

---

٥. الرئيس – كان – أي – يُقرِّبُهُ – من – يفعل – شيء

____

____

Discussion Questions

Al-Ma'arri's ideas were controversial in his time and remain so. His depictions of Heaven and Hell are quite satirical and were offensive to many. Based on your reading, how effective do you think the author has been? Answer the questions below, using al-Ma'arri's text as an example.

١. اتُّهِمَ[8] أبو العلاء المعري بالإلحاد[9] والزَنْدَقة[10]، هل يشير هذا النص لبعض أسباب هذا الاتهام؟ كيف؟
٢. هل ينجح أسلوب التهكّم والسخرية دائمًا في إثارة فكر القارئ وإقناعه بفكرة الكاتب؟
٣. كيف تفسرون هذه المقولة لأبي العلاء: اثنان من أهل الأرض؛ ذو عقلٍ بلا دين وآخر دِيِّنٌ لا عقلَ له.
٤. اختاروا لقبًا جديدًا لأبي العلاء المعري مع التعليل[11].

Research and Presentation

The reading and activities above should give you a clear idea of al-Ma'arri's thoughts. Another area in which he was very involved was in the ethics of dealing with animals. Do some further research about al-Ma'arri and his deep concern for animals and use this as the basis of a 1–2-minute presentation on the following:

8 Was accused
9 Atheism
10 Infidelity, disbelief, atheism
11 Explanation

قضيـة الرفـق بالحيـوان والامتنـاع عـن أكْلِـه عنـد أبي العـلاء المعـري ونظيرهـا[12] في العـصر الحديـث

The following terms are useful in this kind of critical analysis of an argument:

to object to	اعترض على
to criticize	انتقد
to satirize, lampoon	هجا (يهجو)
to disapprove, condemn	استنكر

12 Its similarities

20

Animal Rights—Ikhwan al-Safa

الدرس العشرون – إخوان الصفا

إخوان الصفا وخِلّان الوفا جماعة من المفكرين والفلاسفة. كان أول ظهورهم على الأرجح في أوائل القرن الرابع الهجري (العاشر الميلادي) بمدينة البصرة. وقد اجتهدت هذه الجماعة في التوفيق بين العقائد الإسلامية والحقائق الفلسفية المعروفة في ذلك العهد، فكتبوا قُرابة اثنين وخمسين رسالة عُرفت باسم «تحف إخوان الصفا». وكان الهدف من تلك الرسائل تأسيس مذهب إسلامي ذي طبيعة كونية تحوي المذاهب الدينية والفلسفية كلها وتوحدها معًا. وقد أخذت رسائلهم طابعًا موسوعيًا اشتمل على علوم متفرقة كالمنطق والفلسفة واللاهوت والرياضيات، والموسيقى والفلك والفيزياء. وتعد جماعة إخوان الصفا من أكثر الحركات الإسلامية غموضًا في التاريخ نظرا لعملها سرًّا[1] وفي الخفاء طيلة وجودها، دون إبداء رغبة في سلطة سياسية أو شهرة أدبية.

وقد اختلف الباحثون والعلماء، قديمًا وحديثًا، حول مذهب هذه الجماعة ودورها، فمنهم من نظر إليها نظرة ريبة أو عداء، ومنهم من رآها محل إعجاب وتقدير، ووصفوا أصحابها بأنهم أهل فكر ودعاة إصلاح، ومنهم من زعم أن رسائل إخوان الصفا من تأليف الأئمة، ورفعها إلى مرتبة الكتب المقدسة. كما احتدم الجدل فيما بينهم حول الانتماء المذهبي للجماعة، فاعتقد بعضهم أن الجماعة تنتمي إلى المدرسة المعتزلة، بينما رأي غيرهم أنهم نتاج المدرسة الفاطمية، وذهب آخرون إلى حدّ وصفهم بالإلحاد والزندقة .

1 Secretly

Prediction and Scanning

Based on the context and background given above, record your predictions as to whether you expect to find the following in the story. Be prepared to discuss your predictions with classmates. Then, reading through the excerpts in the next section quickly, without the use of a dictionary, indicate whether your predictions were correct and where (in which lines) you found the answers. Again, be prepared to discuss the results with your classmates.

العبارة	التوقُّع	الدلالة
بَدء الخليقة وتعمير الأرض.		
بعض طوائف الجن دخلت في دين الإسلام.		
يدّعي بعض البشر أن تركيبتهم الجسدية والعقلية تمنحهم الحق في السيطرة على الحيوانات وترويضها.		
تعتقد الحيوانات أن البشر مخطئون في تباهيهم وافتخارهم بالعطايا التي منحها الله لهم.		

From the Writings of Ikhwan al-Safa

رسائل إخوان الصفا، الجزء الثاني، الرسالة الثامنة

The story begins with a brief overview of history:

(١) يُقال إنّه لما توالدت أولاد بني آدم وكثُرت وانتشرت في الأرض برًّا وبحرًا وسهلًا وجبلًا متصرِّفين فيها في مآربهم آمنين . . . (٢) ثم سخَّروا من الأنعام البقر والغنم والجِمال، ومن البهائم الخيل والبغال والحمير . . . (٣) بعث الله محمدًا— صلَّى الله عليه وآله—ودَعَا الإنس والجن إلى الله ودِين الإسلام، فأجابته طائفة من الجن وحسُنَ إسلامُها، ومضتْ على ذلك مدة من الزمان. (٤) ثم إنه وَلِيَ على بَنِي الجانِّ مَلِك منها يُقال له بيراست الحكيم لقبه شاه مردان، وكانت دار مملكته مردان في جزيرة يُقال لها صاغون في وسط البحر الأخضر . . .

The writers then tell how this peculiar case came about:

(٥) ثم إنه طرحتِ الرياح العاصفة في وقت من الزمان مركبًا من سفن البحر إلى ساحل تلك الجزيرة، وكان فيها قوم من التجار والصُّنَّاع وأهل العِلْم وسائر أغنياء الناس، (٦) فخرجوا إلى تلك الجزيرة وطافوا فيها . . . (٧) ورأَوْا فيها أصناف الحيوانات من البهائم والأنعام والطيور والسباع والوحوش والهوامِّ والحشرات أجمع، (٨) وهي كلها متآلِفة بعضها في بعض مستأنِسة غير متنافِرة. (٩) ثم إن أولئك القوم استطابوا ذلك المقام، واستوطنوا وبنَوْا هنالك البنيان وسكنوا، (١٠) ثم إنهم أخذوا يتعرَّضون لتلك البهائم والأنعام التي هناك يُسخِّرونها ليركبوها ويحملوا عليها أثقالَهم . . . (١١) فلمَّا علمتْ تلك البهائم والأنعام هذا الاعتقاد منهم . . . ذهبتْ إلى بيراست الحكيم مَلِك الجن وشكَتْ إليه ما لَقِيَتْ من جَوْر بني آدَمَ . . . (١٢) فبعث ملك الجن رسولًا إلى أولئك القوم ودعاهم إلى حضرته.

Summoned by the king of the Jinn, the leader of the humans makes his case:

(١٣) فقال زعيم الإنس: نقول: إن هؤلاء عبيدٌ لنا، ونحن مواليها، ولنا أن نتحكَّم عليها تحكُّم الأرباب ونتصرَّف فيها تصرُّف الملّاك كيف شاء، فمَن أطاعنا طاعتُه لله . . . (١٤) فقال الملك للإنسي: إن الدَّعاوَى لا تصحُّ عند الحكام إلا بالبيِّنات، ولا تُقبل إلا بالحجَّة الواضحة فيما قلتَ وادَّعَيْتَ. (١٥) فقال الإنسي: إن لنا حججًا عقلية ودلائل فلسفية تدل على صحة ما قلنا. (١٦) قال الملك: ما هي؟ بيِّنها لنعلمها. (١٧) قال: نعم؛ حُسْن صورتنا، وتقويم بنية هيكلنا وانتصاب قامتنا وجَوْدة حواسِّنا ودقة تمييزنا وذكاء نفوسنا ورجحان عقولنا، (١٨) كل هذا يدل على أنَّا أرباب وهُم عبيد لنا. (١٩) فقال الملك لزعيم البهائم: ما تقولون فيما قال الإنسي؟

The leader of the animals then makes a counterargument:

(٢٠) اعلم بأن الله—جلَّ ثناؤه—ما خلقهم على تلك الصورة ولا سوَّاهم على هذه البنية لتكون دلالة على أنهم أرباب . . . (٢١) لما خلق آدم وأولاده عُرَاةً بلا ريش على أبدانهم ولا وَبَر ولا صوف على جلودهم يَقِيهم من الحر والبرد، (٢٢) وجعل أرزاقهم من ثمر الأشجار ودثارهم من أوراقها، (٢٣) وكانت الأشجار منتصبة في جو الهواء، جعل أيضًا قامتهم منتصبة ليسهل عليهم تناول الثمر والورق منها، (٢٤) وهكذا لما جعل أرزاقنا من حشيش الأرض جعل بنية أبداننا منحنية ليسهل علينا تناول العشب من الأرض . . . (٢٥) وأما الذي ذكرتَه من رجحان العقول، فلسنا نرى له أثرًا أو علامة؛ (٢٦) لأنه لو كان لكم عقول راجحة لما افتخرتُم علينا بشيء ليس هو من أفعالكم ولا اكتساب منكم، بل هي مواهب من الله—جلَّ ذِكْرُه—لتعرفوا مواقع النعم وتشكروا له، ولا تعصوه، (٢٧) وإنما العقلاء يفتخرون بأشياء هي مِن أفعالهم من الصنائع المحكمة والآراء الصحيحة والعلوم الحقيقية والمذاهب المرضية والسُّنَن العادلة والطرق المستقيمة، (٢٩) ولسنا نراكم تفتخرون بشيء منها غير دعوى بلا حجة وخصومة بلا بينة.

Despite the animals' convincing argument, the humans eventually win the case.

Vocabulary

بنو آدم	the sons of Adam (a metaphor for humankind)
سخّر	to exploit, make subservient
بهائم	livestock, beasts
البحر الأخضر	the Indian Ocean
سائر	all, other
طاف	walk around, survey
مستأنسة	tame
متنافرة	clashing, conflicting
استطاب	to find pleasing
شكا	to complain
جور	oppression, cruelty

أطاع	to obey
دعوى ج. دعاوى	allegation, case
بيّنة ج. بيّنات	proof, evidence
انتصاب	being upright
رجحان	superiority
جلّ ثناؤه	exalt His Glory (said of God)
عارٍ ج. عراة	naked
ريش	feathers
وَبَر	fur
رزق ج. أرزاق	sustenance
دثار	covering, blanket
منتصب	upright
منحنية	bent over
مواهب	gifts
عَصى	to deny, refuse
خصومة	quarrel, dispute

Comprehension Exercises

A. Answer the following questions in complete Arabic sentences, based on the story:

١. كيف بدأت الخليقة[2] وتزايدت؟

____

____

2 Creation, living persons

٢. مَاذا كان موقف الجنّ من دعوة النبي (ﷺ) لهم؟

____

____

٣. مَن كان على متن السفينة عند وصولها الجزيرة؟

____

____

٤. كيف ردّت الحيوانات على قمع البشر لها؟

____

____

٥. ماذا فعل بيراست الحكيم في شكوى الحيوانات؟

____

____

B. Are the following statements true or not according to the text? If not, why?

١. تكاثرت البشر وانتشرت في كل بقاع الأرض.

____

____

٢. استسلمت الحيوانات للبشر بلا شروط.

---

٣. البشر يراعون حقوق الحيوانات ويحافظون عليها.

---

٤. البشر مميزون عن الحيوانات لهيئتهم وعقولهم.

---

٥. البشر دائمًا في حاجة لبقية المخلوقات.

Interpreting the Text

١. ما أساس حُجّة البشر في تفوقهم على الحيوانات؟

---

٢. كيف فسر زعيم البهائم طبيعة الاختلاف بين البشر والحيوانات؟

____

____

٣. هل يبدو أن ملك الجن متحيّز إلى طرفٍ دون آخر في هذا النزاع؟ لماذا؟

____

____

٤. كيف حوّل زعيم البهائم فخر البشر بأنفسهم إلى دليلٍ ضدهم؟

____

____

٥. لو كنتم في موقع ملك الجن فكيف ستحكمون في هذه القضية؟

____

____

Style and Technique

1. In Line 19, the king of the Jinn addresses the animals using the human plural, as if they are equal to humans: فقال الملك لزعيم البهائم: ما تقولون في قول الإنسي؟ Animals would normally be treated grammatically as feminine singular. This reflects the high degree of respect the Ikhwan al-Safa had toward animals, as well as showing the justice of the king, who treats both sides of the dispute as equal.
2. The word أرباب is repeated three times in this text, in lines 13, 18,

and 20. The word is the plural of ربّ (head, lord). It is common to use the word ربّ in the singular to refer to a leader, such as: الوالد هو ربّ الأسرة (The father is the head of the family). In the plural, the word refers to possession of something, such as:

scholars	أرباب العلم
pensioners	أرباب المعاشات
employers	أرباب العمل

3. In line 23, the meaning of حشيش الأرض refers to all plants that one can eat for nutrition. It is not limited to grass alone.
4. In line 5, the Form I verb طَرَح means here "to throw," equivalent to قذف. However, this verb has a general sense of putting down and can be used in a variety of idioms which would require different verbs in English, such as:

presented, recited	طَرَحَ عليه الأمر
neglected, disregarded	طرحه جانبًا
brought the matter	طَرَح المسألةَ
calling for a vote	طَرْح الثِّقَة بالحكومة على المجلس التشريعيّ
project bidding	طَرْح المشروع في المناقصة
subtract (in math)	طَرَحَ عددًا من آخر
covered him with clothes	طرح عليه الثياب
lessened, eased, relieved	طَرَح عنه الهمَّ

5. In line 15, the word عُرَاة is the plural of (عارٍ – العاري) meaning naked. It is an active participle (اسم فاعل) of the Form I verb (عَرِيَ). In many of its idiomatic uses, the meaning is more metaphorical, in the sense of lacking something. For example:

not true	الخبر عارٍ من الصِحّة
perfect (having no fault)	هو عارٍ من العيوب
bare feet	عاري القدمين
bald	عاري الرأس

Writing Exercises

A. Using vocabulary from the text, express the following in Arabic:

1. It is said that mankind spread out from Africa and settled on every continent.

   ____

2. These people are friends to us, and we are friends to them. (13)

   ____

3. God created the stars to light the night. (21)

   ____

4. I am not finding reason to doubt his story. (29)

   ____

5. If you had more patience, you would not always get angry. (26)

   ____

B. Rearrange the words in coherent sentences, using the text for clues:

١. شعبه – بعثَ – رسالة – إلى – الملك

---

٢. كلامهم – ليس – على – هناك – صحة – دليل

---

٣. السفن – لا – تأتي – تشتهي – بما – الرياح

---

٤. زوجها – سوء – شَكَت – معاملة – من – الزوجة

---

٥. الإنسان – صورة – أحسن – خلق – في – الله

Discussion Questions

The Ikhwan's ideas of animals' rights and the worth of all beings were well ahead of their time. Based on what you have read, what is your opinion on the questions below?

١. ما مغزى[3] اتخاذ[4] الجن حَكَمًا في العلاقة بين البشر والحيوانات؟
٢. لماذا انتصر البشر على الحيوانات في هذا النزاع؟
٣. هل هناك أهداف خفيّة[5] لإخوان الصفا من وراء هذه القصة؟ وضحوا.
٤. ما تقييمكم لجماعة إخوان الصفا من خلال قراءتكم لهذا النص؟

Research and Presentation

Based on your reading above and your own research, prepare a 3–4-minute presentation on the following topic:

هل تشكل حقوق الحيوانات جزءًا أساسيًّا من الأخلاق الإنسانية؟

Some terms to use that may help are:

humane	إنساني
moral, ethical	أخلاقي
responsibility	مسؤولية
natural	طبيعي

3 Significance
4 To take
5 Hidden

Glossary

The first section below presents a consolidated list of the terms in the "Vocabulary" sections of all the lessons. The terms and expressions given in the "Research and Presentation" sections are listed separately after these.

From "Vocabulary" Sections

Arabic Term	Meaning	Lesson
أئمة	imams	4
ابتزّ	to extort	4
أبرويز	Khosrow Parviz, Persian Shah	4
أبطأ	to delay, slow down	18
أَبِه	to take notice of	19
أثيث	abundantly growing	18
أجمر	to burn incense	1
أحاط	to grasp, encompass	3
احتشام	bashfulness, embarrassment	16
احتفل	to celebrate, be interested in	12
أحزان	low spirits, sorrows	14
أحلّ	to permit	19
إِحَن	bad feelings, rancor	5
اختبط	to fumble about	8
اختصم	to quarrel	1
اختلب	to captivate	17
أخزى	to disgrace	1

أذى	harm	18
أرأس	firm	11
ارتجف	to shake, shudder	1
أرسطوطاليس	Aristotle	3
أرغد	most carefree	11
ازدهى	to be roused	17
أزليّ	eternal	6
أزمع	make ready, determine to	17
إساءة	sin, offense, misuse	1
أسباب	here: small items for trading	15
استأهل	to merit, deserve	3
استشهد	here: to cite, mention, quote	6
استأذن	to seek permission	15
استحسان	approval, acclaim	3
استحى	to be ashamed	3
استدرج	to lure, entice	8
استدرك	to set right	16
استطاب	to find pleasing	20
استطالة	arrogance, overbearing	13
استظرف	to consider (something or someone) witty or charming	11
استظهار بـ	appeal for assistance from	13
استعار	to borrow	2
استغاث	to call for help	18
استغاثة	call for help	19
أغنى	to enrich, avail	16
استفظع	to find horrible	6
استقْذَرَ	to consider filthy	6

استكانة	passivity, submission	13
استلاب	pillaging	4
استلب	to steal, wrest away from	11
استمكن	take possession, mastery over	16
استملح	to consider (something or someone) beautiful	11
استنبط	to create, innovate	9
استهان	to devalue, debase	8
استهان	to disparage, dismiss	9
أسقى	to give someone a drink	2
آصف بن برخياء	Asaph son of Berechiah, legendary builder of Hagia Sofia	12
أصل	here: the norm, the natural state	2
أصفى	most serene	11
إضرار	harm, damage	6
اضمحل	to fade away, vanish	7
أطاف	to encircle, surround	12
إطناب	exaggeration, tautology	8
أَطْنب	to exaggerate	12
أطاع	to obey	20
أعاد	repeat, retell	14
أعار	to lend	2
اعتُقِيَ	set free, released from service	10
اعتناء بـ	to care for, look after	5
أغراض	belongings, necessities	15
أغناك الله عني	May God spare you the need. (i.e., "You are not in need for my help.")	2

أفامية	Apamea (in Syria)	10
افتراس	predation, ravening	13
إفرنج	Franks (more generally, Europeans)	10
أفلاطون	Plato	8
اقتناء	acquisition	3
إقدام	enterprise, initiative	16
أقمشة	cloths, textiles	11
أكبَّ	to approach, embrace	2
التحام	cohesion	13
التفت	to turn toward, pay attention to	15
التَمَس	to seek urgently	16
التحى	(classical) to remove bark, peel	4
ألصق	to stick, affix	12
أَلِف	to become acquainted	16
أَلِف	to become used to, familiar with	18
إلفي	out of habit, familiarity	8
إلهيات	theology	8
أمسّ	strongest contact	4
أمعن	to apply oneself to, to focus on	18
إنجيل	the Gospel, the Bible	1
أنبأ	foretell, give warning of	17
انفَرد	to be unique	12
انتدب	to apply oneself	8
انتسب	to associate with (here: introduce)	2
انتصاب	being upright	20
انحدر	to go down to	15
أنداد	equals, rivals	6

آنس	to notice	17
أنساب	predecessors, lineage	3
انشراح	joy, delight	14
أنطاكية	Antioch (now in Türkiye)	10
انعقدت	to clot, coagulate	18
أنفة	rejection, disdain	10
أنفذ إلى	to send someone or something	11
انقرض	extinction, dying out	13
انقمع	deterred	5
إنكار	denial	2
أهدى	to give as a gift	11
أهل القريات	a reference to the people of Sodom and Gomorrah	19
أهواء	whim, bias	8
أهون	easier	16
أُوذِيَ	to be hurt or harmed by someone	1
أوصَتْ / أوصى	to confide, entrust	14
أوطأ	to trample	4
أوقد	to enkindle, light	12
آيا صُوفيا	Hagia Sofia, Cathedral	12
أيقن	to be convinced of	10
باتنجل	A Hindu holy book that al-Biruni translated	6
بادرة ج. بوادر	stirring(s), sign(s)	1
بادٍ	plainly, obviously	17
بارّ	honest, truthful	16
بالٍ	worn out	17
البحر الأخضر	the Indian Ocean	20
بخار	vapor	18

بخس	to depreciate, disparage	3
بدا	to reveal, expose	5
بَرّ	land, ground (as opposed to بحر)	15
بِرّ	charity, goodness	11
بربر	to babble	10
برجاسي	bourgeois	10
بُرهة	a moment, a short time	19
برهن	to prove, demonstrate	18
بسالة	courage	13
بطّأ	to be delayed	16
بَعْر	dung	6
بُغض	hatred	5
بغى	to commit outrage	8
بقراط	Hippocrates	8
بِكْر/ بكارة	virgin/virginity	14
بلاء	good behavior, noble action	16
بنو آدم	the sons of Adam (a metaphor for humankind)	20
بهائم	livestock, beasts	20
بهلة	cursed	19
بهيمي	beastly, animal	3
بوس	kissing	14
بومة ج. بوم	owl	15
بيّنة ج. بيّنات	proof, evidence	20
بيت ج. أبيات	line(s) of poetry	11
بيت الله الحرام	The Holy Kaʿba in Mecca	4
بين يديه	in his presence (lit. between his hands)	11
تأوّه	moan	17

تأويل	interpretation, explanation	19
تباهى	show off, flaunt	7
تثبت	to make certain of	16
تجاهل	to feign or pretend ignorance	2
تجويف	cavity, hollowness	18
تَحَجَّر	to be stiff, adamant (here: uncompromising)	5
تُحْصى	to be counted, be calculated	12
تحريم	prohibiting	4
تحنّث	practice religious piety	1
تُخطئ	to mistake	12
ترجّى	to hope	17
ترقّق	have pity	19
تزوّد	to provision	1
تصادق	to become friends	16
تصافح	to shake hands, greet	16
تصويرٌ	to examine	18
تصويرُ	illustration, painting	12
تعبّد	to engage in worship	1
تعثر بأذيال	to fail, stumble	8
تَعلّق بـ	to hang on	12
تعهد	here: to care for	18
تغافل	to feign or pretend inattention	2
تفرق	to distribute	11
تفريط	negligence	16
تقلّب الدهر	the fickleness, fortunes of time	17

تكلّف	to burden, to assume a responsibility	2
تنازع	to dispute, debate	6
تنصّر	to become a Christian	1
تهافت	incoherence	8
تهوُّر	foolishness, rashness	6
تَوبة	repentance	19
توقّى (توقّي)	to avoid, avoiding	8
تاج ج. تيجان	crown	3
ثِمار	fruits	12
جارية	enslaved woman	11
جائحة ج. جوائح	catastrophe	17
جَذَع	young man	1
جرى	happened	14
جَعبة	case, frame	12
جلّ ثناؤه	exalt His Glory (said of God)	20
جلو	to strip clear	17
جهد	exertion (here: exhaustion, fatigue)	1
جور	oppression, cruelty	20
حاجب بن زرارة	Hajib ibn Zurara (an envoy sent to Korsow, in Persia)	4
حاذق	gifted, clever, brilliant	7
حائز	possessor	4
حبس	holding back, detention (absence)	16
حثّ	to encourage, spur	9
حرّم	to forbid	19
حرَم	a sacred territory or space	12
حرصات	plains, empty land	19

حريز	accomplished	7
حريم	wives, female members of a household	5
حسنات	good deeds	19
حشم	entourage, servants	14
حشوية	literalists	9
حصر	to narrow, restrict (here: meaning to identify)	3
حَلُم	puberty	1
حلاوة روح	survival instinct	15
حماة	Hama (in Syria)	10
حنّ	to feel sympathy, affection for	18
الحنابلة	The Hanbalis (school of religious law)	11
الحنفيّة	Hanifs (believed to be followers of the true religion in Arabia before the coming of Islam)	4
حاجة ج. حوائج	needs	7
حيّز	opportunity, field, area	7
حِيَل	tricks	8
الخاصّ	the elite of society	6
خاصم	to argue, quarrel	10
خاطب	to address, announce	4
خاطر	to risk, hazard	14
خبايا	hidden things (treasures)	17
خبط	to stumble	17
ختان	circumcision	4
خرافة	superstition	6
خَشِنة	ragged, rough	12

خشونة	a tough, rugged lifestyle	13
خشي على	to be afraid, worried for someone	1
خصومة	quarrel, dispute	20
خطّ الاستواء	the equator	18
خطر ببال	to occur to one's mind	15
خلّف	to leave behind	16
خلاء	isolation	1
خلق	a group of people	10
خلية خلية	empty cell	17
خليل ج. خِلّان	loyal friend	15
دَبْر	backside, rear	5
دثار	covering, blanket	20
دجلة	the Tigris River	11
درّ	milk	17
دُرّ	pearls	6
درانة	withered pasture	3
درج	to grow up	8
دعوى ج. دعاوى	allegation, case	20
دعة	tenderness	13
دفائن	hidden	17
دناوةٌ	closeness	4
دَهْر	period of time	2
دهماء	masses, common folk	8
ديباج	brocade	4
ذبَّ عن	to defend	3
ذراع	a unit of measure, a cubit	12, 15
ذم	dispraise	7
رام	to want, demand	7
رامق	perceptive, seeing	17
رائق	bright, clear	17

ربّ العزة	The Lord of Might (i.e., God)	19
ربع	quarter (here: dwelling)	17
ربقة	noose (here: binding)	8
رَثّ	to be raggedy, disheveled	17
رُجْحان	superiority	20
رَجَز	rajaz, a kind of poetry	7
رزانة	poise, calm	8
رزانة	tranquility	17
رزق ج. أرزاق	sustenance	20
رسا/ أرسى	to come to rest\to make anchor	15
رِضوان خازن الجنان	Ridwan, the guardian of the gates of Heaven	19
رعيّة	subjects, citizens	5, 11
رفاهية	luxury	12
رقاب	necks	4
رقعة	piece of cloth, paper	11
ركية	a well	17
رَهط	group, gang	8
روضة ج. رياض	garden	15
ريب المنون	trick of fate	11
ريّس	(naval rank, captain) officer, first mate	15
ريش	feathers	20
رَيم	here: grave	19
زائغ	deviant, not following the right path	6
زجّى	here: to forebear	17
زعم	to claim, say	12, 16
زفّ	to be married	11
زلّة	mistake	16

زِمام ج. أَزِمّة	rein	5
زُمرة	group	17
زَمّل	to cover, wrap (classical use)	1
زُهاء	approximately	19
زِيّ	fashion, ways	10
ساسان	Sassan (ancient Persia)	14
سائر	all, other	20
سائس	ruler, trainer	7
الساعة	here: refers to the Hour of Resurrection	4
سجوف	veils, curtains	3
سخّر	to exploit, make subservient	20
سدف	to darken	3
سرج	lamp, light	12
السروجي	Abu Zayd al-Saruji, the main character in the *Maqamat*	17
سُرِّيَّة ج. سراري	concubine	11
سقالة	scaffold	15
سقائف	booths, sheds	12
سُقراط	Socrates	8
سكّة	road, way	1
سلّ	unsheathe (a sword)	14
سلفنا	our predecessors	18
سمرقند	Samarkand (city in Uzbekistan)	14
سهر	stay up at night	14
سوّلت له نفسه	to be tempted	4
سِوى	except	12
سَوي	(here) straight, unimpaired	17

شاذّ	deviation, not normal	10
شاسع	remote	3
شائن	bad state, disrepute	17
شبل الدولة	ruler of Aleppo (1029–38)	19
شبيهُ عيسى	one who resembles Jesus (a reference to the Muslim belief that Jesus himself was not crucified)	12
شَجَرَ	to fight	1
شحم	fat, grease	2
شرارة	spark	1
شزرًا	looking askance, suspiciously	17
شظف	hardship	13
شظيّة	a splinter, sliver	4
شفاعة	mediation, advocacy	15
شقي	to be miserable	17
شكا	to complain	20
صاع	an old unit of measure for solid items	11
صال	assault	17
صبا إلى	to yearn for	6
صبابة	pittance, small amount	17
الصخرة	The Dome of The Rock in Jerusalem	10
صدر الأول	the earliest period, beginning (of Islam)	9
صَدَقَ	to tell the truth	1
صفر	became empty, void	17
صكّ	document, deed	19

ضانك	(here) to push through, squeeze by	19
ضجّ	make noise, cry out	14
ضِياع	estate, domain	15
ضيم	wrong, harm	13
طاعة	obedience	5
طاف	walk around, survey	20
طاقة	niche in a wall that serves as a window	10
طباهج	cooking	2
طلا	a deer's offspring	18
طلوع	to embark, come up	15
طَهّرَ	to purify	6
طير أبابيل	flock of birds	4
طينة	clay	17
ظاهر	apparent, visible	13
ظبية	deer	18
ظفر	to gain possession of	16
عاج إلى	turns to	13
عارٍ ج. عراة	naked	20
عاشر	to associate with	10, 15
العامّة	the common people	6
عتيق ج. عتق	free slave	10
عِتق	freeing slaves	4
عجّل	hurry	16
عجم	non-Arab (usually Persian)	14
عُذْر	excuse	5
عسير	difficult	16
عشيًّا	in the evening	12
عَصى	to deny, refuse	20

عقد الحُبى	to sit by drawing up the legs under one's garment	17
عقلاء	wise person, rationalist (plural)	2
عكاز	staff, rod	15
علا	to climb (to go up high)	1
عليل	ailing	16
عِلة	weakness, deficiency	3
عمامة	turban	2
عوج	deviance	8
عُودِيَ	to be antagonized by someone	1
عون ج. أعوان	servant, bodyguard	14
عيان	eye witnessing	17
غابر	mortal, perishable, stale	11
غار حراء	the cave of Hira' (outside Mecca)	1
غزار	abundance	8
غشوم	tyrannical	5
غضارة	prosperity, luxury	11, 13
غضاضة	deficiency, stain	13
غطى	to envelop (here: to crush)	1
غفلة	negligence	15
غلال	shackles, fetters	19
غوائل	disasters, ruin	8
غيرة	jealousy (here meant as a good thing), ardency	10
غَيْلَم	male tortoise	16
فتى	young man	17
فداء	redemption, sacrifice	14

فراق	farewell, separation	11
فسخ	to break off, sever	6
فسقية	fountain, well	14
فضائل	virtues	9
فِطْرة	character, instinct	9
فطنة	astuteness, understanding	3, 8
فقهاء	legal scholar (plural)	2
فُلان	so-and-so, unnamed person	19
فلج	to have palsy, paralysis	17
فلق	break of dawn	1
في الأقل	rarely, in the least	13
في هذه الجملة	in all of this (a reference to what he has just discussed)	4
قاسَ على	generalize from, draw conclusions from	10
قاصٍ/ القاصي	distant	3
قِحْف	skull	18
قَدَح ج. أقداح	goblet, drinking vessel	2
قدّس الله روحه	May God sanctify his soul	11
قرار	(here) the bottom	15
قرَعَ	to hammer, strike	17
قرى	to treat hospitably	1
قِرى	hospitality	7
قُصارى	limit, utmost	6
قصر	to lack, fall short of	3
قصعة	tub, large bowl	15
قضيب	branch	4
قَطّ	never, in no circumstance	12

قُطب	pole, axis	5
قلبة	sickness, ailment	17
قلّد	to invest, appoint	5
قَلَنسُوة	cap	2
قَمّ	to sweep	12
قِناع	mask, veil	2
قنطرة	stone bridge, viaduct	11
قنية	acquisition	3
قنينة	flask, bottle	10
قياس	analogy	9
قيان	female singers	11
كاغد ج. كواغد	sheet(s) of paper	12
كزّ	disgusting, repugnant, unpleasant	7
كِساء	garment, cloak	2
كسوة	a type of garment	15
كفّ	palm of the hand	17
كفى	to meet all needs (here, to supply)	2
كمال	(in this use) luxury	13
كوانين	cooking pot, a stove using firewood	15
لا صبر لي على	I cannot bear (something)	19
لا عليك	don't worry yourself	19
لا مطمع في	having no desire for	6
لا يتسع لـ	does not accommodate, suffice (for)	19
لا يخلون	they cannot avoid (i.e., they must)	3
لاح	to make clear, be evident, make apparent	18

لجّج	to reach the depths of the sea	16
لجاج	stubbornness	6
لقّن	instruct, teach	7
لقوة	palsy	17
لم يلبث	did not hesitate	2
لم ينشب	didn't take long, didn't delay	1
لهيب	flame	18
ليتَ	if only . . .	2
ماحية	eraser	19
مباينة	difference, dissimilarity	6
مُبطِل	cancelling, negative	9
متأخر على	subsequent to	18
متأوّل	interpreter	4
متدابرة	opposing, contrasting	8
متلاطم	clashing, crashing	15
متنافرة	clashing, conflicting	20
مثالب	disadvantages, flaw	7
مثبت	asserting, positive	9
مجعول	had put	12
محترز	guardedly	10
محجبين	those hidden or veiled (here, from the knowledge of God)	18
محجوج	overcome by argument, easily rebutted	9
محوجة	deficient	6
محيل	faking, making a trick	17
مدح	praise	7
مُركبة	composed	6
مُرهف	sharp	13

مروَزيٌّ	Mervite (one from Merv)	2
مروءة	generosity	7
مروة	pebble, rock	17
مساوئ	disadvantages	7
مستأنسة	tame	20
مسكين	unfortunate, poor (person)	19
مسيء	offensive	5
مشط	comb	7
مُصرّ	insistent, persistent	7
مصمتة	solid, uniform	18
مضادين لـ	adversaries of	3
مطهر	pure, immaculate	19
معانقة	embrace	14
معتنٍ بـ	concerned with	13
معزّ	Mu'izz (name of the host)	10
معشر	group, troop	16
معصية	disobedience	5
المعقول	that which is reasoned	18
مغزى	intent	9
مفلس ج. مفاليس	bankrupt, penniless (plural)	17
مقتصر على	limited to, restricted to	13
مقتضبة	brief, concise	6
مِقلى	frying pan	2
مقهور	defeated, saddened	14
مكابدة	hardship	2
مُكاشفة	revealing	5
ملّة	community, sect	6
ملّك	to make a king	16
ملاحدة	heretics	8

ملائكة	angels	18
مَلَك	angel	19
ملك	here: property	10
مليج	The term used by Hindus for unclean outsiders	6
مليح	pleasant, delicious (lit: salty)	15
مناقب	merits, advantages	7
منتصب	upright	20
منحنية	bent over	20
مَنزلة	place, position	5
منشأ	growing up, maturing	9
المنقول	that which is passed on (i.e., traditions)	18
منهوك	exhausted, weakened	16
مهلك	death, demise, withering away	16
مؤاكلة	sharing a meal	7, 10
مواهب	gifts	20
موسى	Moses	1
مولاة	lady, consort	11
مؤزرًا	aided, supported	1
مؤنة	supply	2
نابلس	Nablus, city in the West Bank	10
ناسخ	scribe, copier	6
نافذ	powerful, influential	10
نال	to obtain	3
الناموس	the Archangel Gabriel	1
نبّه	to call attention	9
نبوّة	prophethood	4
نجاسة	filth	6

نجدة	auxiliaries	13
نحا	to lead to, to point toward	9
نخوة	honor, dignity	10
ندب	to deputize, entrust	9
ندم	to regret	4
نزّل	to receive hospitably	17
نزع عن	abstain, give up	5
نسخ	here: to abrogate, supersede	4
نشيش	sizzle	2
نصارى	Christians	8
نصرانية	a term for Christianity	6
نظرية	theorical, speculative	9
نعرة	pride (usually in race or group)	13
نفث	spit, expectoration (here, a metaphor for his speech)	17
نفذت صاحبًا	to send someone to accompany	10
نفع	to profit, benefit	15
نفيس	precious	3
نقّح	to correct, improve, revise	6
نقل	here: publication, edition	6
نِقْمة	wrath, grudge	5
نكح	to marry	4
نكير	reproach, blame	10
نهج	to follow, pursue	17
نهر عيسى	a canal connecting the Tigris and Euphrates	11

نهى	to forbid, prevent	9
نوال	favor, blessings	15
نواميس	laws	8
نوائب	ups and downs	17
هاب	to dread, fear	1
هَتَكَ	to divulge	5
هِجاء	spelling	7
هدم	to demolish	1
هذّب	to rectify, refine	6, 8
هرم	old, decrepit	16
هشّ وبشّ	friendly, amiable	17
هلاك	annihilation, destruction	15
هلكة	loss, ruin	13
هوَّن	to make easy, relieve	2
وابل	downpour, barrage	5
واصل	those who have arrived (at the knowledge of God)	18
واظب	to do something persistently, persevere in	7
واغل	deep-rooted	4
معادن	minerals	18
انقدحت	to spark a fire	18
وَبَر	fur	20
وثب	to leap (the first mention – to attack, challenge)	16
وَحشة	loneliness, estrangement	2
ودّع	to bid farewell	15
وزع (يزع)	to restrain	5
وشيك	imminent	7

وصل	here: to associate with	17
وصول	(here, it refers to arriving at an intimate knowledge of God)	18
وطء	sexual penetration	14
وقّف على	to create a waqf (religious endowment) for	11
وقور	dignified	7
وكر	nest	17
وُلي	to be appointed	11
وَهْرِز	Wahrez, a Persian general who conquered Yemen	4
وَهَى	to weaken	1
يسيرة	ease	11

Research and Presentation Vocabulary

(Alphabetical in English)

according to that, because of that	بحسب ذلك
analogy	تمثيل
appropriate	ملائم
argument, evidence	حُجّة
by analogy	على القياس
by way of example	على سبيل المثال
clear evidence	دليل قاطع
conclusion, deduction	استنتاج
despite	رغم أنّ
disproving, negating	مُبْطِل
effect (positive or harmful)	أثر (إيجابي أو مؤذ)

establishing, proving	مُثبِت
humane	إنساني
idealism	مثالية
immediate cause	سبب مباشر
intangible	غير ملموس
integrity	نزاهة
it must be true that	لا بد أنّه صحيح
likewise	ونظير هذا
marginal	هامشي
moral, ethical	أخلاقي
natural	طبيعي
non-essential	غير جوهري
priority	أولوية
private matter	مسألة خاصة
refute	فَنَّدَ
relativism	نسبوية
responsibility	مسؤولية
restrict to	اقتصر على
revealing, exposing	كاشفًا
social custom	العُرف الاجتماعي
standards of behavior	مقياس السلوك
support for	مسند لِـ
the best example of this	خير مثالٍ على ذلك
the end justifies the means	الغاية تبرّر الوسيلة
the public good	الصالح العام
the weight of the evidence, the preponderance of the evidence	رُجْحان الأدلة
there are some exceptions	هناك بعض الاستثناءات
there is no support for . . . except	لا مسند لـ . . . غير
thorny issue	قضية شائكة
to admit, concede (a fact)	اعترف بـ
to assume	افترض
to be given precedence	تُعطى الأولوية

to be in harmony, agreement with	طابَقَ . . . و . . .
to compare	عقد مقارنة بين
to comport with	اتفق مع
to conform to	انسجم مع
to criticize	انتقد
to disapprove, condemn	استنكر
to disprove the expectations	يدحض التوقعات
to express	أعرَبَ عن
to give preference to	فَضَّلَ
to infer (something) (by means of)	استدلّ (على) (بـ)
to infer	استنتج
to lead to	أدّى إلى
to make a comparison between . . . and . . .	وازَنَ بين . . . وبين . . .
to make clear	أوضح
to object to	اعترض على
to reflect	عَكَسَ
to reveal	كشف
to satirize, lampoon	هجا (يهجو)
to some extent	إلى حدٍ ما
underlying cause (of)	سبب كامن (وراء)
unintended consequence	نتيجة غير مرغوبة
universal value	قيمة عامة
weakness (of an argument)	دحوض

Resources for Further Study

We hope the excerpts in this book have sparked your interest in learning more about the works of Classical Arabic Literature, the writers, and their times. In this section, we list some resources you can use for further study and exploration. These resources are also useful for the "Research and Presentation" exercises in the lessons. They include resources in English as well as Arabic. Since some cover many of the writers included in this book, we list those as "general resources" first. Good luck!

General Resources

Cornell University Library: Classical and Medieval Arabic Literature Guide
https://guides.library.cornell.edu/ArabicLiterature/ClassicalIslamic

Library of Arabic Literature (New York University Press): Provides free pdf versions of Classical Arabic works and publishes Arabic–English translations of great works.
https://www.libraryofarabicliterature.org/

Library of Congress—World Digital Library: Contains pdf versions of Classical Arabic books and many original manuscripts.
https://www.loc.gov/collections/world-digital-library/?q=Arabic

Maktabat 'Ayn al-Jama'a: Contains ebook versions of Arabic works in many categories, including philosophy and literature. Large

numbers of texts by the authors featured in this book are available here.
https://ebook.univeyes.com/

Maktabat Noor: A wide variety of Arabic texts available, including general works on Arabic philosophy.
https://www.noor-book.com/

Mu'assasat Hindawi: A non-profit organization providing access to great works of philosophy and literature in Arabic. Many of the works featured in this book and other works from the same authors are available in complete Arabic versions.
https://www.hindawi.org/

Mufakeroon: An Arabic website with biographies and articles about many Arab philosophers
https://mufakeroon.com/

Stanford Encyclopedia of Philosophy: Leading online English-language resource for in-depth information about philosophers and philosophy, including those feature in this book.
https://plato.stanford.edu/

Resources by Lesson

Lesson One: Biography of the Prophet—Ma'mar ibn Rashid:

Ma'mar ibn Rashid. *The Expeditions: An Early Biography of Muḥammad*. Bilingual Arabic–English Edition. Translated by Sean W. Anthony. New York: New York University Press, 2014.

Martin Lings. *Muhammad: His Life Based on the Earliest Sources*. Inner Traditions, 2006.

Links to resources about the life of the Prophet: https://www.kalamullah.com/muhammad.html

Lesson Two: *Adab*—al-Jahiz:

al-Jahiz. *The Book of Misers*. Translated by R.B. Serjeant. Reading, UK: Garnet, 2000.

al-Jahiz. *al-Bukhala' li-l-Jahiz*. Cairo: Dar al-Ma'arif, 1967.

Jamil Jabr. *al-Jahiz fi hayatihi wa-adabihi wa-fikrihi*. Beirut: Dar al-Kitab al-Lubnani, 1974.

Lesson Three: Philosophy—al-Kindi:

al-Kindi. *al-Kindi's Metaphysics: A Translation of Ya'qub ibn Ishaq al-Kindi's Treatise "On First Philosophy."* Albany: State University of New York, 1974.

Peter Adamson. *al-Kindi (Great Medieval Thinkers)*. Oxford: Oxford University Press, 2006.

https://islamonline.net/الكندي-أول-فلاسفة-المسلمين

Lesson Four: Ethnicity in Islam—Ibn Qutayba:

Ibn Qutayba. *The Excellence of the Arabs*. Bilingual Arabic–English Edition. Translated by Sarah Bowen Savant and Peter Webb. New York: New York University Press, 2017.

Overview of Ibn Qutayba's works in Arabic: https://www.almrsal.com/post/848762

Lesson Five: Government and Leadership—Ibn 'Abd Rabbih:

Ibn 'Abd Rabbih. *The Unique Necklace (al-'iqd al-farid), vol. I.* Translated by Issa J. Boullata. Reading, UK: Garnet, 2006.

Works of Ibn 'Abd Rabbih in Arabic: https://al-maktaba.org/author/788

Lesson Six: Anthropology and Religion—al-Biruni:

al-Biruni. ALBERUNI'S INDIA – An account of… India about A.D. 1030, vol. 1, Translated by Edward C. Sachau. London: Kegan Paul, 1910. https://openlibrary.org/books/OL23270588M/Alberuni%27s_India.

Amelia Carolina Sparavigna. "The Science of al-Biruni." Muslim Heritage. https://muslimheritage.com/the-science-of-al-biruni/

Lesson Seven: Education—Ibn Sina:

Michael P. Arya. *The Essential Avicenna (Ibn Sina)*. Maitland, FL: Xulon Press, 2021.

Lenn Evan Goodman. *Avicenna*. New York: Routledge, 1992.

Rachel Hajar. "The Art of History (Part V): Ibn Sina, The Great Physician and Philosopher," *Heart Views* 14:4 (Oct–Dec 2013): 196–201. https://www.ncbi.nlm.nih.gov/pmc/articles/PMC3970379/

"Ibn Sina," *Muslim Philosophy Online*. Links to articles on Ibn Sina http://www.muslimphilosophy.com/sina

Lesson Eight: Religion vs. Philosophy I—al-Ghazali:

al-Ghazali. *The Incoherence of the Philosophers*, 2nd Edition. Bilingual Arabic–English Edition. Translated by Michael E. Marmura. Provo, UT: Brigham Young University Press, 2002.

Ghazali.org A Virtual Online Library. https://www.ghazali.org/

Brian M. Hauglid. "Al-Ghazali, A Muslim Seeker of Truth." *BYU Studies Quarterly* 40:4 https://byustudies.byu.edu/article/al-ghazali-a-muslim-seeker-of-truth/

Lesson Nine: Religion vs. Philosophy II—Ibn Rushd:

Ibn Rushd. *Averroes' Tahafut al-Tahafut (The Incoherence of the Incoherence).* Translated by Simon Van Den Bergh. Oxford: Gibb Memorial Trust, 2008.

Majid Fakhry. *Averroes: His Life, Work and Influence.* Oxford: Oneworld, 2001.

Lesson Ten: Impressions of Europeans—Usama ibn Munqidh:

Usama ibn Munqidh. *The Book of Contemplation: Islam and the Crusades.* Translated by Paul M. Cobb. New York: Penguin, 2008.

Paul M. Cobb. *Usama ibn Munqidh: Warrior Poet of the Age of Crusades.* Oxford: Oneworld, 2006.

Lesson Eleven: Women in the Caliphal Court—Ibn al-Sa'i:

Ibn al-Sa'i. *Consorts of the Caliphs.* Translated by Shawkat M. Toorawa. Bilingual Arabic–English Edition. New York: New York University Press, 2015.

Yasmin Hilloowalla. "Women's Role in Politics in the Medieval Muslim World." *Medievalists.net* https://www.medievalists.net/2015/03/womens-role-politics-medieval-muslim-world/

Gavin R.G. Hambly, ed. *Women in the Medieval Islamic World.* New York: MacMillan, 1998.

Lesson Twelve: Travel Literature—Ibn Battuta:
Ibn Battuta. *The Travels of Ibn Battutah*. Edited by Tim Mackintosh-Smith. London: Picador, 2003.

David DiMeo and Inas Hassan. *The Travels of Ibn Battuta: A Guided Arabic Reader.* Cairo: The American University in Cairo Press, 2016.

Lesson Thirteen: History—Ibn Khaldun:
Ibn Khaldun. *The Muqaddimah: An Introduction to History, Abridged Edition*. Edited by N.J. Dawood. Translated by Franz Rosenthal. Princeton, NJ: Princeton University Press, 2015.

Robert Irwin. *Ibn Khaldun: An Intellectual Biography*. Princeton, NJ: Princeton University Press, 2019.

I.M.N. al-Jubouri. "Ibn Khaldun and the Philosophy of History." *Philosophy Now* (2005). https://philosophynow.org/issues/50/Ibn_Khaldun_and_the_Philosophy_of_History

Lessons Fourteen and Fifteen: Popular Storytelling—*The Arabian Nights:*
The Arabian Nights: Tales from a Thousand and One Nights. Translated by Richard Burton. New York: Modern Library, 2001.

Paulo Lemos Horta, ed. *The Annotated Arabian Nights*. Translated by Yasmine Seale. New York: Liverlight, 2021.

Journal of the 1001 Nights. Blog about the Arabian Nights. http://journalofthenights.blogspot.com/

Lesson Sixteen: Moral Literature–Ibn al-Muqaffa‘:

Ibn al-Muqaffa. *Kalila and Dimna, or The Fables of Bidpai.* Translated by Wyndham Knatchbull. Oxford: Oxford University Press, 1819. https://archive.org/details/kalilaanddimnao00almgoog

Paul Lunde. "Kalila wa-Dimna." *Muslim Heritage* https://muslimheritage.com/kalila-wa-dimna/

Library of Congress. Illuminated manuscript of *Kalila wa-Dimna.* https://www.loc.gov/item/2021667397/

Lesson Seventeen: The *Maqamat*—al-Hariri:

al-Hariri. *Maqamat Abi Zayd al-Saruji.* Arabic Edition. New York: New York University Library, 2020.

al-Hariri. *Impostures.* Translated by Michael Cooperson. New York: New York University Library, 2020.

Lesson Eighteen: Philosophical Novel—Ibn Tufayl:

Lawrence Conrad, ed. *The World of Ibn Tufayl: Interdisciplinary Perspectives on Hayy ibn Yaqzan.* New York: Brill, 1996.

Ibn Tufayl. *Ibn Tufayl's Hayy ibn Yaqzan: A Philosophical Tale.* Translated by Lenn Evan Goodman. Chicago: University of Chicago Press, 2009.

"Ibn Tufayl." *Muslim Philosophy.Com* http://www.muslimphilosophy.com/ip/rep/H030

Taneli Kukkonen. *Ibn Tufayl: Living the Life of Reason.* Oxford: Oneworld, 2014.

Lesson Nineteen: Satire—Abu al-'Alaa' al-Ma'arri:

Abu l-'Ala' al-Ma'arri. *The Epistle of Forgiveness*. Bilingual Arabic–English Edition. Translated by Gregor Schoeler and Geert Jan van Gelder. New York: New York University Press, 2013.

al-Ma'arri on *Geniuses Club*: https://www.geniuses.club/genius/abu-al-ala-al-ma-arri

Books by al-Ma'arri available on Project Gutenberg. https://www.gutenberg.org/ebooks/author/26732

Lesson Twenty: Animal Rights—Ikhwan al-Safa:

Ikhwan al-Safa. *The Case of the Animals versus Man Before the King of the Jinn: A Tenth-century Ecological Fable of the Pure Brethren of Basra*. Translated by Lenn Evan Goodman. Boston: Twayne, 1978.

Godefroid de Callatay. *Ikhwan al-Safa': A Brotherhood of Idealists on the Fringe of Orthodox Islam*. Oxford: Oneworld, 2006.

"The Rasail Ikhwan as-Safa." *Ismaili.Net* https://www.ismaili.net/histoire/history04/history428.html

CPSIA information can be obtained
at www.ICGtesting.com
Printed in the USA
JSHW010528160623
43267JS00001B/1

9 781649 031730